The Jossey-Bass
Business & Management Series

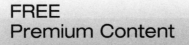

More Praise for *Facilitating with Ease!*

"I have rarely run into a better collection of pragmatic tips, tools, and techniques. If you work with people to accomplish something important, save yourself a lifetime of trial and error: read this book, put its message to use, and start seeing where real collaboration can lead your organization."
—Adriano Pianesi, ParticipAction Consulting, Inc., Washington, D.C.

"Ingrid Bens' masterful book *Facilitation with Ease!* is a must-have for any facilitator regardless of experience. I use it extensively to review processes, tools and techniques before any engagement."
—George F. Smith, CPF, Summit Consultants, Atlanta, Georgia

"*Facilitating with Ease!* is by far the easiest to use, most comprehensive and well structured resource guide I have ever seen! No wonder both new and seasoned facilitators find it invaluable. A must have if facilitation is a skill you need in your toolbox."
—Larry L. Looker, Manager, Global Leadership Development, Amway Corporation, USA

"This book is just excellent! The comprehensive set of practical tools are for everyone engaged in improving how groups work. Helps you to just do it!"
—Ewa Malia, CPF, Polish Insitutute of Facilitation, Warsaw

Facilitating with Ease!

Core Skills for

Facilitators,

Team Leaders

and Members,

Managers,

Consultants,

and Trainers

NEW AND REVISED

Ingrid Bens, M.Ed.

JOSSEY-BASS
A Wiley Imprint
www.josseybass.com

Published by Jossey-Bass
An Imprint of Wiley
One Montgomery Street, Suite 1200, San Francisco, CA 94104-4594
www.josseybass.com

For additional copies/bulk purchases of this book in the U.S. please contact 800-274-4434.
Jossey-Bass books and products are available through most bookstores. To contact Jossey-Bass directly call our Customer Care Department within the U.S. at 800-274-4434, outside the U.S. at 317-572-3985, fax 317-572-4002, or visit www.josseybass.com.

Jossey-Bass publishes in a variety of print and electronic formats and by print-on-demand. Some material included with standard print versions of this book may not be included in e-books or in print-on-demand. If this book refers to media such as a CD or DVD that is not included in the version you purchased, you may download this material at http://booksupport.wiley.com. For more information about Wiley products, visit www.wiley.com.

Library of Congress Cataloging-in-Publication Data

Bens, Ingrid.
Facilitating with ease! : core skills for facilitators, team leaders and members, managers, consultants, and trainers / Ingrid Bens.—3rd ed.
p. cm. — (The Jossey-Bass Business and management series)
Includes bibliographical references.
ISBN 978-1-118-10774-4 (pbk.); 978-1-118-18114-0 (ebk.); 978-1-118-18115-7 (ebk.); 978-1-118-18116-4 (ebk.)
1. Teams in the workplace. 2. Group facilitation. I. Title.
HD66.B445 2012
658.4′022—dc23

2011042749

Printed in the United States of America
THIRD EDITION
PB Printing 10 9 8 7 6 5 4 3 2

Table of Contents

Introduction

It's impossible to be part of an organization today and not attend meetings. Staff meetings, project meetings, task force meetings, planning and coordinating meetings . . . the list is endless. The worst thing about many of these meetings is that they're poorly run and waste valuable time.

Today, there's been a growing recognition that effective meetings happen when proper attention has been paid to the process elements and when proceedings are skillfully facilitated.

For a long time, facilitation has been a rather vague and poorly understood practice, mastered only by human resource types. This is beginning to change. We're now spending so much time in meetings and being asked to achieve so many important goals in teams that there's a growing need for skilled facilitation throughout our organizations and our communities.

> *With its focus on asking instead of telling, listening, and building consensus, facilitation is the essential skill for anyone working collaboratively with others.*

Instead of being relegated to HR, facilitation is fast becoming a core competency for anyone who leads a team, manages a project, heads up a committee, or manages a department. All of these people need to be able to create and manage effective group dynamics that foster true collaboration.

Facilitation is also a central skill for today's managers, who are riding wave after wave of change. New demands are being placed on them. At the same time, the old command and control model of supervision, which worked for decades, is no longer as effective.

To get the most from people today, leaders have to know how to create buy-in, generate participation, and empower people.

To keep pace, today's leaders need to be coaches, mentors, and teachers. At the core of each of these new roles is the skill of facilitation.

The Goal of This Book

This practical workbook has been created to make core facilitation tools and techniques readily available to the growing number of people who want to improve their process skills. It represents materials and ideas that have been collected, tested, and refined over decades of active facilitation in all types of settings. This third edition retains the core tools and instruments that made the first two editions so popular. In addition, new materials have been added to every chapter.

As in the first two editions, *Facilitating with Ease!* remains a practical workbook. While it builds on the theories of organization development pioneers such as Chris Argyris, Donald Schön, and Edgar Schein, this resource doesn't aim to be theoretical. Instead, its focus is on providing the reader with the most commonly used process tools, in a simple and accessible format. This is not so much a book to be read, as one to be used!

The Audience

This workbook contains valuable information for anyone facilitating group interactions. This is a huge constituency, which includes:

- team leaders and team members
- project managers
- any supervisor or manager who holds staff meetings
- community developers
- teachers in traditional classroom settings
- therapists who lead support groups
- marketing consultants who run focus groups
- teachers of adult continuing education programs
- negotiators and conflict mediators

- quality consultants leading process improvement initiatives like Six Sigma
- consultants intervening in conflicts
- anyone teaching others to facilitate
- anyone called on to lead a discussion or run a meeting.

Since facilitation was designed as a role for neutral outsiders, the strategies and techniques in this book are described from the perspective of the external facilitator. Since more and more facilitation is being done by those who have a stake in the outcome of discussions, the third edition includes strategies that help leaders and group members manage the challenges of staying neutral.

Content Overview

The book is organized into ten chapters. Checklists and tools have not been collected in an appendix, but are located throughout each chapter, near the related materials.

Chapter One outlines what facilitation is and its main applications. It differentiates process from content and outlines the core practices. It also addresses facilitation issues such as neutrality, how assertive a facilitator can be, and how to balance the role of the group leader with that of the facilitator.

Chapter One also describes what facilitators do at the beginning, middle, and end of discussions. It provides information about the language of facilitation, the principles of giving and receiving feedback, plus a thumbnail sketch of the best and worst practices of facilitators.

At the end of the chapter, there are two observation sheets and a four-level skills self-assessment, useful to anyone hoping for feedback on current skills.

Chapter Two focuses on how facilitation can be managed by leaders. This is a major new addition and reflects the growing awareness among leaders of the importance of process management.

This new chapter explores the challenges leaders face when they facilitate and provides strategies that help leaders effectively manage group process. This chapter also discusses the issues encountered when the facilitator feels he or she lacks authority or is working with people of senior rank.

Chapter Three explores the stages of designing and managing a facilitation assignment. It describes the importance of each step in the facilitation process: assessment, design, feedback, refinement, and final preparation. Helpful checklists are also provided to guide the start, middle, and end of any facilitation session.

Chapter Four focuses on knowing your participants and provides information about the four most commonly used needs-assessment techniques. Sample assessment questions and surveys are provided. This chapter also discusses the differences between facilitating groups and facilitating teams and passes along strategies for getting any group to behave more like an effective team. The creation of team norms is discussed, along with an overview of the team growth stages and the corresponding facilitation strategies that work best at each stage.

Chapter Five begins with a frank discussion of the many reasons people are often less than enthusiastic to be involved in a meeting or workshop and provides tested strategies for overcoming these blocks, including ideas on gaining buy-in. High participation techniques are also shared, along with a training plan to encourage effective meeting behaviors in members.

Chapter Six delves into the complexities of decision making. Facilitators are introduced to the types of discussions and the importance of clarifying empowerment. Various methods for reaching decisions are described and differentiated. The pros, cons, and uses of each approach are explored, along with an expanded discussion of consensus building. Chapter Six also offers an overview of the behaviors that help decision effectiveness and provides the steps in the systematic consensus-building process. The chapter ends with a discussion of poor decisions: their symptoms, causes, and cures. A survey is provided with which a group can assess its current decision-making effectiveness.

Chapter Seven deals with facilitative strategies for handling both conflict and resistance. It begins with an overview of the difference between healthy debates and dysfunctional arguments. It goes on to share techniques that encourage healthy debates and the steps in managing any conflict. Special attention is paid to strategies for venting emotions. The five conflict-management options are also explored and placed into the context of which are most appropriate for facilitators.

Chapter Seven also provides a three-part format for wording interventions that tactfully allows a facilitator to redirect inappropriate behavior. Also described are the two approaches a facilitator can choose when confronted with resistance and why one is superior. At the end of the chapter, nine common facilitator dilemmas and their solutions are presented.

Chapter Eight focuses on meeting management. There's a useful checklist and meeting effectiveness diagnostic that lets groups assess whether or not their meetings are working. There's also a chart that outlines the symptoms and cures for common meeting ills. The fundamentals of meeting management are outlined, with special emphasis on the role of the facilitator as compared to the traditional chairperson role. Both mid-point checks and exit surveys are explained, and samples are provided. Since virtual meetings are on the rise, strategies are offered for using facilitation techniques during distance meetings.

Chapter Nine contains some of the process tools that are fundamental to all facilitation activities. These include: visioning, sequential questioning, force-field analysis, brainstorming, gap analysis, root cause analysis, decision grids, affinity diagrams, needs and offers dialogue, systematic problem solving, survey feedback, multi-voting, and troubleshooting. Each tool is described, and step-by-step directions are given for using it.

Chapter Ten pulls it all together by providing twelve sample process designs, complete with facilitator notes. These notes describe each meeting design in detail and set an example for how facilitators should prepare their design notes. The twelve samples are some of the most commonly requested facilitations and provide the reader with graphic illustrations of the level of detail a facilitator needs to consider before stepping in front of any group.

After years of experience as a consultant, project manager, team leader, and trainer, I'm convinced that it's impossible to build teams, consistently achieve consensus, or run effective decision-making meetings without highly developed facilitation skills. The good news is that these skills can be mastered by anyone! I hope you find the third edition of *Facilitating with Ease!* to be a valuable resource in your quest to gain this important skill.

January 2012 **Ingrid Bens, M.Ed., CPF**

Questions Answered in This Book

What is facilitation? When do I use it?

What's the role of the facilitator?

What are the main tools and techniques?

What are the values and attitudes of a facilitator?

How neutral do I really need to be?

How assertive am I allowed to be?

How can facilitation be used in the classroom?

How can those who have a stake in the group's decisions facilitate?

How can I facilitate when I'm not the official facilitator?

How do I get everyone to participate?

Can facilitation techniques be used to manage distance meetings?

How do I overcome people's reluctance to open up?

What's the difference between a group and a team?

How can I get a group to act like a team?

What do I do if a group is very cynical?

What do I do if I encounter high resistance?

What if there's zero buy-in?

What are my options for dealing with conflict?

What if a meeting falls apart and I lose control?

What decision-making techniques are available?

Why is consensus building most effective for arriving at a group decision?

What can go wrong in making decisions?

How do I make sure that discussions achieve closure?

How can facilitation be used to manage conference calls?

How do I balance the roles of chairperson and facilitator?

What facilitation tools are available?

How do I design an effective process?

How do I know whether the meeting is going well?

What are the elements of an effective meeting design?

Some Definitions

Facilitator: One who contributes structure and process to interactions so groups are able to function effectively and make high-quality decisions. A helper and enabler whose goal is to support others as they pursue their objectives.

Content: The topics or subjects under discussion at any meeting. Also referred to as the task, the decisions made, or the issues explored.

Process: The structure, framework, methods, and tools used in interactions. Also refers to the climate or spirit established, as well as the style of the facilitator.

Intervention: An action or set of actions that aims to improve the functioning of a group.

Plenary: A large group session held to share the ideas developed in separate subgroups.

Norms: A set of rules created by group members with which they mutually agree to govern themselves.

Group: A collection of individuals who come together to share information, coordinate their efforts, or achieve a task, but who mainly pursue their own individual goals and work independently.

Team: A collection of individuals who are committed to achieving a common goal, who support each other, who fully utilize member resources, and who have closely linked roles.

Process Agenda: A detailed step-by-step description of the tools and techniques used to bring structure to conversations.

Project: A collaborative enterprise, frequently involving research or design, that is carefully planned to achieve a particular aim.

Process Improvement: A series of actions taken by a process owner to identify, analyze, and improve existing processes within an organization to meet new goals and objectives.

Lean: A production practice that considers the expenditure of resources for any goal other than the creation of value for the end customer to be wasteful, and thus a target for elimination. Basically, lean is centered on preserving value with less work.

Six Sigma: A business management strategy that seeks to improve the quality of process outputs by identifying and removing the causes of defects or errors and minimizing variability. A six sigma process is one in which 99.99966 percent of the products manufactured are statistically expected to be free of defects (3.4 defects per million).

Chapter One
Understanding Facilitation

If you look up the word facilitator in the dictionary, you'll see it described as someone who helps a group of people understand their common objectives and assists them to achieve these objectives without taking a particular position in the discussion.

The goal of facilitation is enhanced group effectiveness.

This role basically did not exist until the middle of the last century, when theorists in the emerging field of behavioral science identified the need for a leadership style that contributed structure to complex group interactions instead of direction and answers.

The work of these behavioral pioneers led to the emergence of a new and important role in which the person who manages the meeting no longer participates in the discussion or tries to influence the outcome. Instead, he or she stays out of all conversations in order to focus on how the meeting is being run. Instead of offering opinions, this person provides participants with structure and tools. Instead of promoting a point of view, he or she manages participation to ensure that everyone is heard. Instead of making decisions and giving orders, he or she supports the participants in identifying their own goals and developing their own action plans.

What Is Facilitation?

A meeting without a facilitator is about as effective as a sports team trying to play a game without a referee.

Facilitation is a leadership role in which the decision-making power resides in the members. This frees the facilitator to focus on creating a climate of collaboration and provide the group with the structure it needs to be effective.

Instead of offering solutions, facilitators offer group members tools they can use to develop their own answers. Facilitators attend meetings to guide members through their discussions, step-by-step, encouraging them to reach their own conclusions.

Rather than being a player, facilitators act more like referees. They watch the action, more than participate in it. They help members define their goals. They ensure that group members have effective rules to guide interaction. They provide an orderly sequence of activities. They keep their fingers on the pulse and know when to move on or wrap things up. They keep discussion focused and help group members achieve closure. They do all of this while remaining neutral about the topics under discussion so as not to interfere with the decision-making authority of the group.

What Does a Facilitator Do?

Facilitation is a helping role.

Facilitators make their contribution by:

- conducting background research to understand the needs of the group and what they hope to achieve
- helping the group define its overall goal, as well as its specific objectives
- preparing a detailed agenda that includes process notes describing how the interaction will unfold
- helping the group create rules of conduct that create an effective climate
- making sure that assumptions are surfaced and tested
- questioning and probing to encourage deeper exploration
- offering the right tools and techniques at the right moment
- encouraging participation by everyone
- guiding group discussion to keep it on track
- making accurate notes that reflect the ideas of members
- helping members constructively manage differences of opinion
- redirecting ineffective behaviors
- providing feedback to the group, so that they can assess their progress and make adjustments
- helping the group to achieve closure and identify next steps
- helping the group access resources from inside and outside the group
- providing a means for evaluation the meeting and seeking improvements

Facilitators bring structure to interactions to make them productive. They plan carefully and then adapt as things unfold. For more on how facilitators organize and manage their work, refer to Chapter Three on the stages of the facilitation process.

What Do Facilitators Believe?

Facilitators operate by a core set of principles. At the heart of these is the belief that two heads are better than one and that, to do a good job, people need to be fully engaged and empowered.

Facilitators believe that two heads are better than one.

All facilitators firmly believe that:

- people are intelligent, capable, and want to do the right thing
- groups can make better decisions than any one person can make alone
- everyone's opinion is of equal value, regardless of rank or position
- people are more committed to the ideas and plans that they have helped to create
- participants can be trusted to assume accountability for their decisions
- groups can manage their own conflicts, behaviors, and relationships if they are given the right tools and training
- the *process*, if well designed and honestly applied, can be trusted to achieve results

In contrast to the traditional model of leadership, in which the leader is viewed as the most important person in the room, the facilitator puts the members first. Members decide the goals, make the decisions, implement action plans, and hold themselves accountable for achieving results. The facilitator's contribution is to provide structure and offer the right tools at the right time.

Facilitating is ultimately about shifting responsibility from the leader to the members, from management to employees. By playing the process role, facilitators encourage group members to take charge.

What Are Typical Facilitator Assignments?

Neutral, third-party facilitators are asked to design and lead a wide variety of meetings:

- strategic planning retreats
- team-building events
- sessions to clarify objectives and create detailed results indicators
- priority-setting meetings
- regular staff meetings
- program review/evaluation sessions
- communications/liaison meetings
- meetings to negotiate team roles and responsibilities
- problem-solving/process improvement sessions
- meetings to share feedback and recommend improvements
- focus groups for gathering input on a new program or product

Differentiating Between Process and Content

The two words you'll hear over and over again in facilitation are process and content. These are the two dimensions of any interaction between people.

The *content* of any meeting is *what* is being discussed: the task at hand, the subjects being dealt with and the problems being solved. The *content* is expressed in the agenda and the words that are spoken. Because it's the verbal portion of the meeting, the content is obvious and typically consumes the attention of the members.

A facilitator's job is to manage the process and leave the content to the participants.

Process deals with *how* things are being discussed: the methods, procedures, format, and tools used. The *process* also includes the style of the interaction, the group dynamics, and the climate that's established. Because the *process* is silent, it's harder to pinpoint. It's the aspect of most meetings that's largely unseen and often ignored, while people are focused on the *content*.

When the person leading the meeting offers an opinion with the intent of influencing the outcome of discussions, he or she is acting as the "content leader." When a facilitator offers tools and focuses on managing member interaction, he or she is acting as the "process leader."

CONTENT	PROCESS
What	**How**
The task The subjects for discussion The problems being solved The decisions made The agenda items The goals	The methods How relations are maintained The tools being used The rules or norms set The group dynamics The climate

It is important to note that, while facilitators are totally unassertive about the content under discussion, they are very assertive in the way they manage the process elements. This assertiveness is needed to deal with conflict, make interventions, and help the group when it gets stuck.

At first glance, facilitation may seem like a rather vague set of "warm and fuzzy," people-oriented stuff. But as you'll learn, it's actually a highly structured and assertive set of practices with a rich set of tools and techniques. Once you understand these techniques and learn how to apply them, you'll immediately see substantial improvement in the overall performance of any group.

Facilitation Tools

As a facilitator you'll have an extensive set of tools at your disposal. These tools fall into two categories: the *Core Practices* and the *Process Tools*.

The *Core Practices,* which are rooted in the manner, style, and behavior of the facilitator, include:

- Staying Neutral
- Listening Actively
- Asking Questions
- Paraphrasing Continuously
- Summarizing Discussions
- Recording Ideas
- Synthesizing Ideas
- Keeping on Track
- Testing Assumptions
- Managing the Climate

Facilitation has a rich set of tools and techniques.

The *Process Tools,* which are structured activities that provide a clear sequence of steps, include:

- Visioning
- Force-Field Analysis
- Brainstorming
- Priority Setting
- Surveys
- Root-Cause Analysis
- Gap Analysis
- Decision Grids
- Systematic Problem Solving

Understanding each of these tools and how to use them is a vital part of any facilitator's job.

Core Practices Overview

Regardless of the type of meeting they're managing or the specific process tool being used, facilitators make constant use of the following core practices. Of these, the first five are foundational. These are in constant use during facilitation, regardless of what other tool are also deployed.

The core practices are the foundation of the facilitator's style.

1. Facilitators stay neutral on the content. Staying neutral on the content of discussions is the hallmark of the facilitator role. Facilitators are neutral outsiders who have no stake in the outcome of discussions. They are there only to provide structure and create a climate of collaboration. When facilitators ask questions or make helpful suggestions, they never do this to impose their views or impact decisions.

2. They listen actively. This is listening to understand more than judge. It also means using attentive body language and looking participants in the eye while they're speaking. Eye contact can also be used to acknowledge points and prompt quiet people to take part.

3. They ask questions. Questioning is the most fundamental facilitator tool. Questions can be used to test assumptions, probe for hidden information, challenge assumptions, and ratify for consensus. Effective questioning encourages people to look past symptoms to get at root causes.

4. They paraphrase continuously. Facilitators paraphrase continuously during discussions. Paraphrasing involves repeating what group members say. This lets people know they are heard and acknowledges their input. Paraphrasing also lets others hear points for a second time and provides an opportunity to clarify ideas.

5. They summarize discussions. Facilitators summarize ideas shared by members at the end of every discussion. They do this to ensure that everyone heard all of the ideas that were put forth, to check for accuracy, and to bring closure. Facilitators also summarize in the midst of discussions to catch everyone up on the conversation and refresh the topic during conversation lulls. Summarizing is also useful to restart a stalled discussion, since it reminds group members of the points already made and often sparks new thinking. In many decision-making discussions, consensus is created when the facilitator gives the group a clear and concise summarization of key points.

In addition to the five techniques described above, there are several additional facilitator techniques that make up the core practices.

Facilitators record ideas. Groups need to leave meetings with complete and accurate notes that summarize discussions. Facilitators quickly and accurately record what's being said. Whether they are using a flip chart or electronic whiteboard, they are careful to use the key words that people suggest and organize the notes into related groupings. There is more on recording group ideas later in this chapter.

They synthesize ideas. Facilitators ping-pong ideas around the group to ensure that people build on each other's ideas. In non-decision-making conversations they do this to build conversation and create synergy. In decision-making conversations they ping-pong ideas to allow each person to add his or her comments to the points made by others until they have synthesized a statement everyone can live with.

They keep discussions on track. When discussions veer off track or when people lose focus, facilitators notice this and tactfully point it out. They place a Parking Lot sheet on a wall and offer participants the option of placing extraneous topics on it for later discussion.

They test assumptions. Facilitators outline the parameters, empowerment levels, and other constraints that apply so that they are understood by all. They are always on the lookout for situations in which misunderstanding are rooted in differing assumptions and probe carefully to uncover these.

They manage the group climate. Facilitators help members set behavioral norms or group guidelines. Then they intervene tactfully when they notice that members are not adhering to their own rules. (See later chapters for more on both norms and making interventions.)

They make periodic process checks. This involves tactfully stopping the action whenever group effectiveness declines. Facilitators can intervene to check whether the purpose is still clear to everyone, the process is working, and the pace is effective or to find out how people are feeling.

They give and receive feedback. Facilitators always have their fingers on the pulse of the group and offer their perspective to help the group make adjustments. They are also receptive to input and invite members to point out anything that needs adjustment. At the end of each meeting, facilitators create mechanisms such as written evaluations or exit surveys to capture feedback for ongoing improvement.

What Does Neutral Mean?

Facilitation was created to be a neutral role played by an unbiased outsider. The role of this neutral third party is solely to support group decision making without exerting influence over the outcome. Facilitators, therefore, always focus on process and stay out of the content.

One of the most difficult things about learning to facilitate is staying within the neutrality boundary because facilitators often have insight into the subject under discussion. The issue of neutrality is further complicated by the fact that a lot of facilitation isn't done by disinterested outsiders, but by someone from within the group who has a real stake in the outcome.

This question of whether or not leaders can facilitate their own teams is so significant that an entire chapter of this book has been devoted to exploring this issue. For now, the discussion of neutrality will focus on the assumption that the facilitator is indeed a third-party outsider.

It's important to note that staying neutral is a challenge, even for neutral outsiders! Sometimes group members say things that are obviously incorrect or they miss important facts. In these instances it's very difficult for the facilitator to hold back and maintain body language that hides a bias.

Regardless of the situation, it's important to understand that neutrality can still be maintained by applying specific techniques.

1st Strategy—Ask Questions

Even though the role is dispassionate, it's important to realize that facilitators don't want to enable bad decision making! If the facilitator has an idea that might help the group, he or she should not withhold it.

If the facilitator thinks that the group is overlooking an idea, the facilitator can introduce that idea as a question that sparks thought. For example, if the group is spinning its wheels because they can't afford new computers, the facilitator can ask: *"What are the benefits of renting new computers as an interim strategy?"*

Through questioning, group members are being prompted to consider another option, but are not being told whether to accept or reject it. The facilitator's neutrality is maintained because he or she hasn't told the group what to do and decision-making control remains with the members.

Neither asking questions nor offering suggestions oversteps the boundaries of neutrality.

2nd Strategy—Offer Suggestions

If the facilitator has a good content idea that the group should consider, it's within the bounds of the neutral role to offer the group a suggestion for their consideration. He or she might say: *"I suggest that you consider researching the pros and cons of renting computers."* Although this sounds like the facilitator has strayed into content, it's still facilitative if the content sounds like an offering, not an order. As with questioning, making suggestions doesn't violate neutrality as long as group members retain the power to decide.

External parties can more easily remain neutral than leaders or peers.

3rd Strategy—Take Off the Facilitator's Hat

If the group is about to make a serious mistake and all of the questioning and suggesting in the world has not worked to move them in the right direction, facilitators sometimes step out of their neutral role to share information that will move the group to a higher quality decision.

In these rare cases, it's important for the facilitator to clearly indicate that he or she is stepping out of the role and explain that he or she is now playing a content role. The facilitator might say: *"I need to step out of the role of facilitator for a minute and tell you that the office location you're considering is not close to any of the rapid transit corridors planned for the next twenty years."*

Since leaping in and out of the facilitator role causes confusion and distrust, taking off the neutral hat should be done very selectively. This role shift is justified when the facilitator is convinced that the group is in danger of making a major mistake and he or she has information or advice that will save the day.

Leaping in and out of the neutral role sends the message to participants that the facilitator is not to be trusted in the neutral role and that their ideas may be overturned at any time.

There's also a huge difference between a neutral, external party asking a question or making a suggestion and a leader who's facilitating doing these things. When an outsider asks questions or offers a suggestion, members feel helped in their decision-making process. When their leader does the same thing, members likely hear an order. Therefore, staying neutral while questioning and suggesting should take into account the power relationship between the players.

Learn to Say *"Okay"*

Learn to say "okay" instead of "good."

When a group member says something that seems like an excellent point, facilitators can be tempted to congratulate that person by saying *"Good point."* or *"Great idea."* Unfortunately, this is a sure way to lose your neutrality, since it makes it appear that you're straying into the content and trying to influence the group's opinion. To avoid this common pitfall, substitute the word *"Okay"* for *"Good point." "Okay"* allows you to acknowledge that you heard the point, but does not indicate any approval on your part.

Whenever you're tempted to say *"I like that idea,"* substitute *"Do the rest of you like that idea?"* After all, you're not there to judge member suggestions, but to help them do that.

When to Say *"We"*

Another of the dilemmas related to neutrality concerns whether or not to say *"We"* and include oneself in the conversation. Here is the simple rule:

Include yourself and say *"We"* when referring to the process:

> *"How are we doing on time?"*
> *"Does this approach we're taking seem to be working?"*
> *"Do we need a break?"*

Use "We" when referring to the process and "You" when reviewing the content.

Use *"You"* when referring to the content:

> *"Let me read back what you've said so far."*
> *"Here are the issues in the order you ranked them."*
> *"Are you satisfied that this has been discussed enough?"*

Saying *"We"* about the content gives the impression that you also own the ideas being generated, while saying *"You"* reinforces their ownership of the meeting and the ideas that emerge from it.

How Assertive Can a Facilitator Be?

Consider this scenario. You're facilitating a meeting in which a key decision has to be made; however, two of the members get embroiled in a conflict. They take turns interrupting one another. Neither one is listening or acknowledging the other. Tempers rise. As the conflict escalates, you stand by helplessly saying nothing, in the mistaken belief that staying neutral means staying totally removed.

This scenario addresses a common misconception that taking a neutral stance on the content of meetings means being passive. This is far from the case. In fact, if you operate on the belief that your role is basically unassertive, you'll be in danger of ending up as nothing more than a note taker or scribe, while conflicts rage around you.

While it's true that facilitators should be non-directive on the topic being discussed, they have to be assertive on the process aspects of any meeting. It's within the parameters of the facilitator role to decide all aspects of the meeting process, including informing members how agenda items will be handled, which discussion tools will be used, who will speak in which order, and so on.

Don't make the mistake of thinking that being neutral on the content also means being neutral about the process!

This doesn't mean that you shouldn't collaborate with members on the session design. Gaining member input is always a good idea since it enhances buy-in. It does mean that process is the special expertise of the facilitator. In matters of process, it's appropriate for you to have the final say.

Just how appropriate and necessary a high level of assertiveness is can be best understood when a group becomes dysfunctional. In these situations, facilitators need to be firm and act like referees, stepping into the fray to restore order to the proceedings.

A high level of assertiveness on process is especially critical whenever there are personal attacks or other rude behavior. All facilitators are empowered to interrupt and redirect individuals so that their interactions become more appropriate. In the section on facilitating conflict, you'll find more on techniques and language you can use for making interventions and managing stormy meetings. By following these practices, you'll be behaving in a way that's anything but passive.

Some assertive actions facilitators take, when the situation warrants it, include:

- insisting on meeting norms
- calling on quiet people
- stopping to check on the process
- calling time-outs and breaks
- intervening to stop rude behavior
- asking probing questions
- challenging assumptions
- adjusting the meeting design
- summarizing discussions
- insisting on closure
- insisting on action plans
- implementing evaluation activities

Mastering the language of facilitation will help you avoid sounding critical or judgmental.

The Language of Facililtation

A specific style of language has evolved that lets facilitators manage interactions without sounding critical or judgmental. The main language techniques are:

- paraphrasing
- reporting behavior
- describing feelings
- perception checking

Paraphrasing involves describing, in your own words, what another person's remarks convey.

> *"Do I understand you correctly that . . ."*
> *"Are you saying . . ."*
> *"What I'm hearing you say is . . ."*

Facilitators paraphrase continuously, especially if the discussion starts to spin in circles or if the conversation becomes heated. This repetition assures participants that their ideas are being heard.

Reporting behavior consists of stating the specific, observable actions of others without making accusations or generalizations about them as people, or attributing motives to them.

> *"I'm noticing that we've only heard from three people throughout most of this discussion."*
> *"I'm noticing that several people are looking through their journals and writing."*

By describing specific behaviors, facilitators give participants information about how their actions are being perceived. Feeding this information back in a non-threatening manner opens the door to improve the existing situation.

New facilitators often make the mistake of not paraphrasing enough.

Descriptions of feelings consist of specifying or identifying feelings by naming the feeling with a metaphor or a figure of speech.

> *"I feel we've run out of energy."* (naming)
> *"I feel as if we're facing a brick wall."* (metaphor)
> *"I feel like a fly on the wall."* (figure of speech)

Facilitators always need to be honest with group members by saying things like: *"I feel exhausted right now"* or *"I feel frustrated."* This lets other people know that it's okay for them to express feelings.

Perception checking is describing another person's inner state in order to check whether that perception is correct.

> *"You appear upset by the last comment that was made. Are you?"*
> *"You seem impatient. Are you anxious to move on to the next topic?"*

Perception checking is a very important tool. It lets the facilitator take the pulse of participants who might be experiencing emotions that get in the way of their participation.

Conversation Structures

One of the most important mental models in facilitation is that conversations fall into two distinct categories: they are either decision making in nature or not. Each type of conversation has distinct features that dictate the techniques used to manage it. Facilitators who understand these two distinct conversation structures can use them to structure and manage discussions.

Non-Decision-Making Conversations

Non-decision-making conversations are those in which group members simply share ideas or information. Examples of non-decision-making conversations include:

- a brainstorming session in which ideas are generated but not judged
- an information sharing session in which group members describe their experiences or update each other
- a discussion aimed at making a list of individual preferences or key factors in a situation

Always know whether you're facilitating a decision-making conversation or one in which no decisions are being made.

During non-decision-making discussions, members state ideas, but there is no element of judging or ranking the ideas. The facilitator simply records ideas as they are presented without the need to check with others to test their views.

Decision-Making Conversations

Decision-making conversations are those discussions in which group member ideas are combined to arrive at either an action plan or a rule that all members must feel they can implement or accept.

Facilitators need to manage decision-making conversations differently because they need to help members arrive at a shared agreement. This involves clarifying ideas, ping-ponging ideas around so others can add their thoughts, making summary statements that summarize the discussion, and recording the group opinion.

In non-decision-making conversations facilitators record what individuals think. In decision-making conversations they record what the group thinks. In summary:

Non-Decision-Making	**Decision-Making**
Conversations in which no action plans or norms are identified or ratified	Discussions in which action plans or norms are identified and ratified
Information sharing	Interactive discussions where members arrive at a decision
Brainstorming	List making
One-way dialogue	Interactive dialogue
Facilitator records individual ideas	Facilitator records group opinion

Starting a Facilitation

Anyone who attends meetings knows that things can easily go off track or be stalled if there's the slightest confusion about the goal, how the discussion will be managed, or the empowerment level of the group. That's why facilitators always ensure that there's clarity regarding the scope of the conversation before they allow people to start discussing agenda items. They create this clarity by using a Start Sequence.

Facilitators clarify the scope of every conversation by ensuring that there's a Start Sequence in place.

Start sequences have three components:

1. The Purpose—a statement that clearly describes the goal of the facilitated discussion. This is what will be discussed. This can take the form of a simple goal statement or it can be more detailed and include a description of the desired outcomes.

2. The Process—a statement of how the session will be conducted. This helps the participants understand how decisions will be made, the speaking order, and any structuring tools that will be used. The process description should also clarify whether members are making the final decision or are simply being asked for input about a decision to be made elsewhere.

3. The Timeframe—a statement of how long the entire discussion will take. In more complex conversations, timeframes should also be provided for segments within the overall discussion.

Start Sequence Variations

Start sequences can be simple or they can be more complex. They can be created ahead of time by getting input from group members, then feeding that input back at the beginning of a discussion. In other situations the start sequence is created at the start of a discussion. In these instances the facilitator can invite group members to make a statement about the purpose of the session and then test that statement with everyone to ensure a shared understanding.

While group member input is almost always sought to define the purpose, facilitators usually provide the process. This is because group members typically don't have enough experience with process design to propose an approach. Describing the process is important because it helps the participants understand how the topic will be managed.

Clearly defining the timeframe for a specific discussion is always a good idea. One of the biggest problems in meetings is that they can drag on. By engaging members in a discussion about time, the facilitator can help members set boundaries. Once members have agreed to timeframes, it's also easier for the facilitator to intervene if agreed to timeframes are being violated.

While it isn't always necessary, it is a good practice to write the details of the start sequence on a flip chart and post this in clear sight. This helps to minimize confusion as the discussion unfolds.

Start Sequence Examples

A Simple Start Sequence

Purpose: To make recommendations to the committee empowered to renovate staff common areas.
Process: Brainstorming of ideas by the large group. Multi-voting to rank the ideas.
Time: 25 minutes.

A Complex Start Sequence

Purpose: To discuss the recent new product launch campaign in order to identify the lessons learned. To leave with a clear list of the things that we did well, the things that we did not execute well, and specific strategies for overcoming the things that we did not execute effectively to improve our next launch.
Process: (1) In a large group, identify all of the things that went well and the contributing factors at every step of the launch. Tell success stories to celebrate the positives and isolate what made each element work.
(2) Individually write all the things that did not go well at each launch stage on index cards. Post these on the walls. (3) Hold a plenary to read all the posted issues aloud. (4) Use multi-voting to rank the execution issues. (5) Break into small groups to apply the steps of systematic problem solving to the four top-ranked items. (6) Hold a plenary to hear the top-ranked recommendations for action from each team and ratify these in the large group.
Timeframe: (1) 35 min, (2) 40 min, (3) 30 min, (4) 30 min (with break), (5) 60 min, (6) 45 min. Total = 240 minutes or 4 hours.

Learn to differentiate between simple and complex start sequences.

During a Facilitation

Once a discussion is underway, it can easily get side-tracked or stuck, even when there's a clear start sequence in place. This can happen for any number of reasons, including that:

- the topic may be more complex than anticipated
- the conversation may have drifted onto another topic
- the process tool being used may not be the right one for the discussion
- the original timeframes may not have been realistic
- individuals may be feeling tired or lose focus

Sometimes there are obvious signs that these things have happened, but there are also lots of times when there are no outward signs that meeting effectiveness is declining. That's why it's vitally important that facilitators periodically stop the action and conduct what is known as a process check.

Process checking is a type of intervention designed to test effectiveness even when there are no outward signs of problems. As with all interventions, the sole purpose of process checking is to restore the effectiveness of the group.

A useful metaphor for process checking is a stop sign. That's because conducting a process check involves stopping the action to shift member focus to the process or how things are going.

Process Checking Structure

There are four basic areas of inquiry in process checking. Facilitators can check just one element, two, three, or all four.

Make it a routine to conduct process checks, even when there are no signs of problems.

1. *Progress:* Ask the members if they think the goal of the meeting is being achieved. Do they think that the purpose is still clear. Do they think that the discussion is still on topic. Do they feel that they're making progress.

   When to check for progress: If few ideas are emerging, when the conversation goes in circles, at periodic intervals, or at points of closure.

2. *Process:* Ask members whether they feel that the tool or approach being used is working. Ask whether any progress is being made using this approach. Ask how much longer they're willing to keep using that approach. Offer other tools.

   When to check the process: When the tool being used isn't yielding results, when it's evident that the designated process isn't being followed, or at periodic intervals.

3. *Pace:* Ask members if things are moving at the right pace.

   When to check the pace: When timelines are not being met or at periodic intervals.

4. *People:* Ask people how they are feeling. Ask whether anyone has lost the thread of the conversation.

   When to check the people: When the meeting has been going on for a while, when people grow silent and withdraw, or when people look tired or frustrated.

Why Process Checks Are Important

Process checks are like an early warning system that lets the facilitator detect problems while there's still time to take corrective action. This avoids the pitfall of finding out at the end of a meeting that things had been off track since the early stages.

Ending a Facilitation

One of the biggest meeting pitfalls is ending without real closure or detailed next steps. When members leave a meeting without action plans, the entire meeting can feel like a waste of time.

Whether ending a short discussion or an extended meeting, facilitators always provide a summary of key points to ensure that there's a shared view of the outcome.

Even if the session was a non-decision-making session, facilitators should provide a concise summary of what was discussed.

Ending a Non-Decision-Making Session

It's essential to bring proper closure to all discussions.

At the end of a discussion during which people shared information, brainstormed ideas, or made lists, it is a facilitator best practice to provide a summary of the points discussed. This allows people to add any points that were missed and it brings closure.

Ending a Decision-Making Session

At the end of a session during which group members made one or more decisions, the facilitator needs to not only recap what was decided, but also ratify the outcome and ensure that clear action steps are in place. This can include:

- reviewing the details of the decision(s)
- checking the decision(s) for clarity and completeness
- ratifying the decision by asking each member whether he or she can live with the outcome to reduce the risks of post-meeting loss of commitment
- identification of next steps and creation of detailed action plans
- troubleshooting the action plan by asking and answering questions like:

"What sudden shifts could change priorities or block implementation?"

In addition to helping group members summarize and plan for action, facilitators also do some or all of the following to end a facilitation:

- round up Parking Lot items and help members identify how to deal with them in the future
- help members create the agenda for their next meeting
- decide on a means of follow-up: either written reports, emails, or personal report-back session
- help members decide who will transcribe the flip-chart sheets
- allow group members to take digital snapshots of flip charts if they have an immediate need for notes
- help members evaluate the session
- thank group members for the privilege of facilitating

For more on ending a facilitated session, refer to page 57.

It's essential to record member ideas so everyone can see the progress being made.

Effective Note Taking

Facilitation has always been very closely linked with those awkward three-legged easels that are the trademark of the profession. Flip charts were invented by the first facilitators, who were looking for a way to enable group members to see what was being said during discussions.

Today, flip charts are quickly being eclipsed by all manner of electronic boards and sticky wall coverings. While this trend is likely to continue, don't be surprised if those gawky flip-chart stands stick around as well.

Writing on a flip chart or electronic board requires slightly larger handwriting than normal so people can see the words across the room. Writing while also asking questions, listening to new comments, and monitoring group body language can be quite a challenge. Don't be surprised if your handwriting suddenly looks like kindergarten scrawl and even familiar spelling is impossible to recall.

Since very few people are able to create flawless flip charts, it's best to relax about spelling and penmanship as long as the main ideas are captured so that the main ideas are clear. This relaxed attitude is especially important when encouraging group members to try their hand at facilitating. Just point out that every piece of flip-chart paper has an imaginary spell-check button that automatically corrects all mistakes.

Install an imaginary spell check button on each piece of flip-chart paper. Ask people to accept that hitting the button corrects all mistakes!

The Rules of Wording

Since facilitators always strive to be neutral to ensure that group members control outcomes, it's important to accurately record what people say without editing too much. If the facilitator changes too many words or adds words that he or she personally prefers, group members will feel that the facilitator has taken control of the proceedings. The first rule of recording ideas is, therefore, to faithfully record what people are saying.

Since people say much more than we can record in a few crisp statements, facilitators are always challenged to create a short, concise summary of the dialogue. This is tricky because it necessitates editing, which can lead to inadvertently changing the meaning of what is said.

Skillful facilitators are good at editing so that the shortened statement still manages to be faithful to the original idea. They do this by following these rules:

Rule 1—Use their words—Listen carefully for the key words that participants use and ensure that these words are included in what is written on the flip chart. Reinforce this by saying things like:

"I'm writing the word 'disaster' because you emphasized it."
"Let me read you back what I wrote to check whether I accurately captured your point."

Be very careful about the words that are recorded.

Rule 2—Ask permission to change words—If participants struggle to articulate a point or are at a loss to find the right words, offer wording, but get member approval to ensure that what's recorded reflects what people intended to say. Say something like:

"I've shortened what you said to this... Is this okay?"
"Can I use the word...?"
"Is it okay to record that this way?"

Recording Tip

A great technique to keep up your sleeve is to ask people to dictate the exact words they want to see recorded. This is useful if you don't understand what they're saying or lost focus momentarily and can't remember what they said. In these situations say something like:

"Tell me what you want me to write down."
"Give me the exact words you need to see on the page."

This technique also works when people have rambled or shared long, convoluted ideas. Rather than taking on the task of creating a summary of their comments, ask them to take responsibility for doing this. Say something like:

"I want to be sure that I capture the important parts of your idea. Shorten that down to one or two crisp sentences that I can record."

Managing the Flip Chart

A flip chart may look innocent enough, but remember that these three-legged beasts can trip you, make your handwriting look like kindergarten scrawl, and make even familiar spelling impossible to recall. Here are some definite *do's* and *don'ts* about flip charts.

These do's and don'ts are as relevant to electronic recording devices as they are to paper flip charts.

DO	DON'T
Write down exactly what members say. While their comments have to be edited somewhat, always use their key words. Check to make sure that what is written captures the meaning expressed.	Write down your personal interpretation of things. These are their notes. If unsure, ask, *"What should I write down?"*
Use verbs and make phrases fairly complete. For example, writing "work group" is not as helpful as "work group to meet Monday at 10 a.m." Always be sure the flip chart can convey meaning, even to someone who was not at the meeting.	Worry about spelling. If you make a fuss, it will inhibit members from getting up and taking a turn at facilitating.
Talk and write at the same time. This is necessary in order to maintain a good pace. Practiced facilitators can write one thing and be asking the next question.	Hide behind the flip chart or talk to it. Unless you are writing, stand squarely beside it, facing the members when reading back notes.
Move around and act alive. There is nothing worse than a facilitator who acts as though he or she is chained to the flip chart. If an important point is being made, walk closer to the person who is talking so you can better pay attention.	Stand passively at the flip chart while a long discussion is going on without writing anything down. Ideas don't need to be in complete sentences before recording them. Make note of key words and ideas. Comprehensive statements can be formulated later.
Write in black, blue, or some other dark color. Use fairly large letters so it can be read from the back of the room.	Use script unless you have great handwriting. Avoid red and pale pastels that are impossible to see from any distance.
Post flip sheets around the room so that people can keep track of what has been discussed.	Monopolize the flip chart.
Whenever appropriate, let others take over both large and small group facilitation. This builds commitment and reinforces the idea that this isn't the facilitator's meeting.	Monopolize managing the meeting process.

Focus on Questioning

The importance of knowing how and when to ask great probing questions can't be stressed enough. In fact, effective questioning is the key facilitative technique. As a facilitator, you need to ask the right questions.

Questions invite participation. They get people thinking about issues from a different perspective. Even when acting as a neutral facilitator, you can share your good ideas by turning them into questions. Questions are also essential for getting feedback from participants about how things are going.

Facilitating is essentially a questioning activity.

Effective questioning means:

- **Asking the right questions at the right time**—select the right type of question and phrase it so that it solicits the best possible response. Then, direct it to the right person.

If You Want to ...	Then ...
Stimulate everyone's thinking	Allow people to respond voluntarily or avoid putting an individual on the spot.
Direct the question to the group	Ask a question such as *"What experiences have any of you had with this problem?"*
Stimulate one person to think and respond	Direct the question to that individual. *"How should we handle this, Bill?"*
Tap the known resources of an expert in the group	Direct the question to that person. *"Mary, you have had a lot of experience in applying these regulations. What would you do in this case?"*

Praising ideas or responding to direct questions will take you out of the facilitator role.

- **Handling answers to questions**—if a group member directly asks you for your opinion about the content, you have three options:
  - Redirect the question to another group member or refer it to the whole group.
  - Defer any questions that are beyond the scope of anyone present and commit to getting back to the group with an answer later.
  - Provide the answer yourself only after signaling that you are no longer playing the process role and are now providing expert input.

- **Responding to comments**—Facilitators often lose neutrality by praising an idea put forward by a member. Be careful when acknowledging the efforts of any respondents. Instead of praising the content by saying, *"That was a good idea!"* switch to praising the process instead by saying something like, *"Thank you for offering that idea."*

Be aware that responding to direct questions can take you out of the facilitator role.

Open-ended questions are used more often and are superior to closed questions.

Question Types

There are two basic question types:

1. **Closed ended**
2. **Open ended**

Each has its uses:

TYPE OF QUESTION	DESCRIPTION	EXAMPLE
Closed	Requires a one-word answer. Closes off discussion. Usually begins with Is, Can, How many, or Does.	*"Does everyone understand the changes we've discussed?"*
Open Ended	Requires more than a Yes or No answer. Stimulates thinking. Usually begins with What, How, When, or Why.	*"What ideas do you have for explaining the changes to our customer?"*

Here are some questioning do's and don'ts:

DO	DON'T
Ask clear, concise questions covering a single issue. Ask challenging questions that will stimulate thought. Ask reasonable questions based on what people know. Ask honest and relevant questions.	Ask rambling, ambiguous questions that cover multiple issues. Ask questions that don't provide an opportunity for thought. Ask questions that most people can't answer. Ask trick questions designed to fool them.

Questioning Formats

When selecting questions to ask, there is a broad range to choose from. It's important to understand how each of these question formats achieves a slightly different outcome.

Different types of questions create specific responses.

Fact-finding questions are targeted at verifiable data such as who, what, when, where, and how much. Use them to gather information about the current situation.

e.g. *"What kind of computer equipment are you now using?"*
"How much training did staff receive at the start?"

Feeling-finding questions ask for subjective information that gets at the participants' opinions, feelings, values, and beliefs. They help you understand views and they contain words like *think* or *feel.*

e.g. *"How do you feel about the effectiveness of the new equipment?"*
"Do you think the staff felt they received enough training?"

Tell-me-more questions can help you find out more about what the participants are saying. They encourage the speaker to provide more details.

e.g. *"Tell me more." "Can you elaborate on that?"*
"Can you be more specific?"

Best/least questions help you understand potential opportunities in the present situation. They let you test for the outer limits of participants' wants and needs.

e.g. *"What's the best thing about receiving a new computer?"*
"What's the worst thing about the new equipment?"

Third-party questions help uncover thoughts in an indirect manner. They're designed to help people express sensitive information.

e.g. *"Some people find that computer training is too time-consuming. How does that sound to you?"*
"There is some concern about overly autocratic managers in many factories. Can you relate to that concern?"

"Magic wand" questions let you explore people's true desires. Also known as "crystal ball" questions, these are useful in temporarily removing obstacles from a person's mind.

e.g. *"If time and money were no obstacle, what sort of a computer system would you design for the department?"*

Sample Probing Questions

The following sample questions are designed to delve more deeply into a problem situation.

- How would you describe the current situation in this department?
- How would your most important customer describe it?
- How would a senior manager describe it?
- How long has this situation been going on?
- What makes it worse? . . . better?
- To what extent are people aware of the problem?
- How do people feel about the situation?
- Why hasn't the problem been solved?
- Who wants change to take place? Who does not?
- Who contributes to the problem?
- How do *you* contribute to the problem?
- If the problem were totally resolved, what would the ideal situation look like?
- On a scale of 1 to 5, how serious would you say this problem is?

1	2	3	4	5
not serious at all		somewhat serious		very serious

- What are the most significant barriers to solving this problem?
- What are the parameters of this initiative? (time, money, materials)
- Are any solutions going to be taboo or unacceptable?
- How would you rate the overall level of commitment to making changes that have been agreed to?

1	2	3	4	5
Low		Medium		High

- What are some boundaries that you would suggest for this initiative?
- What would be the best possible outcome of this initiative? . . . The worst?
- What are the things that will help this initiative succeed?
- What are the potential blocks to success?
- What rules or guidelines would you like to suggest to guide the group interaction?

Best and Worst Facilitator Practices

Some of the best things that a facilitator can do:

- carefully assess the needs of the members
- probe sensitively into people's feelings
- create an open and trusting atmosphere
- help people understand why they're there
- view self as serving the group's needs
- make members the center of attention
- speak in simple and direct language
- work hard to stay neutral
- display energy and appropriate levels of assertiveness
- champion ideas he or she does not personally favor
- treat all participants as equals
- stay flexible and ready to change direction if necessary
- listen intently to fully understand what's being said
- make notes that reflect what participants mean
- periodically summarize related ideas into a coherent summary
- know how to use a wide range of process tools
- make sure every session ends with clear steps for the next meeting
- ensure that participants feel ownership for what has been achieved
- end on a positive and optimistic note

Some of the worst things a facilitator can do:

- remain oblivious to what the group thinks or needs
- never check member concerns
- fail to listen carefully to what's being said
- lose track of key ideas
- take poor notes or change the meaning of what's said
- try to be the center of attention
- get defensive
- get into personality battles
- put people down
- avoid or ignore conflict
- let a few people or the leader dominate
- never check how the meeting is going
- be overly passive on process
- push ahead on an irrelevant agenda
- have no alternative approaches
- let discussions get badly sidetracked
- let discussions ramble without proper closure
- be oblivious about when to stop
- be insensitive to cultural diversity issues
- use inappropriate humor

Facilitator Behaviors and Strategies

Regardless of whether you're a facilitator from within the group or from outside, the team's leader or a member, the following are parameters for facilitator behaviors.

Be Informed—Successful facilitators always gather extensive data about their prospective participants in order to fully understand both their business and their needs. They survey and interview participants, read background reports, and use prepared questions to build a complete picture of the group's situation.

Be Optimistic—Facilitators don't let disinterest, antagonism, shyness, cynicism, or other negative reactions throw them off. Instead, they focus on what can be achieved and strategies to draw the best from each participant.

Be Consensual—Facilitation is fundamentally a consensus-building process. Facilitators always strive to create outcomes that reflect the ideas of all participants equally.

Be Flexible—Successful facilitators always have a process plan for all meetings, yet at the same time are always ready to toss it aside and change direction if that's what is needed. Really great facilitators possess a wide repertoire of process tools and come prepared with alternative strategies.

Be Understanding—Facilitators need to understand that there are great pressures on employees in today's workplace and that antagonistic or cynical behaviors may be a result of high stress levels.

Be Alert—Accomplished facilitators are expert people watchers. They pay careful attention to group dynamics and notice what's going on at all times. They are attuned to noticing both how people interact and how well they're achieving the task.

Be Firm—Good facilitation is not a passive activity, but one that calls for substantial assertiveness. Facilitators should always be ready to step in and redirect an ineffective process.

Be Unobtrusive—The facilitator should do as little talking as possible. The participants should be doing all of the talking. The facilitator says only enough to give instructions, stop arguments, keep things on track and sum up. Trying to be the center of attention or make yourself look important is a misuse of your position.

Facilitating should be an egoless activity. The purpose is to make the group succeed, not to make you look really important and clever. An effective facilitator will leave a group convinced that *"We did it ourselves!"*

Facilitation Cue Card

WEB

To start a facilitation

- Welcome participants
- Introduce members
- Explain your role
- Clarify session goal
- Explain the process
- Set time frames
- Appoint timekeeper
- Create parking lot
- Start the discussion

Remember to:

- Stay neutral
- Listen actively
- Ask questions
- Paraphrase continuously
- Provide summaries
- Record ideas
- Synthesize ideas
- Keep on track

During a facilitation

- Check the purpose
- Check the process
- Check the pace
- Test assumptions
- Maintain the climate

Conflict Management

1. *Vent concerns and feelings*
2. *Solve problems*

To end a facilitation

- Summarize discussions
- clarify and ratify decisions
- Create action plans
- Force-field analysis
- Round up leftover items
- Help create next agenda
- Clarify follow-up process
- Evaluate the session
- Systematic problem solving

Toolkit

Visioning
S.W.O.T/S.O.A.R.
Brainstorming
Multi-voting
Gap analysis
Root cause analysis
Decision grids

Be soft on people—hard on issues!

Practice Feedback Sheets

An excellent way of improving your facilitation skills is to ask a colleague to observe you in action and give you feedback. On the following pages are two different observation sheets for feedback purposes. The first focuses on core practices, while the second emphasizes the key elements in an effective process.

Learning to facilitate takes practice.

Regardless of which sheet is used, the following steps are suggested:

1. First describe what you think you did well. Ask yourself: *"What did I do effectively? What were my strengths?"*
2. Next, invite the observer to offer specific observations of the things that he or she saw you do well.
3. Finally, have the observer provide concrete suggestions for improvements that would enhance your facilitation effectiveness.

Notes

Core Practices Observation Sheet

WEB

Facilitator:

Behaviors that help

__ listens actively
__ maintains eye contact
__ helps identify needs
__ gets buy-in
__ surfaces concerns
__ defines problems
__ brings everyone into the discussion
__ uses good body language and intonation
__ paraphrases continuously
__ accepts and uses feedback
__ checks time and pace
__ provides useful feedback
__ monitors and adjusts the process
__ asks relevant, probing questions
__ keeps an open attitude
__ stays neutral
__ offers helpful suggestions
__ is optimistic and positive
__ manages conflict well
__ takes a problem-solving approach
__ stays focused on process
__ ping-pongs ideas around
__ makes accurate notes that reflect the discussion
__ effectively uses humor
__ looks calm and pleasant
__ is flexible about changing the approach used
__ skillfully summarizes what is said
__ knows when to stop

Behaviors that hinder

__ is oblivious to group needs
__ no follow-up on concerns
__ poor listening
__ strays into content
__ loses track of key ideas
__ makes poor notes
__ ignores conflicts
__ provides no alternatives for structuring the discussion
__ gets defensive
__ doesn't paraphrase enough
__ lets a few people dominate
__ never checks how it's going
__ is the center of attention
__ lets the group get sidetracked
__ projects a poor image
__ uses negative or sarcastic tone
__ talks too much
__ puts people down
__ doesn't know when to stop

Additional Observations:

Process Flow Observation Sheet

WEB

Facilitator:

Clarifies the purpose

Creates buy-in if needed

Checks assumptions

Makes sure there are norms

Establishes the process

Sets time frames

Stays neutral and objective

Paraphrases continuously

Acts lively and positively

Makes clear notes

Asks good probing questions

Makes helpful suggestions

Encourages participation

Addresses conflict

Sets a good pace

Checks the process

Moves smoothly to new topics

Makes clear and timely summaries

Knows when to stop

Facilitation Skill Levels

Mastering the art of neutrality, keeping notes, and asking questions at meetings is not all there is to facilitating. Being a true facilitator means developing your competency at four distinct levels.

Review the skills needed at each of the four levels described below. Then complete the facilitation skills and needs assessment instrument that follows to identify your current strengths and future training needs.

Level 1

Understanding concepts, values, and beliefs; use of facilitative behaviors such as active listening, paraphrasing, questioning, summarizing; managing time; encouraging participation; keeping clear and accurate notes; using basic tools like problem solving and action planning.

Level 2

Mastering process tools; designing meetings; skilled at using the right decision-making method, achieving consensus, and getting true closure; handling feedback activities and conducting process checks; using exit surveys; good at managing meetings in an effective manner; able to help a group set goals and objectives that are measurable; skilled at checking assumptions and challenging ideas.

Level 3

Skilled at managing conflict and making immediate interventions; able to deal with resistance and personal attacks; make design changes on the spot; size up a group and use the right strategies for its developmental stage; manage survey feedback exercises; able to design and conduct interviews and focus groups; design and implement surveys; consolidate ideas from a mass of information into coherent summaries.

Level 4

Design and implement process interventions in response to complex organizational issues; use tools to promote process improvement, customer intimacy, and overall organizational effectiveness; able to support teams in the various stages of team development.

Facilitation Skills Self-Assessment

Assess your *current* skill levels by rating yourself according to the basic skill areas outlined below.

Rank your *current* skill level using the five-point scale below.

1	2	3	4	5
skills lacking		some skills		total mastery

Level 1 **Rating**

1. Understand the concepts, values, and beliefs of facilitation __________
2. Skilled at active listening, paraphrasing, questioning, and summarizing key points __________
3. Able to manage time and maintain a good pace __________
4. Armed with techniques for getting active participation and generating ideas __________
5. Keep clear and accurate notes that reflect what participants have said __________
6. Familiar with the basic tools of systematic problem solving, brainstorming, and force-field analysis __________

Level 2 **Rating**

1. Knowledge of a wide range of procedural tools essential for structuring group discussions __________
2. Able to design meetings using a broad set of process tools __________
3. Knowledge of the six main decision-making approaches __________
4. Skilled at achieving consensus and gaining closure __________
5. Skilled at using feedback processes. Able to hear and accept personal feedback __________
6. Able to set goals and objectives that are measurable __________
7. Able to ask good probing questions that challenge own and others' assumptions in a non-threatening way __________
8. Able to stop the action and check on how things are going __________
9. Able to use exit surveys to improve performance __________
10. Able to manage meetings in an orderly and effective manner __________

Level 3 **Rating**

1. Able to manage conflict between participants and remain composed __________
2. Able to make quick and effective interventions __________
3. Able to deal with resistance non-defensively __________
4. Skilled at dealing with personal attacks __________

5. Able to redesign meeting processes on the spot ______
6. Able to size up a group and use the right strategies for their developmental stage ______
7. Able to implement survey feedback exercises ______
8. Able to design and conduct interviews and focus groups ______
9. Knowledgeable about survey design and questionnaire development ______
10. Able to integrate and consolidate ideas from a mass of information and create coherent summaries ______

Level 4 **Rating**

1. Able to design and implement process interventions in response to complex organizational issues ______
2. Able to facilitate process improvement, customer intimacy, and other organization development activities ______
3. Able to support teams in their forming, storming, and performing stages ______

My current skills (Include all the items you ranked as 4 or 5)

______

______

______

______

______

The skills I most need to work on (Choose the ones most immediately important from all the ones ranked as 1 or 2)

______

______

______

______

______

Chapter Two
Who Can Facilitate

Once the need for facilitation has been identified, there's often confusion about who should take on the role. Should it be an internal staff member, a paid outsider, or the leader of the group?

When to Use an Internal Facilitator

In many organizations, facilitators are considered such an important resource as to warrant the development of a full-time in-house cadre. These are paid organization development consultants who are available to help any team needing assistance.

Facilitators are not always neutral outsiders.

Some organizations that are unable to maintain full-time facilitators maintain a group of part-time volunteer facilitators. These are employees who are interested in developing their group process expertise and who voluntarily take on facilitation assignments in other parts of their organization.

Whether they're full-time professionals or part of a volunteer group, internal facilitators enjoy several advantages over external ones, such as:

- they understand the organization's history and culture
- they have a stake in the health and success of the organization
- they're on hand and easy to access
- they're on salary, so are less costly than hiring outsiders
- they're aware of the resources available within the organization
- they can follow the outcomes of their work and ensure continuity

Despite the many benefits of using internal facilitators, there are also some drawbacks, such as:

- internal facilitators may lack experience with specific facilitation tools or processes
- even when they're very experienced, they may not be seen as credible inside the organization
- they may have a history with some co-workers, who consequently do not see them as neutral
- they may be stretched too far if there are only a few of them to deal with all of the needs of a large organization
- some discussions may simply be too risky to be tackled by an insider, who then has to stay around and live with the fallout

When to Use an External Facilitator

It's advantageous to use an outside facilitator in a number of situations, most notably when total neutrality is essential and the discussions require the full participation of all members. In addition, external facilitators enjoy several advantages, including that:

- they're assumed to be credible
- they may have more experience leading some types of specialized discussions
- people are more likely to trust their neutrality
- they're unencumbered by political or emotional baggage
- they can often afford to take more risks
- they can walk away from the repercussions of sensitive interventions
- they are paid for their efforts, so much can be asked of them

External facilitators are automatically given greater credibility.

Using the services of an external facilitator also has drawbacks, including that:

- they lack data about the group and the organization, such as its history, and therefore need to do considerable research
- they don't fully understand the personalities involved
- they need to build rapport with the client to establish trust
- they don't get to see the initiatives of the group unfold
- they can be costly to hire, especially for longer projects
- they may be unavailable for follow-on work

Organizations that have internal facilitators will still bring in externals for selected assignments. This is usually done for assignments that the internal facilitators feel are too sensitive to tackle or that they lack the expertise to conduct. External facilitators are also brought in to allow the internal team to experience a new technique. Regardless of whether facilitators are external or internal, they all work according to a well-defined set of steps, outlined in Chapter Three.

When Leaders Facilitate

It was established in the last chapter that the facilitation function was designed to be performed by a neutral third party. This neutrality exists to ensure that the person facilitating is able to focus all of his or her attention on providing structure and to encourage people to speak freely. It's important to note that when an internal facilitator takes on an assignment within the organization, he or she is nonetheless operating as a neutral outsider in relation to the internal client.

Most meetings do not have neutral parties on hand to facilitate.

Unfortunately, neutral parties simply aren't available every time there's a need for effective process. As a result, the task of designing and managing meetings almost always falls to leaders. This begs the question: *"Can a leader, who has an interest in the outcome of a discussion, effectively facilitate the members of his or her own team?"*

The simple answer is yes: leaders who have a stake in the decisions being made by their teams can, nonetheless, provide effective process leadership. The catch is that they have to approach the facilitator role very differently. There are two main reasons for this.

First, leaders have a degree of power over the members of their teams. This means that, even when the leader claims to be neutral, team members may be reluctant to speak up and voice opinions that could be contrary to what they think the leader might want to hear.

Second, many leaders have a difficult time switching into the neutral mode. They may want the input of staff, but may be so used to solving problems and making decisions that they can't hold back their opinions.

Given the great need for effective process in every meeting, it's clear that leaders need strategies to provide process to their teams. This means learning to do a delicate balancing act. While it's definitely easier for a neutral party to facilitate, leaders can manage the facilitator role if they're aware of the challenges they face and have strategies to overcome them.

Leaders can facilitate their own people but must use specific strategies.

Facilitation Strategies for Leaders

Challenge 1—Leaders often choose the wrong discussions to facilitate. For example, they may mistakenly try to be neutral during a discussion about a topic on which they have most of the expertise. Also they may try to facilitate an entire meeting, instead of chairing the main portions of the meeting in the usual manner and then selectively facilitating those topics where it's most effective to gain staff input.

Strategy 1—Leaders need to pick the right topics to facilitate. Here are some guidelines about when to facilitate and when to stay in the traditional chair role.

BE DIRECTIVE AND ACT LIKE A MEETING CHAIR TO:	BE FACILITATIVE FOR THE SECTIONS OF THE MEETING IN WHICH IT'S IMPORTANT TO:
give clear instructions	gain the input of team members
share your expertise	create more buy-in and commitment
tell people about decisions that have already been made	encourage staff to take the lead
there's no room for input in non-negotiable situations	accountability can be shared
accountability cannot be shared	the ideas of staff are needed and can actually be implemented
there's no possibility that staff ideas will be implemented	

Challenge 2—Staff may not understand the role of facilitator and could therefore be confused when the leader starts to act in a new way.

Strategy 2—The first few times a leader facilitates, he or she should clearly explain what a facilitator does, the reason for choosing to facilitate at this point in the meeting, and the length of time he or she will be in the role.

The leader needs to be clear that the honest opinions and insights of the members are being sought and that no decision has been made about the matter under discussion. Once group members understand that their leader really is looking for their ideas on a specific topic, they are more likely to accept their leader in the role of a facilitator.

Leaders need to clarify empowerment so that group members understand how much decision-making power they are being given.

Challenge 3—Group members are going to be justifiably leery of taking part in decision making if they sense that the decision is actually going to be made elsewhere anyway.

Strategy 3—When leaders facilitate, they need to be very clear about the empowerment level of the group members. Leaders need to tell followers who will be making the final decision, whether they are making a recommendation that needs final approval or they are merely being asked for their ideas as input to a decision that will be made by someone else. When the decision-making context is clarified, people will be more likely to engage.

Also, a leader who feels he or she needs to retain the power to make the final decision on a matter can tell people that he or she is using Level II empowerment. In this mode, the leader gathers input from staff, but clearly signals to them that they are not making the final decision. This allows the leader to be both the facilitator in the meeting and the decider after the meeting. The key is to be totally open that this is what is happening.

A chart that's useful for clarifying decision authority is the Empowerment Chart below. Leaders should share this chart with their teams and then clarify the specific level that applies to each agenda item before they start to facilitate that topic.

Empowerment Chart

Level I. Telling	Staff are being told about an outcome and have no input
Level II. Consulting	Staff are being consulted for their input, but the final decision will be made elsewhere.
Level III. Participating	Staff are being asked for their ideas and can create action plans, but these plans need approval before they can be implemented.
Level IV. Delegating	Staff can made decisions and act on their ideas without any further approvals.

* For more information on using the Empowerment Chart, refer to page 99 in Chapter Six.

Challenge 4—The leader sets out to facilitate, but the moment group members propose an idea that seems flawed, he or she falls out of the role and takes control.

Strategy 4—Leaders need to accept that facilitating can result in the group coming up with ideas that have flaws. Rather than stepping in to overturn their suggestions, leaders must help group members apply critical thinking skills so that they can discover the gaps themselves.

The leader can help members identify the traits of an effective solution, then have group members use those criteria to test their proposal. Another approach when members seem to be making a low quality decision is to help members objectively list both the upside and downside of their ideas. The leader can then facilitate discussions to help members find solutions to overcome the weaknesses they identified in their own proposal.

Leaders need to learn to ask questions in a very neutral way.

Challenge 5—When a leader asks a question, their staff will naturally try to figure out whether there's a motive behind the question or guess what the leader might have in mind.

Strategy 5—Leaders must ask questions is such a neutral manner that no one can possibly guess at a motive behind them. For example, a leader can ask two questions at once: one that goes in one direction and one that goes in the other. This can sound like: *"Tell me why this is a good idea, then I want you to tell me why this might be the worst thing to do."*

Another strategy is to attribute probing questions to someone else: *"A customer might ask. . . .?"* Leaders can also try to distance themselves from the question by saying: *"I don't necessarily think this is the way to go, but what about . . .?* Finally, the leaders can make a clear disclaimer before asking a question: *"I want you to know that I have no fixed idea about what should be done, so please see my questions as pure fishing expeditions."*

Challenge 6—People may not want to speak up with the leader in the room or say things that they think the leader won't like.

Strategy 6—Leaders have to be on the lookout for opportunities to choose techniques that don't require open discussion. These techniques allow for ideas to be shared both silently and anonymously.

- One example of this is using written brainstorming to gather input from members on slips of paper, then using a form of multi-voting to prioritize suggestions and arrive at the best course of action.
- Another example is using the walls to post issues and then allowing people to wander from topic to topic, sharing views with only the members of the small groups gathered at the same topic.
- Another very neutral approach to making decisions is to have group members anonymously provide their rating of an idea on a decision grid.

For many of these processes, the leader can set up the exercise and then participate as a group member, since no discussion actually takes place. For more information about how to use the process tools mentioned above refer to Chapter Nine.

Challenge 7—The group needs structure to effectively discuss a complex topic, but the leader needs to be in the discussion and no one else is available to facilitate.

When a leader can't facilitate he or she should at least establish the start sequence and offer process tools.

Strategy 7—When the input of the leader is essential to the discussion, he or she may only be able to step into the neutral facilitator role for the start of the discussion to help the group clarify purpose, the process, and the time.

Once the start sequence is in place, the leader can announce that he or she is stepping out of the facilitator role to take part in the discussion. While this is far from ideal, having a clear structure for a discussion is better than operating without having a process in place.

Challenge 8—The group needs structure, but the group is too small to lose someone to play the neutral role.

Strategy 8—In situations when no one is available to facilitate, the group can use a strategy known as *shared facilitation*. This involves taking the roles that a facilitator would normally perform and dividing them among the members so that everyone has at least one facilitation role to play.

After the leader has established the start sequence, he or she divides up the tasks that the facilitator would normally perform, such as keeping track of time, recording ideas, pointing out digressions and parking them, calling on quiet people, summarizing points, identifying when the group is stuck, and so forth.

To deploy this strategy, access the free tool called Shared Facilitation on the website established for this book (www.josseybass.com/go/ingridbens). There you will find detailed role cards and instructions about how to engage the whole team in sharing facilitation roles.

Challenge 9—The leaders' expertise is always in demand, so they are seldom free to step into the facilitator role.

One definition of a leader is someone who creates leaders.

Strategy 9—Whenever leaders facilitate, they should help their people learn to facilitate so that facilitation duties can be rotated. The best way to do this is for leaders to model facilitation and then debrief the various functions so that members can understand the techniques involved. By modeling facilitation techniques, leaders can teach others how to facilitate so that they can share the role and won't always have to stand outside the group.

Once all team members have mastered the basics, the facilitator role can be rotated so that everyone learns to use process tools and becomes skilled at managing complex group interactions. This will do a great deal to build the leadership capacity of all members.

Best and Worst Facilitation Practices for Leaders

WEB

BEST THINGS TO DO	WORST THINGS TO DO
Select the specific discussions that need to be facilitated.	Facilitate when you feel like it.
Tell people you are facilitating and explain the role clearly.	Let people guess at whether you're facilitating or not.
Clearly state the empowerment level of staff in each discussion.	Neglect to clarify whether members are deciding or just being consulted.
Be consistent once in the role: don't leap back and forth.	Periodically make strong points while facilitating.
Avoid leading questions.	Ask the questions that lead people to the ideas you like.
Use tools that create objectivity and anonymity.	Make people stand up and take a stand publicly.
Use neutral body language.	Let how you feel about their ideas show through.
Always set up a start sequence, even when not facilitating.	Have discussions without clear parameters.
Manage group effectiveness, even when not facilitating.	Fail to notice how people are interacting.
Share facilitation tasks with group members.	Be the only skilled facilitator on your team.
Teach others to facilitate.	Do not teach anyone else.

Facilitation As a Leadership Style

Leaders can shift their styles by facilitating more and directing less.

Centuries of directive leadership have created a culture in many organizations where those at the front line are viewed only as doers and totally underutilized as thinkers. This directive leadership style may still work in some settings, but is largely ineffective in today's knowledge-driven organizations.

Workplaces need to harness the intelligence, commitment, and energy of all their members. This level of engagement can only be fostered by a shift in leadership—from telling to asking and from controlling to facilitating.

When leaders shift their approach from controlling and directing to facilitating and empowering, they may feel as though they're giving up control. In reality, there's a substantial amount of power and control built into the role of facilitator. The difference is that this power is exerted indirectly, through the application of process, rather than through control over content.

Consider the following examples of how process can be used to manage in specific situations:

SITUATION	DIRECTIVE APPROACH	FACILITATIVE APPROACH
Members argue.	Give them a pep talk about getting along.	Have members create rules to manage disagreements.
A poor decision is made.	Overturn it, then explain later.	Have members critique their decision using objective criteria.
Members overstep their authority.	Rein them in, supervise more carefully.	Expand empowerment to meet the needs of specific situations.

Facilitative leaders can often get people to do things that directive leaders cannot. When using a facilitative approach, leaders can:

- help groups to identify and commit to achieving ambitious goals
- build and maintain high-performance teams
- run efficient and highly effective meetings
- engage groups in creative thinking
- settle conflicts between groups
- help staff to resolve complex problems
- manage interpersonal dynamics

Facilitation techniques give leaders new tools for managing groups.

Once a leader begins to use facilitation with his or her staff, he or she comes to appreciate that stepping into the neutral role is actually very freeing. When leaders stop giving all the answers, staff must draw on their own resources. Instead of coming with questions, they learn to bring answers. Instead of complying with orders, they participate in creating strategies and plans. When given more decision-making authority, they weigh options more carefully. When a leader adopts a more facilitative approach, group members are challenged to take on more. This develops their autonomy and brings out their leadership potential.

One of the most important outcomes of leaders taking a facilitative approach is that it encourages dialogue. When leaders ask questions, they foster conversation. This give staff an opportunity to vent, to challenge, and to explore new ideas. The net result is a greater sense of partnership. Staff are listened to and feel their views count. Nothing is needed more in these changing times than this capacity in leaders.

Additional Role Challenges

Both internal and external facilitators encounter situations in which they feel that they lack the authority to effectively manage the group's process. For the external facilitator this can be when the client second-guesses the design and meddles throughout the assignment. For internal facilitators this lack of authority often stems from the fact that they're facilitating staff whose rank is higher than their own. Here are some common role dilemmas and solutions.

The Difficult Client

One definition of leadership is someone who creates leaders.

They hire you for your expertise, but then they meddle in your design. Sometimes they may do this in advance, or they may try to change the design in the middle of the meeting. You make interventions, but they don't listen. They just expect you to adjust to whatever they throw at you.

What's going on? They want you to do what they want you to do. They are not very good at following while others lead. They feel they hired you, so you must do as they dictate.

What to do about it: During the assessment phase interviews, ask each group member for suggestions about the rules of conduct that should be in place during the facilitation. Ask individuals to tell you about the things that happen in the group that can make them less than effective. Ask for specific suggestions or norms that could be put into place to eliminate these behaviors.

At the start of the facilitation share the rules that were suggested by the group members during the interviews. Ratify these rules and post them in clear sight so that you can use them to intervene if people violate them.

When presenting the design for the meeting to the group, clarify that you will be leaving the content totally to them, but that you must be in control of the process. Explain that you may consult them about how things are going, but that the decision to use a specific tool or approach needs to rest with you. Gain a firm commitment to this and post this commitment along with the group norms. If people start to meddle, thank them for their input, then politely remind them that the design is your area of expertise.

This will help you avoid clashes between the role of the content leader and role of the process leader during the session.

Facilitating Senior Managers

You' re asked to facilitate for a group of senior managers. This group needs your help, but then resists your efforts to provide structure. They second-guess your approach, are distracted by laptops, go off on tangents, argue, and run in and out. Because they're all senior to you, you don't feel that you can intervene or assert the process.

What's going on? The hierarchy of the organization is spilling over into the facilitation arena. The managers are not used to being facilitated and do not have a clear understanding about the role of a neutral third party.

What to do about it: Clearly explain the role of the facilitator to the group members during the design phase. Help group members understand that you're only neutral about the content and that it is within the boundaries of your role to be assertive about the process.

As with the previous example, also engage the members in setting very specific norms to govern behavior at the session. Ratify these rules at the start of the meeting and then immediately negotiate some power for yourself.

Facilitators need to negotiate specific powers when dealing with senior management groups.

Ask questions like:

- *"What is it okay for me to say or do if I notice that the group's not following its own rules? Can I stop the action and point it out? Can I suggest what would be better?"*
- *"What if I sense that a techniques or approach is not working? Can I change it?"*
- *"Can we agree that you're in charge of the content of the discussion, but that I'm managing how the meeting is run?"*

When group members agree to these things, they are essentially giving you the power you need to manage the group dynamic. This green light from them protects you from recrimination later since the group agreed to your actions in advance.

It's important to note that facilitators don't actually need approval to intervene or manage the process. Facilitators already have that authority in the job description. Asking the group for specific powers to intervene and manage the process is simply done to make it less risky to facilitate senior people assertively.

Facilitating Colleagues

You sit through meeting after terrible meeting. You wish someone would facilitate, but no one steps up to the plate. You wish that you could just start to facilitate, but worry that you do not have the official authority to step in.

What's going on? There's a total lack of process at the meetings. The leader has no idea about how to provide structure. No one at the meeting has any idea that the group needs facilitation.

What to do about it: You can work at three levels to provide structure. The first level is the most covert. Simply provide facilitation support from your seat as it's needed. Periodically mention the time, ask quiet people for their ideas, ask probing questions, point out digressions, help people understand differing views, and so forth.

At the second level, you can speak up and offer the group help when they're struggling. Offer a tool or technique. Wait until they agree that they want your help. Then step in to structure the discussion. At the end of that activity, rejoin the group. The general rule is that if you offer facilitation and members accept, you have been given the role.

At the third level, approach the leader and ask him or her to allow you to facilitate all or specific portions of an upcoming meeting. If the leader is reluctant, tell him or her that learning to facilitate is one of your personal learning objectives and that practice is essential.

Manage the session according to the steps outlined in Chapter Three. At the end of the facilitation activities, help the group evaluate the outcome of your work. Hopefully, this will raise their awareness about the need for a more structured approach to their meetings.

Facilitating Tiny Groups

There are lots of meetings attended by only three or four people. If four people are making a decision and one of them assumes the facilitator's role, this removes a valuable resource from the conversation.

Sometimes it's necessary to wear more than one hat and balance the role of facilitator and group member.

What's going on? There is no neutral outsider available and the group is too small to be able to afford to lose a person to the process role.

What to do about it: There are a number of solutions to this dilemma. The person who offers to facilitate can do any of the following:

- set out the process, establish the start sequence, and then rejoin the group. Then divide the facilitator role among members with one person watching the time, the other noticing digressions, someone recording ideas, and so forth, using the shared facilitation tool mentioned earlier.
- stay in the facilitator role, but write down ideas and give them to a colleague to represent.
- stay in the role and balance the role of facilitator and group member by adding comments only after others have offered their ideas.
- facilitate, but take off the facilitator hat periodically to step out of the role to add comments.

Since all group interactions are more effective when attention has been paid to the process, it's very important that facilitation should not be withheld just because the conditions are less than ideal. There will never be a time when there's a neutral third party available to run every meeting, so leaders and team members who understand facilitation will need to find ways to add process elements to their meetings.

Notes

Chapter Three
Facilitation Stages

One of the biggest mistakes a facilitator can make is to come to a meeting without assessing the needs of the group or preparing design notes for the session. Before facilitating any meeting, be aware of the specific stages involved to ensure proper planning and implementation.

While the following steps were originally designed to be followed by external facilitators, these steps are equally relevant for internal facilitators.

Preparation is almost as important as the facilitation itself.

Stages in Conducting a Facilitation

1. Assessment and Design
2. Feedback and Refinement
3. Final Preparation
4. Starting a Facilitation
5. During a Facilitation
6. Ending a Facilitation
7. Following Up on a Facilitation

While thorough preparation is absolutely essential, experienced facilitators will tell you that most agendas rarely run exactly as planned. Some discussions will inevitably take longer than planned or it may become evident that agenda items need to be addressed in a different order. Any number of things can result in the need to adjust the design mid-stream. In fact, making adjustments on the fly is an art that all facilitators need to master.

Over-prepare, then go with the flow!

1. Assessment and Design

The first step in ensuring success in any facilitation is to make sure the meeting design is based on sufficient and adequate information. If you're coming from outside, ask the group's leader to send a letter to all members, informing them that an external facilitator has been hired and that you will be contacting them to gather background information for the agenda.

It's common practice to start by interviewing the person who asked you to facilitate the meeting. It's important, however, not to stop there and assume that that person is necessarily aware of all the needs and interests of the rest of the group. If you also gather information from a cross-section of group members, you will be able to build a more complete picture of the situation, as well as check out the key assumptions.

Any experienced facilitator will tell you that there's nothing worse than basing the design of a meeting on what one person has told you, only to find that no one else in the group agrees with that assessment!

To assess the needs and status of the group, you can use one or more of the following techniques:

- one-on-one interviews
- surveys
- group interviews
- direct observation

Details about each technique are shown on page 59 in Chapter Four.

Any time you gather data about a group, a summary of that information *must* always be fed back to the members. This can be done by providing the members with a written summary of the assessment notes or by writing key points on a flip chart and reviewing them briefly at the start of the session.

Ensure that the members understand and ratify the meeting design.

Facilitators also review any data they collected at the start of the facilitation to help everyone understand how the final agenda was created. If you've done a good job of interpreting the input of group members, the design of the meeting should sound as if it flows directly from the information gathered.

Once all relevant background information has been collected and tabulated, and once you feel confident that you understand the group's needs, you can create a preliminary design. This includes identifying the objectives of the session and writing an agenda with detailed process notes. In Chapter Ten you will find examples of process notes that show the format and level of detail that is needed.

2. Feedback and Refinement

Once you've created a proposed agenda for the session, share the design with group members to gain their approval. Sharing the details about how the process will unfold will help group members understand the structure of the meeting. If your design is intended for a large group or a complex event, such as a planning retreat, this feedback activity will need to be more formal. It's common to meet with a representative subgroup of members so that they can hear the feedback from the data gathering and review the proposed design being presented. If the design is for a smaller, less complex meeting, it may suffice to discuss your agenda ideas with the leader and/or representative member.

Don't back down too easily if you feel the group really needs to discuss certain items.

There are many situations in which the group's members may not like what you've designed. There's often a gap between what a group wants and what the facilitator thinks they need.

If a disagreement about the design arises, you need to ensure that all viewpoints are heard and that optional designs are considered. If the group has valid reasons for not wanting to do an exercise (that is, the content is too sensitive to discuss, the objectives have changed, etc.), respect that concern.

On the other hand, you should stand firm and assertively promote your design, especially if meeting members are reluctant to use participatory techniques or have a history of dysfunction. In these cases, listen to their objections, then help them understand your recommendations. Sometimes what they want is not what they need.

Once agreement on a final workshop design has been reached, you can write a brief summary of both the feedback and final version of the design and send it to the group's representatives. This written memorandum will help reduce the potential for misunderstanding.

3. Final Preparation

Professional facilitators spend as much time preparing for a facilitation session as they do leading the actual event. The industry standard for session leaders is one day of preparation for each day of facilitation. Some complex sessions even have a ratio of two days of preparation for each day of facilitation.

Here are common time allocations for facilitation assignments:

Workshop/ Meeting Length	Interview Time	Design Time		Total Time
1-day workshop (18 people)	1/2 day	1/2 day	→	2 days
2-day workshop (18 people)	1 day	1 day	→	4 days
2-day retreat (60 people)	1 day	3 days	→	6 days

Facilitators spend as much time planning as they spend in front of groups.

Establishing Behavioral Norms

Meetings run best when there are clear rules or norms to follow. These are sometimes difficult to set at the start of the meeting. People may feel reluctant to speak up and suggest rules or there may be pressure to start discussing the agenda items.

For these reason, it's a good strategy to ask group members to suggest norms during the assessment phase. This can be done during one-on-one interviews or via emails. The suggested norms can them be shared and ratified at the end of the feedback meeting.

If you do not build norms during the data collection, you can build a set of norms at the meeting to discuss and ratify the agenda. Simply ask members specific norming questions like: *"What rules will ensure that this meeting runs smoothly?" "What should the rule be about laptops and handhelds?" "What about people coming and going?" "What about side conversations?" "What should the rule be about bringing up topics not on the agenda?"*

Combine member responses into a coherent set of meeting guidelines. Bring these forward for at the start of the facilitated session.

For more about setting norms see page 67 in Chapter Four.

Negotiating Personal Power

It is also important during the final preparation phase to negotiate for sufficient power to be able to manage the dynamics of the group. This is especially important for internal facilitators.

Lack of power comes from a number of sources. The most obvious power vacuum is experienced by staff who are asked to facilitate a meeting filled with upper-level managers. To gain the power needed to manage the interactions of powerful groups, facilitators always negotiate for what they need.

Facilitators have no real power, so they need to negotiate for whatever power they need.

In addition to helping the group set norms during the feedback session, ask members pointed questions about what it's okay for you to say and do during the facilitation. Make sure they understand that you may need to come across as assertive to keep things on track. Prompt conversation with questions such as:

- *"If people start to side-chat, run in and out, or talk over each other, what is it okay for me to say and do? Is it okay for me to tactfully point these things out and steer people back?"*
- *"What if there are arguments or someone goes on for too long? Can I point these things out and suggest what would be better?"*

In most cases the group members will tell you that they want you to be assertive and will give you the permission you need to intervene whenever necessary. In some cases they may even go further and ask you to stop them if they fall into ineffective patterns.

Strictly speaking, facilitators do not need the approval of group members to intervene. Managing group interaction is, after all, the job of the facilitator. The reason for negotiating the right to assertively intervene is to set group member expectations. Once members have stated that they want you to assertively manage the meeting dynamics, it gives you the green light you need to step in. In fact, you can start these interventions by saying something like: *"I'm going to remind you that you asked me to stop you if this happened."*

Gaining the group's permission to intervene assertively creates a group norm that protects the facilitator from being seen as overstepping traditional boundaries. Negotiating the right to intervene assertively gives facilitators the green light to do their jobs and protects them from having career-limiting moments.

Final Preparations

Here is a checklist of the things that should be part of the final preparation:

__ finalize the design and share it with group members
__ clarify the things that you are responsible for doing, as well as the things that the group will take care of
__ negotiate the power that you need to be able to manage effectively
__ check the suitability of the meeting location

__ help the meeting organizer prepare a letter detailing meeting logistics and the final agenda for distribution
__ identify all needed materials and supplies
__ write all workshop materials and handouts
__ print all materials and handouts
__ prepare important flip-chart sheets ahead of time or program that data into the electronic board you will be using

The members of the group are typically responsible for sending notices, arranging and paying for logistics such as accommodations, ensuring that a suitable meeting room is available, arranging and paying for printing, keeping clear minutes of the proceedings, transcribing all flip-chart notes, monitoring to ensure follow-through on all action plans, and evaluating the results.

Be the first to arrive and pay attention to room set-up.

4. Starting a Facilitation

As the facilitator, you should always be the first person to arrive for any meeting. This ensures that there's time to make last-minute seating changes in the room, post the agenda and survey data, test the equipment, and so on. Arriving early also allows you to greet participants as they arrive. Chatting informally with members not only helps break the ice, but it gives people an opportunity to get to know you.

Room set-up is critical for facilitated discussions. A large room with modular furniture works best for both large group and subgroup settings. Huge boardroom tables, on the other hand, are detrimental to creating an atmosphere conducive to dialogue. A long table also tends to reinforce hierarchical patterns and discourage eye contact between members. When facilitating large groups, it's best to seat people at round tables spaced evenly around the room. Small table groups of five to eight are ideal.

Start each discussion by specifying:
- ***Purpose,***
- ***Process,***
- ***Time.***

If using flip charts, make sure there's ample wall space for posting the notes that will be generated throughout the day. If the design calls for breaking into small group discussions, you will need to arrange for an easel for each subgroup in addition to the one you will be using at the front of the room.

Over time you'll develop your own personal approach for beginning a session; here's a checklist to get you started:

__ introduce yourself and give a brief personal background

__ clarify the role you'll be playing as the facilitator

__ clarify the roles to be played by any other members

__ go around the room and have members introduce themselves by name and perhaps position, especially if there are people present who don't know each other

__ take care of all housekeeping items

__ conduct a warm-up activity to relax the group; make sure this fits with the time available and activity focus

__ review any data collected from members; have key points posted for all to see and answer questions about the data

__ review the agenda: clarify the objectives and desired outcomes of the entire meeting and also of subsections

__ review the behavioral norms or meeting guidelines that will be in effect during the session

__ remind members of the powers that they have given you to intervene

__ if the group already has a set of meeting guidelines, review these and invite members to add any new norms that may be needed. If the group does not have norms, either help them create a new set of norms for the session or ratify the ones that were developed during the design phase. Post the norms on a wall within clear view of all members

__ set up a parking lot sheet on a side wall to keep track of digressions

__ make a clear statement about the purpose of the each agenda item; describe the expected outcome of each agenda item

__ describe the process tools and techniques to be used in each discussion

__ set out the timeframe for each agenda item; in some settings set a timer or appoint a timekeeper

__ start the discussions

Once the preliminaries have been dealt with, start the first discussion. Remember to begin each new agenda item with a clear start sequence. Refer to page 18 in Chapter One for more on start sequence components.

5. During a Facilitation

The key contribution of the facilitator during any meeting is to provide the necessary structure and guidance so that discussions are consistently effective. Facilitators do not act like passive scribes while members discuss agenda items.

Facilitators actively monitor how the discussion is going.

Remember that facilitators are only neutral about the content of discussions. They are not neutral about the process or how things are unfolding. The best facilitators continually monitor group interaction and intervene whenever they see group productivity decline.

On page 127 in Chapter Seven you can find an overview of the way facilitators use language to make interventions when they see ineffective behavior. This is an essential tool for helping maintain group effectiveness.

In addition to making interventions, facilitators also periodically make process checks. Refer to page 20 for a more detailed description of the four elements of every process check. These are either made at the halfway point of any discussion or are conducted whenever there are signs that things are not going well.

During all discussions be sure to:

__ ensure that all members participate
__ ask probing questions to further the conversation
__ paraphrase continually to acknowledge and clarify ideas
__ monitor time and maintain an appropriate pace
__ keep track of ideas by making concise notes
__ make periodic summaries to restart or end conversations
__ encourage members to adhere to their ground rules
__ make interventions if behaviors become ineffective
__ keep the group on track and park off-topic items
__ help members objectively discuss differences of opinion
__ make periodic process checks to test overall effectiveness
__ stop the action if the discussion spins its wheels and ask members why they are stuck and what will move them forward
__ adjust the process and offer additional tools when needed
__ maintain a high energy level and positive tone

Discussions that end without closure waste everyone's time!

6. Ending a Facilitation

A common problem in many meetings is lack of closure. Lots of things are discussed, but there's no clear path forward. One of the facilitator's key contributions is to ensure that decisions are reached and detailed action steps are in place before moving to the next topic or adjourning the meeting.

Here are some ways you can help bring effective closure to a meeting:

__ provide summary statements about what has been decided and record these on a flip chart or electronic board
__ ensure that each action item is accompanied by detailed action plans
__ round up items not discussed at the meeting, including those placed in the parking lot, and help members create a plan of action for each
__ help the group create an agenda for the next meeting
__ decide on a means of follow-up: written reports/group session
__ clarify your role in any follow-up meetings
__ help members decide who will transcribe notes
__ make digital snapshots of all flip-chart notes as a back-up
__ post an exit survey to get member views about the session
__ hand out a written evaluation so that group members can provide more detailed comments about the session and offer you feedback on your work
__ thank the participants for the opportunity to facilitate

7. Following Up on a Facilitation

No matter how formal or informal the facilitation process has been, following up with the group is always a good idea. If the facilitation consisted of a brief meeting, you might simply call the group leader to determine the extent to which the session helped the group become more effective. If the session was a major decision-making workshop or retreat, encourage the group leader to send out a written follow-up workshop evaluation to the members.

Unless it was formally agreed that you would conduct the follow-up activity, you can leave any post-session reports to the group's members. This ensures that they, not you, assume accountability for the implementation of the ideas emerging from the session. Your role may be to merely remind the group about the need for follow-up and to provide them with a format for reporting results later. In some cases, you may negotiate with the group to facilitate a follow-up meeting at which post-meeting progress is discussed and evaluated.

Seek personal feedback to support your growth as a facilitator.

Seeking Feedback on Your Facilitation

When an outside facilitator works with a client, it's routine procedure for him or her to seek feedback about his or her personal performance from the person who made the contract. This is done to ensure that the client is satisfied and helps preserve the client relationship.

It's equally important for internal facilitators to seek feedback. They may not be worried about cultivating a client, but should be thinking about whether or not their work contributed to the overall health of the organization.

Gaining detailed and specific feedback is essential to all facilitators seeking to increase their personal effectiveness. The feedback process can be done in person or over the phone. The format is often as simple as asking fundamental questions like:

- *"What did I do well?*
- *"What was my most valuable contribution?"*
- *"What did I do during the session that was especially effective?"*
- *"What did I not do well?"*
- *"In what instances could I have done something differently?"*
- *"What specific improvements could I make to my facilitation work to become even more effective?"*

Chapter Four
Knowing Your Participants

Getting to know the people you'll be working with is an essential first step in designing any effective meeting. Before you facilitate, you need to know whether the people coming to the meeting are:

___ total strangers who have never met before and won't be together again after this single, special-purpose meeting
___ total strangers or people who only have a passing acquaintance with each other, but who will be working together again after this meeting
___ a group of people who know each other, have interacted for some time, and get along well
___ a group in turmoil who meet periodically and either spin their wheels in frustration or become embroiled in conflicts that are rarely resolved
___ a high-performance team with a solid track record of achievements, made up of members with highly developed people skills who are good at managing their internal group dynamics

Always take the time to get to know your participants.

Conducting an Assessment

Experienced facilitators never take a group or situation for granted! They know that surface appearances may not be accurate. They also know that what they are initially told may not be totally accurate.

It's very important therefore to do careful background research and design a process that matches the group's actual circumstances. This research is done using one or more of the following techniques:

- *One-on-one interviews*—These allow you to question people about the state of the group and member interactions. This is the best way to get people to be open and candid when there are sensitive issues.
- *Group interviews or focus groups*—This is an effective strategy when the subject is not sensitive and when there are too many people to interview singly. Group interviews let you observe the group dynamics before the actual facilitated session.
- *Surveys*—These allow anonymous gathering of information from all group members. They make it possible to compile answers to the same questions from each member. They also generate quantifiable data.
- *Group Observation*—This involves attending a group meeting to watch people interact. This is the best way to learn about the interpersonal dynamics of members. Group observation is most helpful when conducting team interventions in mature groups.

Assessment Questions

Whether you are asking questions in one-on-one interviews or in survey format, the following questions will be helpful in preparing for a facilitated session:

It's essential to ask the right probing questions to really get to know a group.

What's the history of the group?

What's the proudest achievement of the members?

How familiar are members with each other?

Are there clear goals?

Are there team rules or norms?

In meetings, does everyone participate or do a few dominate?

To what extent is there a high level of openness and honesty among members?

Do members listen to and support each other's ideas?

How does the group handle differing views or conflict?

How are important decisions made?

Do people usually leave meetings feeling like something has been achieved?

How would you describe the group atmosphere?

Are meetings thoroughly planned and structured or are they basically freewheeling?

Does the group ever stop to evaluate how it's doing and make corrections?

What's the best thing about the group? What's the worst?

How do people feel about being part of this group?

Describe a recent incident that illustrates how members typically interact.

Are there any reasons why members might not be open and say what they really think?

Why do you need facilitation support? Is there any opposition to this?

What's the worst thing that could happen at this meeting? What could be done to ensure that this doesn't happen?

What advice would you give me in planning this session? Is there a particular pitfall that I need to be aware of?

On the following page, you will find a survey that can be used to assess the internal climate of any group.

Group Assessment Survey

1. How familiar are members of this group with each other?

1	2	3	4	5
We are passing acquaintances		Some of us know each other		We are a high-performance team

2. Are there clear goals for the group?

1	2	3	4	5
We have no stated goals		Not sure about the goals		We have clear goals

3. Does the group have a clear set of rules to manage interactions?

1	2	3	4	5
No norms exist		We have but don't use our norms		We have and use our norms

4. Describe the typical participation pattern.

1	2	3	4	5
A few people dominate		Participation varies from topic to topic		Every voice is heard

5. How much honesty and openness is there in this group?

1	2	3	4	5
People hide what they really think		We are somewhat open		We are very open and honest

6. How good are members at listening, supporting, and encouraging each other?

1	2	3	4	5
We don't do this at all		We try but don't always succeed		We are consistently supportive

7. How do members typically handle differences of opinion?

1	2	3	4	5
Lots of emotional arguing		It varies		We always debate objectively and respectfully

Group Assessment Survey, cont'd

While all trout are fish, not all fish are trout! Likewise, all teams are groups, but not all groups are teams.

8. How are important decisions usually made?

1	2	3	4	5
Lots of voting and giving in		Our approach varies		We strive for consensus

9. Does the group usually end its meetings with a sense of achievement and clear action plans?

1	2	3	4	5
Never		Sometimes		Always

10. How would you describe the atmosphere between members?

1	2	3	4	5
Hostile and tense		Satisfactory		Totally relaxed and harmonious

11. How would you describe the group's meetings?

1	2	3	4	5
Unstructured: waste of time		Satisfactory		Well planned and productive

12. Does the group ever stop and evaluate how it's doing and then take action to improve?

1	2	3	4	5
Never		Sporadically		Consistently

Note: Refer to the instructions about how to do survey feedback on page 192 in Chapter Nine.

Comparing Groups to Teams

In order to design appropriate meeting processes, it's important for you to be aware of the differences between groups and teams, as well as the significant differences between teams at the forming, storming, norming, and performing stages of their development.

Teams have a common goal created by the members.

What Is a Group?

A group is a collection of people who come together to communicate, tackle a problem, or coordinate an event. Even though they may meet often, they're a group and not a team because they have specific traits. In most groups. These include:

- individual members operate under their own separate parameters and work to achieve individual goals
- groups usually operate by externally set procedures such as the traditional rules of order
- group members usually have separate roles and responsibilities and tend to work on their own
- individuals in groups operate at various levels of empowerment depending on their position in the organization
- little or no time is devoted to building relationships, and issues of cohesion and trust are rarely addressed
- groups rarely focus on feedback between members to improve group effectiveness
- leadership and decision-making power typically lie with the leader

Since group members typically pursue their own individual goals, groups tend to exhibit "I"-centered behavior when debating. This generally makes a group more competitive and argumentative than a true team. When each person strives to obtain what's best for him- or herself, conflict tends to be handled in a more adversarial manner.

How Is a Team Different?

In contrast to a group, a team is a collection of people who come together to achieve a clear and compelling common goal that they have participated in defining. To the members of a true team, that goal is more important than their own individual pursuits. It's this factor that gives a team its cohesion.

A team also creates a set of norms or rules of conduct that define the team's culture. While groups tend to be run by a chairman, according to pre-published rules of order, a team runs itself by guidelines created by the members.

It's important to know whether you're facilitating a team or a group.

Team members also jointly plan work and coordinate roles much more than groups. Their work lives are linked together, and they depend on each other.

When team members have differences of opinion, they tend to debate the ideas rather than argue points of view. They aren't out to gain personal victory, but to arrive at the best solution for the good of the whole.

While the members of a group generally have only the level of authority inherent in their positions within the organization, teams seek and attain higher levels of empowerment. Drawing on each other to make better decisions, a team typically evolves toward greater autonomy in managing its work.

There is a definite sequence of stages a team goes through in order to reach high performance levels. A group does not tend to follow this pattern. One reason is that team membership is more permanent. While a group can operate with members coming and going, the membership of a team needs to be more consistent. In fact, if a member leaves a team, the team may need to return briefly to the forming stage in order to integrate a new member.

Whether teams are created to stay together for just a few meetings or for years, they tend to develop more trust and openness than do most groups. Members have bought into the idea of working together and have made a commitment to common action. This helps create the comfort that many people need before they can freely express their ideas and concerns.

Group/Team Comparison Chart

A GROUP	A TEAM
Individual "I" focus	Collective "We" focus
Individual purpose	Common goal
Operates by external rules of order	Operates by own set of team norms
Operates alone	Has linked roles and responsibilities
Individuals have position authority	Seeks and gains empowerment
Meets irregularly	Meets regularly
Focuses on information sharing and coordinating	Focuses on problem solving and process improvement
Has a fixed chairperson	Shares leadership role
Fights to be right	Debates to make sound decisions
Is closed	Open and trusting
May like each other	Shares a strong bond

Do All Groups Need to Become Teams?

The simple answer is no. While teams have some distinct advantages over groups, not all groups should be developed into teams. A group should stay a group if:

- the members will only be together for a short time
- it's only supposed to do one simple task
- its purpose is solely to share information
- the same people don't come to every meeting
- there's no regular or frequent pattern of meetings
- there's no real common goal or need for linked roles
- work is best planned and managed by isolated individuals
- there's no intent to empower
- there's no support for teamwork in the organization
- leadership styles are controlling and directive

Conversely, it is advantageous to do team building with any group if:

- there's a need to create a high level of cohesion and commitment to a common goal
- there's an ongoing task for the group to accomplish
- a consistent set of people will be working closely over an extended period
- members need to link and coordinate their roles closely
- higher empowerment levels would improve effectiveness and performance

Not all groups need to become teams, but all groups can be encouraged to act like teams.

As a facilitator, you should be aware that you will probably work with more unstructured groups than with real teams who have been through a team-building process. This is one of the things that makes facilitation a challenge, as unschooled groups are likely to be unstructured, more argumentative, and less skilled at effective interpersonal behaviors.

Getting a Group to Act Like a Team

Even when a group isn't destined to become a team, it's a good idea to take some tips from rudimentary team building and get members to at least act like a team while they're working together. This can be achieved by incorporating the following key team-building activities right into the agenda. These activities include:

___ getting people to participate in creating a clear goal for the session or topic being discussed

___ creating a set of norms or rules to guide conduct, posting these rules, and encouraging members to use them to maintain effective behaviors

___ clarifying roles and responsibilities for all action plans generated by the group

___ clarifying all accountabilities to ensure that everyone is clear about expected results

___ training members in effective behaviors such as how to handle conflict and make decisions

___ conducting process checks, building in feedback loops and other evaluation mechanisms so that members can take responsibility for improving how the group functions

Understanding Team Stages

If you're working with a true team, you need to know that teams develop through four distinct stages. Each of these stages has unique characteristics and must be facilitated differently.

Forming—The Honeymoon Stage

Forming teams requires context setting and relationship building.

Forming is the first stage of team development. It starts when members are first brought together. In the forming stage, members tend to be optimistic, and expectations are usually high. At the same time, there's also anxiety about fitting in and being able to achieve the task. Despite these early anxieties, forming is generally a honeymoon for most teams.

Members of forming teams are usually shy. They hold back until they know each other better. People are guarded with their comments. No one is sure exactly how he or she fits into the new team.

This stage is also characterized by an overdependence on the leader. Members want to be given a clear mandate, structure, and parameters.

Forming can last anywhere from a few weeks to several months, depending on how often the team meets and how quickly the team completes the team formation agenda.

Facilitating the Formation of a Team

When facilitating a new team, you need to be optimistic and encouraging in order to ease anxieties. You also need to:

__ make sure there's clarity about the mandate and parameters for the new team

__ help the members collaborate to create a goal that achieves the stated mandate

__ break the ice with activities that create comfort and disclosure

__ help members develop norms or rules of conduct

__ identify tasks and specify roles and responsibilities

__ provide structure for all discussions

__ manage participation so that everyone has an equal say

__ provide training in decision making and effective behaviors

Creating Team Norms

A major difference between groups and teams is that teams have clear norms or rules set by the team's members. These rules are used by the members to control their own and their peers' behaviors.

Developing norms is essential at the forming stage. Once they're in place, the norms are posted, referred to when behaviors become less than desirable, and amended as the team matures.

Norms are always developed by team members. It only makes sense that bringing in guidelines from outside and asking the members to adhere to them will be largely ineffective. Members will be more likely to follow rules that they've created together.

People are more likely to buy in to rules that they have created together.

Norms will vary somewhat with each team, but these are some of the most common. When you facilitate a discussion to generate a set of norms, you can ask questions to prompt members to consider adding to these rules.

- We will listen actively to all ideas
- Everyone's opinions count
- No interrupting while someone is talking
- Anyone can call time out if he or she feels the need for a break
- We will be open, yet honor privacy
- All team discussions will remain confidential
- We will respect differences
- We will be supportive rather than judgmental
- We will give helpful feedback directly and openly
- All team members will offer their ideas and resources
- Each member will take responsibility for the work of the team
- We will respect team meeting times by starting on time, returning from breaks promptly, and avoiding unnecessary interruptions
- We will stay focused on our goals and avoid getting sidetracked
- When we have a difference of opinion, we'll debate the facts of the situation and not personalities
- We will all work to make sure there are no hidden agendas and that all issues and concerns can be dealt with openly by all members

Once a set of norms is in place, they can be used as the basis for making interventions. When group members violate one of the rules that they set, you can point this out and ask them to honor their agreements. Suggestions about how to word these types of interventions can be found on page 130 in Chapter Seven.

Storming—The Potential Death of the Team

Storming is a natural stage of team development and not necessarily a sign that a leader is being ineffective. In this stage, members experience a discrepancy between their initial hopes for the team and the realities of working together. Conflict arises and everyone knows that the honeymoon is over. Storming can take place for a variety of reasons, including:

Many factors contribute to storming.

Problems with the task: Some aspect of the work may be too difficult for members. Work loads may be unrealistic. Members may be resisting taking on more power and responsibility. The task itself may be unclear, or the members may not have bought into the task.

Problems with the process: There may be generally unstructured approaches to work. Meetings may lack process and tend to be ineffective.

Lack of skills: People may be lacking some of the skills they need to do their jobs. This can result in them not doing their part or in others having to do parts of their work for them. Often teams also lack basic problem-solving and meeting-management skills. As a result they are unable to make complex decisions or handle interpersonal conflicts.

Ineffective leadership: If a team leader is overly controlling while the members are trying to flex their muscles, members may challenge the leader in order to gain more power. If a leader is disorganized, communicates badly, or fails to follow through on commitments, these things can throw the team into storming. Additionally, many traditional leaders don't know how to build and maintain a high performance team and hence are unable to manage the stages of team growth.

Interpersonal conflict: People may discover that they like some members, but dislike others. Cliques can form. People may also clash over personal styles. Some people may not be pulling their weight. Others may talk too much or try to dominate. All of these interpersonal challenges contribute to team storming.

Organizational barriers: There may be a variety of systemic blocks and barriers that can cause team strife. These can include lack of funding, understaffing, shifting priorities, lack of true support for team initiatives, and lack of adequate empowerment to get things done.

Dysfunctional behavior is often a symptom of storming rather than its cause.

Beware of the Iceberg!

Many people mistakenly think that storming is essentially caused by interpersonal conflict. While conflict is a reliable sign of storming, think of it more as a symptom rather than the cause. In other words, people may be in conflict as a result of problems with the task, lack of process, skill gaps, ineffective leadership, or organizational barriers.

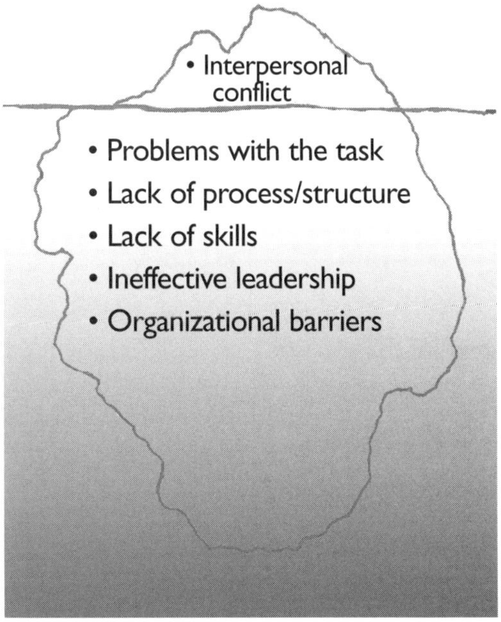

It's important not to take storming personally.

Reacting to Storming

One of the most reliable signs that a team has entered the storming stage is for members to feel dissatisfied with their dependence on someone else's authority, most often that of the team leader. It's not unusual for members to challenge or even reject the leader at this stage. Power struggles can also take place as team members compete for authority.

Due to these power struggles, team members can become distracted. As people become embroiled in interpersonal stress, productivity plummets. Frustration increases. This is accompanied by a corresponding decline in morale. There's a feeling of ineffectiveness, and there may be meetings during which little is achieved. People start to wonder whether the team is a good idea, since so much time seems to be wasted.

If you find yourself facilitating a team that is storming, be careful not to take this personally. Check to see whether you're thinking:

- *"This is awful. Things are falling apart!"*
- *"They're not being very nice."*
- *"I can't facilitate these people!"*

Storming is the hardest state to facilitate.

In order to survive storming, you need to believe:

- *Storming is okay. It's a normal stage."*
- *"They don't hate each other; they're just storming."*
- *"This is energy I have to channel into solutions."*

Signs of Storming

Use the following checklist to raise your awareness of storming. It can help you determine whether the team you're working with is in this sensitive state:

___ the team isn't achieving its goals
___ people express frustration with blocks and barriers
___ people say the team makes them feel drained of energy
___ people no longer think the team is a good idea
___ there's no attention to process or how the team functions
___ there's a tendency toward arguing viewpoints instead of debating ideas
___ people don't listen actively or support each other's ideas
___ the team is divided into factions
___ members vie for power with and against each other
___ members demonstrate their lack of respect for the leader
___ meetings go in circles; little is achieved
___ there's a tendency to complain and second-guess decisions
___ people are often late, absent, or don't do their homework
___ no one wants to take responsibility; follow-through is poor
___ some people have withdrawn; they no longer participate
___ members go to each other after meetings to air their concerns
___ people express frustration with blocks and barriers
___ people say the team makes them feel drained of energy
___ people no longer think the team is a good idea

Facilitating a Team in Storming

Storming is the most difficult stage to facilitate because feelings are running high. Facilitators need to handle storming carefully in order to remain absolutely neutral and not take sides in any debates. Storming also demands a high degree of assertiveness. Facilitators need to:

___ expect and accept tension as normal
___ stay totally neutral and calm
___ create an environment in which people can safely express feelings
___ honestly and openly admit that there's conflict
___ help members identify issues and solve them together
___ invite input and feedback
___ make interventions to correct dysfunctional behaviors
___ assertively referee heated discussions
___ train members in group skills
___ facilitate communication

When a Team Storms

Consider the best and worst things to do during storming:

BEST ACTIONS	WORST ACTIONS
→ Surface all problems to get them on the table to be solved	→ Ignore problems
→ Create norms that make it safe to discuss problems. Encourage members to debate ideas in a non-personal way	→ Avoid all arguments
→ Offer clear options and encourage members to take control	→ Take back control
→ Help members identify strategies and action plans	→ Tell people what to do
→ Help members identify their problems and resolve them	→ Take a punitive attitude

The outcome of storming depends on you!

The Facilitator's Role in Storming

If you're facilitating a group that's storming, you will need to intervene. This means stopping the team's work to draw members' attention to the process.

During this phase it's more important than ever to stay totally neutral and offer the group tools with which they can solve their own problems. It is also important to recognize that receiving feedback and addressing issues are scary activities. One of the first things that the facilitator needs to do, therefore, is to help members identify the rules of the feedback activities that will ensure that everyone stays safe. Refer to page 86 in Chapter Five for details on how to establish what are known as safety norms.

Key facilitator strategies include:

- helping members create ground rules for giving and receiving feedback that ensure everyone stays safe
- offering feedback and inviting input
- encouraging problem identification and problem solving
- offering training and support to team members
- further sharing of power
- mediating in personality clashes
- coaching and counseling individuals
- encouraging others to take on leadership roles
- supporting members while they make improvements

Norming is the gateway out of storming to high performance.

Norming—The Turning Point

By now you will be familiar with the idea of norming as an activity to set team rules. In addition to that, norming is also a transitional stage that a team must move through to get past storming and into performing. In the norming stage, the team confronts its problems and resolves them. New rules or norms are set. When team members adhere to these new norms, the team is able to transcend storming.

During norming, members face their issues, accept feedback, and act on it. This results in improved team performance. It is a sad truth that most team leaders do not understand the stages of team development and, thus, are not able to comprehend that when a team storms, this is the cue to help the team engage in norming activities to get through storming to high performing.

There are four distinct types of norming activities to help a team that has entered the storming phase:

___ ***Survey feedback:*** This involves creating and circulating a survey that probes into the problems the group is experiencing. This could be a meeting effectiveness survey, a team effectiveness survey, or a project progress survey. Survey results are returned to the members for their analysis. Members use the data to identify problems and generate ideas to resolve them

As a team exits storming and enters the norming phase, they stop to assess how they're doing in order to make improvements.

___ ***Force-field analysis:*** Team members engage in a frank discussion during which they analyze what's working well and what's not. They them generate solutions for each item identified in the not-working category.

___ ***Interpersonal feedback:*** Team members give each other constructive feedback about what they're doing that's effective and what they could do better using tools that are designed to keep them safe. This includes peer feedback and dialogue with the leader.

___ ***New norm development:*** In some cases team members can simply be engaged in reviewing their existing norms and adding any new norms that could help them be more effective. This can be aided by turning the existing norms into a survey that allows members to rate the extent to which each norm is being successfully applied.

Performing—The Ultimate Team Growth Stage

If norming is managed successfully, team members will create new norms and action steps that help them perform more effectively. Once the main blocks and barriers have been removed, members will be ready to focus on their work without distraction. Everyone wins here. Productivity goes up. So does morale.

Once the a team reaches the performing stage, you will notice that:

- time and resources are used efficiently; more work is done
- everyone behaves in a supportive way
- everyone shares power by rotating leadership roles
- members take turns facilitating
- members feel committed and bonded
- the official leader is treated as a valued member
- the team evaluates and corrects continuously
- decisions made are typically of high quality
- conflicts are seen as constructive debates, rarely getting heated or emotional

It's important to know that every team that reaches the performing stage exhibits these traits. They all have:

1. A clear team goal that has been created by the team and that dovetails with organizational targets.
2. Established ground rules or norms to monitor and improve the team.
3. Detailed work plans that define tasks, clarify roles and responsibilities, lay out a schedule of events, and specify the performance expectations of the team.
4. Clearly defined empowerment so that members know which decisions they can make.
5. Clear and open communication between members and with those outside the team.
6. Well-defined decision-making procedures that help the team know which decision-making approach to use
7. Beneficial team behaviors that reflect good interpersonal skills and positive intent to make the team successful
8. Balanced participation so that everyone is heard and the team's decision making isn't dominated by one or two strong personalities
9. Awareness of group process along with regular initiatives to improve how the team functions
10. Well-planned and executed meetings with detailed agendas

Know the signs of performing.

Facilitating a Performing Team

You'll find that the easiest group to facilitate is a high-performance team whose members have learned to manage their own conflict and who have highly developed interpersonal skills. But that doesn't mean your job's over yet. When facilitating a high-performance team, facilitators must:

___ collaborate with members more to obtain their input
___ share facilitation duties
___ offer expertise to the team
___ help the team reward and celebrate success
___ offer to observe and give feedback to further improve the team

Adjourning—The Final Stage

In today's fast-paced world, teams are always coming together to take on projects and just as quickly adjourn. When a team completes its work, it is essential that there be some closure on the experience. This phase is also an opportunity for the team leader and the members to learn from their experience so that they will be even better team members on their next project.

Successfully adjourning a team involves:

__ helping members conduct a retrospective to identify the critical success factors of the team

__ helping members identify the weaknesses or mistakes the team made in order to learn lessons that can be applied to future ventures

__ allowing members to speak to the whole team about their personal experiences and to express appreciation for fellow team mates

__ encouraging team members to celebrate their success

Facilitating Team Adjournment

High-performance teams are the easiest to facilitate.

The main role of the facilitator in the adjournment phase is to provide process tools that allow the team to reflect on past experiences. This can include facilitating some or all of the following activities:

__ a team retrospective meeting such as described on page 223 in Chapter Ten

__ a team closure meeting during which members say goodbye and celebrate their success

WEB

Facilitation Strategies Chart

Use the following quick reference chart to match facilitator approaches with the team-development stage being experienced by the group or team.

Stage	Key Elements	Facilitator Strategies
Group	May be strangers	Warm-up exercises
	"I" focused individuals	Create a common goal
	Lack of compelling goal	Create and use norms
	Lack of norms	Clarify and link roles
	Roles loosely linked	Define accountabilities
	Individual accountabilities	Provide clear process
		Encourage participation
		Evaluate meeting effectiveness

Main Strategy—To provide structure and support

With effective structure, any group can act like a team.

Stage	Key Elements	Facilitator Strategies
Forming	Members unsure	Build buy-in
	Uncertainty	Disclosure exercises
	Low trust	Create a common goal
	Need direction	Create and use norms
	Commitment low	Define accountabilities
	Group skills unrefined	Clarify roles and responsibilities
	Overdependence on leader	Provide clear process
		Encourage participation

Main Strategy—Build team spirit and comfort while providing lots of structure for activities

Forming lays the foundation for team effectiveness.

Stage	Key Elements	Facilitator Strategies
Storming	Problems with the task	Expect and accept tension
	Lack of process	Stay neutral and calm
	Lack of skills	Create safety for expressing feelings
	Ineffective leadership	Honestly admit there's conflict
	Blocks and barriers	Help members identify and solve issues
	Cliques form	
	Conflict emerges	
	Frustration sets in	Invite input and feedback
	Animosities develop	Make interventions
	Leader is rejected	Assertively referee conflict
	Power struggles	Encourage communication

Main Strategy—To listen, address conflict, referee assertively, and resolve issues collaboratively

Storming is the "make it or break it" stage.

Norming requires honesty and disclosure.

Stage	Key Elements	Facilitator Strategies
Norming	Members "own" problems Conflicts are resolved Power issues are resolved Team redefines its norms Performance problems corrected Create empowerment plans	Offer methods for feedback Help solve problems Invite personal feedback Offer further training Support members while they make improvements Share power Mediate personality clashes Coach and counsel individuals Share the leadership role

Main Strategy—To help the group refocus and support team improvement efforts

Performing teams can manage their own process.

Stage	Key Elements	Facilitator Strategies
Performing	High productivity Conflicts managed by members High commitment to goal Roles and responsibilities clear Members behave in a facilitative manner Team continuously improves itself Members feel committed and bonded	Collaborate with members on process Rotate facilitation duties Offer your expertise Help the team recognize and celebrate success

Main Strategy—To build agendas together, share facilitation responsibilities, collaborate, act as a resource

Stage	Key Elements	Facilitator Strategies
Adjourning	Reviewing outcomes Sharing feedback Celebrating success	Support member candor Express thanks Provide feedback tools that offer safety Enjoy the team's celebration

Main Strategy—To encourage candor, provide safe tools for review and feedback, help members celebrate success

Team Effectiveness Survey

Provide your candid opinion of your immediate work team by rating its key characteristics on the five-point scale shown below. Circle the appropriate number on each scale to represent your evaluation. Do not put your name on this. Return the survey in the envelope provided.

Administer a team survey periodically, then use the steps of the survey-feedback process to identify improvement strategies.

1. Goal Clarity

Are goals and objectives clearly understood and accepted by all members?

1	2	3	4	5
Goals and objectives aren't known, understood, or accepted.				Goals and objectives are clear and accepted.

2. Participation

Is everyone involved and heard during group discussions or do only the views of a few dominate?

1	2	3	4	5
A few people tend to dominate.				Everyone is active and has a say.

3. Consultation

Are team members consulted on matters concerning them?

1	2	3	4	5
We are seldom consulted.				Team members are always consulted.

4. Decision Making

Is the group both objective and effective at making decisions?

1	2	3	4	5
The team is ineffective at reaching decisions.				The team is very effective at reaching decisions.

5. Roles and Responsibilities

When action is planned, are clear assignments made and accepted?

1	2	3	4	5
Roles are poorly defined.				Roles are clearly defined.

6. Procedures

Does the team have clear rules, methods, and procedures to guide it? Are there agreed-upon methods for problem solving?

1	2	3	4	5
There is little structure and we lack procedures.				The team has clear rules and procedures.

Team Effectiveness Survey, cont'd

7. Communications

Are communications between members open and honest?

1	2	3	4	5

Communications are not open. — Communications are open.

8. Confronting Difficulties

Are difficult or uncomfortable issues addressed or are conflicts avoided?

1	2	3	4	5

Difficulties are avoided
Little direct conflict management. — Problems are attacked openly and directly.

9. Openness and Trust

Are team members open and candid or are feelings mostly hidden?

1	2	3	4	5

Individuals are guarded and hide motives. — Everyone is open and speaks freely.

10. Commitment

How committed are team members to meetings and other team activities?

1	2	3	4	5

Team committments often missed. — There is total commitment.

11. Support

Do members help and support each other?

1	2	3	4	5

Little evidence of support. — Lots of support.

12. Risk Taking

Do individuals feel that they can try new things and take risks?

1	2	3	4	5

There is little support for risk. — There is lots of support for risk.

13. Atmosphere

Is the team atmosphere informal, comfortable, and relaxed?

1	2	3	4	5

The team spirit is tense. — The team is comfortable and relaxed.

Team Effectiveness Survey, cont'd

14. Leadership

Are leadership roles shared, or do the same people dominate and control?

1	2	3	4	5

A few people dominate. — Leadership is evenly shared.

15. Evaluation

Does the team routinely stop and evaluate how it's doing in order to improve?

1	2	3	4	5

We rarely evaluate. — We routinely evaluate.

16. Meetings

Are meetings orderly, well planned, and productive?

1	2	3	4	5

They're unstructured and unproductive. — They're well organized and productive.

17. Fun

Is there an "esprit de corps," or sense of fun, on this team?

1	2	3	4	5

No fun here! — We have lots of fun on this team!

Administer a team survey periodically, then use the steps of the survey-feedback process to indentify improvement strategies.

Notes

Chapter Five
Creating Participation

Imagine yourself at the start of a meeting with a group of people you barely know and nothing is working. No one is answering questions. Some people look bored. Others seem openly uncomfortable. Everyone looks nervously at the leader whenever you ask a serious question. You start to wonder how you're going to get through the rest of the session!

Anticipate the potential blocks to active participation and come armed with strategies to overcome them.

Given the pressures of today's workplace, it would be naive to go into most meetings assuming that people will automatically be enthusiastic and engaged.

The first step in getting people to participate actively is to understand why they may be holding back. Consider these barriers to participation:

- ____ people may be tired from attending too many meetings
- ____ some participants may be exhausted from overwork
- ____ some members may be confused about the topic being discussed
- ____ there may be a lack of commitment to the topic of the meeting
- ____ some people may be insecure about speaking in front of others
- ____ talkative members may shut down quieter people
- ____ junior staff may be reluctant to speak up in front of those they consider to be their superiors
- ____ there may be a low level of trust and openness in the group
- ____ some traumatic event may have occurred recently that has left people feeling stressed or withdrawn
- ____ the organization may have a history of not listening to or supporting employee suggestions

When planning any facilitation session, it's important to assess how participative the members are likely to be. Before the meeting or workshop, find out:

- ____ whether or not the participants are used to group discussion
- ____ whether or not members have well-developed group skills such as listening, debating, decision making, etc.
- ____ how committed people are to the topic
- ____ how the members feel about speaking in front of their leader and each other
- ____ whether relationships between participants are healthy or strained
- ____ if there has been a recent layoff, personal tragedy, or other event that might distract participants
- ____ if members have well-developed group skills such as listening, debating, decision making, etc.
- ____ whether the organization is likely to support the ideas of the group

Understand what it takes for people to open up.

Creating the Conditions for Full Participation

All facilitators need to understand the basic prerequisites for full participation. In general, people will participate fully if they:

- ____ feel relaxed with the other participants
- ____ understand the topic under discussion
- ____ have had some say in the planning process
- ____ feel committed to the topic
- ____ have the information and knowledge needed for fruitful discussion
- ____ feel safe in expressing their opinions
- ____ aren't interfered with or otherwise unduly influenced
- ____ trust and have confidence in the facilitator
- ____ are comfortable and at ease in the meeting room
- ____ feel that the organization will support their ideas

A good rule is that the more resistant a group is likely to be, the more necessary it is to hold interviews or focus groups with members beforehand to let them voice their concerns and so that you can become aware of blocks.

Removing the Blocks to Participation

Ensuring that people participate actively is a primary facilitator responsibility. There's no excuse for running a meeting that a few people dominate or in which half the group sits in silent withdrawal. Here are some strategies to encourage involvement.

Break the Ice

Even in a group in which members know one another, they need to engage in icebreakers to set a warm and supportive tone. With groups of strangers, warm-up exercises are even more important. They help people get to know each other and they help to remove barriers to speaking in front of strangers.

Books of icebreakers abound. Do your homework so that you have at least four to six simple warm-up exercises handy at all times.

Be clear about your role, especially with groups unaccustomed to working with facilitators.

Clarify Your Role

In situations when people seldom work with outside facilitators, they may hold back if they're confused about your role. Near the beginning of any facilitation, tell participants why you're there and what you'll be doing. Be clear about your neutrality and explain that your role is to make sure everyone is committed to the work of the group and that discussions stay on track. This will help people feel that you are there to support them.

Share your hopes for a successful meeting, so people know you intend to help make it a productive session. Don't be afraid to brag about yourself a bit. Some participants will be more likely to speak up if they have confidence in your skills.

Clarify the Topic

At the start of each discussion, take pains to ensure that each topic is clearly defined. For example, if the meeting is being called to solve a problem, ensure that there's a clear problem statement. Regardless of the type of session, a clear statement that describes the purpose of the meeting is a must. Refer back to page 18 in Chapter One for an outline of a clear start sequence.

You add to topic clarity by having a well-defined outcome statement for each discussion. This means helping the group to agree on what they hope to achieve. This aligns the participants.

Clarify the purpose and outcome of each discussion.

You can ensure topic clarity by:

____ reviewing the history of the situation so that everyone understands the need for the meeting

____ sharing any input members gave during surveys, focus groups, or interviews to emphasize member participation in creating the agenda

____ engaging participants in ratifying a purpose statement to ensure understanding and commitment

____ stating the goal of the facilitation so everyone is clear about the desired outcome

Always be alert to the fact that even a crystal-clear purpose can quickly become cloudy. Members can become sidetracked or bring in new elements that obscure the purpose of the meeting. Performing effectively in your role means checking often to make sure that members remain clear about the goal and haven't become confused.

Even a clear purpose can become obscure.

It's quite common for facilitators to have to redesign a session in midstream. That's what makes facilitating such a challenge! The wise facilitator is always open to making changes. Forcing a group to continue a discussion that no longer makes sense, just because it's on the agenda, is a sure formula for disaster.

Create Buy-In

In today's work environment, it's folly to run any meeting without gaining buy-in from the participants.

Never assume that people have automatically bought in!

In many organizations, speculation about layoffs is rampant. People may also be weary after wave upon wave of new initiatives. These and other forms of turbulence have left people cynical. They may be feeling vulnerable. They are often working longer hours than in the past. In many organizations, employee morale is low, while distrust levels are high.

Facilitators who naïvely think that people are automatically going to be keen and enthusiastic about coming to their session are in for a shock. These days it's especially important to check with your group to determine how many of the following harsh realities are going to be a factor:

Incorporate a buy-in process at the start of major meetings.

____ people are working extra hours and don't know how they'll find the time to attend the session

____ facilitated meetings usually generate many action plans; this is extra work no one wants

____ the organization may not support the ideas generated by employees; priorities could shift tomorrow

____ a feeling that the improvements gained will only benefit the organization

On the simplest level, getting people to commit is achieved by asking them to answer the universal buy-in question: *"What's in it for me?"* The most basic buy-in exercise is to pair participants at the start of a session and ask them to spend several minutes discussing two questions in relation to the purpose of the meeting:

"What's the gain for the organization?"
"How will you personally benefit?"

After the partner discussion, participants can recount their own or their partners' responses. Record all comments on a flip chart or electronic board. The responses to the second question amount to the participants' psychological buy-in to the session. This process seems simple and is actually very effective.

You will need to vary the buy-in question for different situations. To create buy-in for a process-improvement exercise, ask members: *"How will your work life be made easier if we manage to simplify this process?"*

To create buy-in for joining a team, ask group members: *"What are the benefits for you personally if you become a member of this team?"*

To create buy-in for learning a new skill, ask group members: *"How is learning to operate the new software going to benefit you?"*

If the pre-workshop diagnostics reveal that participants feel that there are lots of reasons for them not to participate, you'll need to spend more time on the buy-in activity.

Some leaders need to be coached ahead of time not to dominate.

In these cases of heightened levels of resistance, you can add two additional questions to the partner buy-in exercise:

"What's blocking me personally from participating? Why might I be reluctant?"
"What will it take to overcome these blocks? Under what conditions, and with what support, will I consider giving this my total commitment?"

When you record member responses to the two questions above, you'll actually be negotiating group member participation. People may say they'll participate if they receive assurances of senior management support or that they'll participate wholeheartedly if they receive training or other needed assistance. Having their conditions on the table lets you assess the extent to which participants are feeling blocked.

The problem with identifying the blocks is, of course, that you may not be in a position to negotiate some of these items. If you anticipate strong resistance, it's best to surface the blocks in the planning phase. This allows the time that may be needed to negotiate support issues before the session. The results of these negotiations can then be presented at the beginning of the session to help relieve concerns and help people move forward with commitment. In high-resistance situations, managers and even senior managers may have to be present at the start of a meeting to respond to the needs expressed by the members.

For more on dealing with resistance, refer to page 134 in Chapter Seven.

Identify Organizational Support

If the pre-workshop interviews reveal that people are worried that the session might be an exercise in futility, be sure to express these concerns to the appropriate manager. There's nothing worse than having members balk at the start of a workshop because they feel that their ideas won't be supported. If organizational barriers can be dealt with before the session, that will help create a much more positive environment.

Recognize past frustrations that members have had with organizational blocks.

Another common strategy is to have a senior manager attend the kick-off portion of the meeting to offer his or her personal assurance of support for the group's efforts. If this isn't possible, a memo or letter from the senior manager expressing strong support is a help.

If there's no senior management support and barriers are a major concern, it's important to surface these issues and discuss them, rather than pretend they don't exist. Set aside time at the end of the workshop to identify the barriers, analyze them, and generate solutions for getting around them. This way, members will feel that the discussions have been honest and that they have strategies for dealing with the realities they face.

Manage the Participation of Leaders

If you're acting as an external facilitator, you'll often be asked to plan and manage meetings in which the group's leader is present. This leader may be the person who contacted you and may consider him- or herself to be your client.

Leaders are accustomed to influencing the outcome of meetings. For this reason it isn't unheard of for a leader to ask a facilitator to lead a discussion in the direction of a predetermined outcome that he or she favors. The harsh reality is that some people see facilitation as a sophisticated tool for manipulating others.

To avoid misunderstandings, the facilitator and leader need to meet ahead of time to discuss a number of key points. The leader needs to be tactfully told that:

- while the leader is very important, a facilitator's client is always the whole group, including the leader
- facilitation is a democratic undertaking in which the leader agrees to accept decisions made by the whole group

- the facilitator needs to be able to contact participants before the session via interviews or surveys to gain their input

If the pre-session interviews with staff reveal that the leader is domineering or that staff are reluctant to speak in the leader's presence, it's a wise strategy to speak with the leader before the session and ask him or her to hold back. Every experienced facilitator can recount stories of situations in which the group leader had to be taken aside at a break and asked to temper his or her participation.

One strategy is to have the leader attend a kick-off session, pledge support, and then leave while the staff work. At the end of the session, the leader returns to hear final recommendations, give any needed approvals, and offer to act as an ongoing sponsor of member activities.

If you're lucky enough to have a group whose leader is open and regarded as a valuable colleague by team members, encourage him or her to play an active role in the entire discussion. After all, one of the reasons leaders bring in facilitators is so they can participate and offer their expertise to the group.

Help Participants Prepare

People may not participate if they haven't done their homework.

People often hold back at meetings because they aren't prepared. To prevent this from happening in your sessions, make sure that the purpose of each meeting is clearly communicated ahead of time so that people have time to prepare. If a meeting is expected to be complex, identify who needs to do which portion of the homework. When people do adequate pre-work, they gain confidence and participate more actively.

Create Targeted Norms

Some discussions require special, targeted norms.

All groups need guidelines to ensure a cooperative and supportive climate. As mentioned many times in this book, all groups should have a set of core norms that were created with the input of all the members. Having a basic set of norms may not, however, be sufficient to handle the task of getting through a sensitive conversation.

If the conversation the group is about to have is sensitive in nature, the group will need to create specific, targeted norms to ensure that members feel safe enough to participate freely. Safety norms are an example of targeted norms. In this case, norms are created to reduce the risk to participants for speaking out.

Help members create safety norms by asking these questions:

"What rules are needed for today's conversation to ensure that everyone can confidently share what's on his or her mind?"

"Under what conditions are you going to be able to speak freely?"

Some examples of safety norms are

- everything will be said with positive intention to improve the team and the workplace

- all ideas will be listened to with respect
- all discussions will be held strictly confidential: what's said here stays here
- both people and issues will be handled with sincerity
- there will be no retaliation on the basis of anything that is said during this meeting
- no one will personally attack another person
- all feedback must be phrased in a constructive manner and be aimed at helping the other person or the team
- if anyone feels emotionally stressed, he or she can call time out or request a change in how a topic is being handled
- everyone will use neutral body language and avoid things like finger-pointing, eye rolling, or sighing
- instead of arguing personal points, we will listen to and acknowledge each other's ideas first
- anyone can call a time out if he or she is confused about the topic or feels that the discussion is going off track

Creating the right norms will encourage people to participate.

We all know that these rules will be most effective if they're suggested by the group members themselves. There's one exception to this general rule, however. If you are conducting an intervention with a group of people who are not only extremely dysfunctional, but unlikely to suggest effective rules for themselves, you will have to suggest the rules. In these types of circumstances, clearly state that you will be unable to facilitate unless these rules are accepted by each member. Read the rules aloud at the start of the session and then go around the entire group and ask each person if he or she is willing to adhere to the rules. This will not only set the right climate, but will provide you with the leverage you need to intervene if people act inappropriately.

Targeted norms may also be necessary in a variety of other situations.

If conflict is anticipated, ask a norming question such as:
"What rules are needed today to ensure that we have healthy debates instead of heated arguments"?

If any members of a group are *reluctant to participate*, ask:
"What would encourage participation and make everyone feel that their ideas are important?"

If the group has trouble *staying on track*, ask:
"How do we ensure that this meeting stays on track and on time?"

Make Eye Contact

Use eye contact to include quiet people.

This is a simple but very important technique to improve participation. Facilitators need to make eye contact with everyone, not just the active participants. By looking directly at quiet people, you're telling them that they haven't been forgotten. Sometimes your glance will prompt them to speak up. The eye contact must, of course, be friendly and encouraging, not piercing and intimidating.

Humor needs to be in proper proportion.

Use Humor

Everybody enjoys a good laugh, and humor is a great way to create an open atmosphere. You can introduce humor into your sessions by having people reveal amusing anecdotes about themselves, showing cartoons, or stopping periodically for a team game. Running jokes and amusing comments are all useful as long as they're in proper proportion and don't detract from the focus of the session.

Room setup is important in encouraging conversation.

Set Up the Room to Encourage Participation

It's a factor that may not seem major at first mention, but how you arrange a room will greatly affect how group members interact. Theater-style seating is the worst possible arrangement for facilitating an interactive discussion. People automatically assume that they'll be spoken at. It also discourages people from looking at each other.

Large boardroom tables have an especially stifling effect on people. This is very unfortunate, as many large companies have huge boardroom tables stuck squarely in the middle of many of their best meeting rooms. If a boardroom-style space is your only option for your session, break people into pairs, trios, and foursomes as often as possible to keep everyone talking.

If you have any choice in the matter of seating, select a large room with smaller, modular tables. Small tables arranged in a large horseshoe for whole group sessions is a good arrangement for groups with more than twelve members.

When a group has more than twelve people, it's important to break it into small groups of five to six people. People can sit in their small groups, even when the whole group is in session. Small groups always help break the ice and create a more private forum for discussions.

High-Participation Techniques

Many excellent techniques are available to get even the most reluctant and shy participant to play an active part. These techniques offer anonymity to members and generate lots of energy.

Discussion Partners

This simple technique can be used as a way of starting any discussion. After posing a question to a large group, ask people to find partners to discuss the question or topic for a few minutes. (The term for a pair of people is a dyad.) Have people report what they talked about. You can use this with threesomes or triads as well.

Tossed Salad

Place an empty cardboard box or an inexpensive plastic salad bowl on the table or in the middle of the room. Give out small slips of paper and ask people to write down one idea per slip. Have them fold and then toss the slips into the box or bowl. When people have finished writing, have someone toss the salad. Pass the bowl so that each person can take out as many slips as he or she tossed in. Go around the table and have people read the ideas on the slips they drew. Discuss and refine the ideas as a group.

Issues and Answers

When faced with a long list of issues to tackle, rather than attempting to problem solve all of them as a whole group, which may take too long, post the problems around the room. Put only one issue on each sheet of flip-chart paper or section of the electronic board.

Use dyads or triads to get people talking.

Ask all members to go to one of the issue sheets and discuss that problem with whoever else was drawn to that topic. Make sure people are distributed evenly, with at least three people per issue. You can use chairs, but this works best as a stand-up activity.

Allow up to five minutes for the subgroups to analyze the situation. Have them make notes on the top half of each flip-chart sheet. Periodically ask everyone to move to another flip-chart sheet. When they switch, ask them to read the analysis made by the first group and to add any additional ideas. This round is often shorter than five minutes. Keep people circulating until everyone has added ideas to all of the sheets.

Once the analysis round is complete, ask everyone to return to the original issue he or she started with. Ask them to generate and record solutions to their respective issue on the bottom half of the sheet. Once again circulate people until everyone has added ideas on all of the sheets.

Use the walls to engage everyone is working on problems.

To end the process have everyone walk by each sheet, read all of the solutions, and check off the one to three ideas he or she thinks are best.

Talk Circuit

This technique works best in a large crowd because it creates a strong buzz and lets people get to know each other. Start by posing a question to the group and then allow quiet time for each person to write his or her own response.

Ask everyone to sit "knee to knee" with a partner and share ideas. Have one person speak while the other acts as the facilitator. After two to three minutes, stop the interaction and have partners reverse their roles. After two to three more minutes, stop the discussions.

Partner people with those they know the least.

Ask everyone to find a new partner and repeat the process, but in slightly less time. Stop the action and then have everyone repeat the process with a third partner.

In the final round allow only one minute per person. When the partner discussions are over, share the ideas as a whole group and record them.

Use anonymous brainstorming.

Pass the Envelope

Give each person an envelope filled with blank slips of paper. Pose a question or challenge to the group, and then have everyone write down as many ideas as they can within the given time frame and put the slips into the envelope. Tell people to pass the envelopes, either to the next person or in all directions, and when the passing stops, ask them to read the contents of the envelopes they received.

Place participants in pairs and have them discuss the ideas in their envelope. What ideas did they receive? What are the positives and negatives of each idea? What other ideas should they add? Combine pairs to form groups of four and ask them to further refine the contents of their respective envelopes into practical action plans. Hold a plenary to collect ideas.

Group Participation Survey

Please review the following statements and rate how your group currently manages the participation of members. Be totally honest. Remember that this survey is anonymous. The results will be tabulated and fed back to the group for their assessment.

1. At our meetings people feel free to express any idea regardless of who's present.

1 totally disagree	2 disagree somewhat	3 not sure	4 agree somewhat	5 totally agree

2. Everyone feels totally relaxed.

1 totally disagree	2 disagree somewhat	3 not sure	4 agree somewhat	5 totally agree

3. The members of our group are always clear about the purpose of discussions.

1 totally disagree	2 disagree somewhat	3 not sure	4 agree somewhat	5 totally agree

4. Our people always do their homework and come to meetings prepared.

1 totally disagree	2 disagree somewhat	3 not sure	4 agree somewhat	5 totally agree

5. Members listen to and respect each other's views.

1 totally disagree	2 disagree somewhat	3 not sure	4 agree somewhat	5 totally agree

6. Members appreciate each other's different strengths. Everyone is valued for his or her specific skills.

1 totally disagree	2 disagree somewhat	3 not sure	4 agree somewhat	5 totally agree

7. Members recognize and accept individual differences.

1 totally disagree	2 disagree somewhat	3 not sure	4 agree somewhat	5 totally agree

8. The organization fully supports the work of the group.

1 totally disagree	2 disagree somewhat	3 not sure	4 agree somewhat	5 totally agree

Never continue facilitating a session in which people behave dysfunctionally!

Encouraging Effective Meeting Behaviors

Sometimes you'll find yourself working with groups whose members behave as though they were being paid bonuses for rudeness. People interrupt. Members run in and out. People dismiss ideas before they've really tried to understand them, and so on.

Producing outcomes is a battle in these situations. Sometimes the wisest thing to do is stop the proceedings and raise member awareness about effective meeting behaviors.

This mini-training session is simple, quick, and surprisingly effective. It consists of the following steps:

1. Introduce the idea that certain behaviors are less effective than others. Hand out the sheets on the next two pages, which describe effective and ineffective meeting behaviors. Review each behavior. Answer any questions.

2. Ask all members to act as observers for the rest of the meeting. Give each person an observation sheet and ask everyone to make note of all occurrences of the listed behaviors. This means keeping track of both the names of people and the specific thing done or said.

3. At the end of the session, set aside some time to share observations.
   - *"Were there more effective or ineffective behaviors displayed?"*
   - *"Which ineffective behaviors were in evidence?"*

4. At the end of this discussion, help group members to write new norms by asking:
   - *"What new rules should be added to the existing norms to overcome these behaviors?"*

Group Behaviors Handout

Behaviors That Help Effectiveness

Behavior	*Description*
Listens Actively	looks at the person who is speaking, nods, asks probing questions and acknowledges what is said by paraphrasing point(s) made
Supports	encourages others to develop ideas and make suggestions; gives them recognition for their ideas
Probes	goes beyond the surface comments by questioning teammates to uncover hidden information
Clarifies	asks members for more information about what they mean; clears up confusion
Offers Ideas	shares suggestions, ideas, solutions, and proposals
Includes Others	asks quiet members for their opinions, making sure no one is left out
Summarizes	pulls together ideas from a number of people; determines where the group is and what has been covered
Harmonizes	reconciles opposing points of view; links together similar ideas; points out where ideas are the same
Manages Conflict	listens to the views of others; clarifies issues and key points made by opponents; seeks solutions

Behaviors That Hinder Effectiveness

Behavior	*Description*
"Yeah But's"	discredits the ideas of others
Blocks	insists on getting one's way; doesn't compromise; stands in the way of the team's progress
Grandstands	draws attention to one's personal skills; boasts
Goes Off Topic	directs the conversation off onto other topics
Dominates	tries to "run" the group through dictating, bullying
Withdraws	doesn't participate or offer help or support to others
Devil's Advocate	takes pride in being contrary
Criticizes	makes negative comments about people or their ideas
Personal Slurs	hurls insults at other people

Observing Group Behaviors in Action

EFFECTIVE	INEFFECTIVE
Actively listens	*Yeah but's*
Supports	*Blocks*
Probes	*Grandstands*
Clarifies	*Goes off topic*
Offers ideas	*Dominates*
Includes others	*Withdraws*
Summarizes	*Devil's advocate*
Harmonizes	*Criticizes*
Manages conflict	*Personal slurs*

Peer Review Instructions

WEB

At times group members need to receive feedback from each other. This may be necessary when they're experiencing conflict or when individuals are letting down the team.

The peer feedback format consists of two areas of focus, both of which have a positive intent. The first lets people praise each other. The second offers supportive advice to help the other person improve. These areas are:

1. *"What you do that's really effective. Keep on doing it!"*
2. *"What you could do that would make you even more effective."*

Harness the power of peer feedback to manage member behaviors.

Here's how everyone can participate in this powerful feedback exercise:

Step 1: Each member writes his or her name at the top of a blank Peer Review Worksheet like the one on the next page and then passes it to the right.

Step 2: Each member answers both questions about the person whose name is at the top of each sheet.

Step 3: Sheets are passed around the table until everyone has written comments about every other member.

Step 4: Each person eventually receives back the sheet with his or her own name on it, completely filled out with comments from all of the other members.

Step 5: The process can stop here, with each person keeping his or her own feedback, or you can ask people to:

- pass the completed sheets around again, and have people read aloud the positive comments they wrote about the other person. This is called a "strength bombardment."
- Have members choose partners to discuss what they learned from their feedback and create action plans for personal change. End with members sharing their action steps with the group.

This form of peer review is non-threatening, because no one receives negative comments, as both feedback questions are positive and forward-looking.

This exercise is extremely effective because the coaching advice is coming from peers. It subtly reminds members of the importance of meeting each other's needs and expectations. If tensions develop between people, this feedback method allows them to safely request what they need from each other. Since peer feedback often resolves interpersonal conflicts before they flare up, it's a good activity to do periodically as a preventative measure.

Peer Review Worksheet

Name: ______________________ **Date:** ____________________

What you do that's really effective. Keep on doing it!

What you could do that would make you even more effective.

Chapter Six
Effective Decision Making

Helping groups make high-quality decisions is one of the most important functions of a facilitator. It's also one of the most difficult! There are a number of things that make decision making such a challenge:

- people may be trying to make a decision without having done their homework or being in possession of all of the important facts
- the key stakeholders or decision-makers may not be present
- individuals in the group may have a solution or position in mind that they spend their time advocating without being open to further input
- a few people may dominate while others hold their ideas back
- there may be real confusion about the purpose of the decision-making conversation or whether the group is empowered to decide the issue under discussion
- there may be no process in place to give the conversation structure, so the group engages in unstructured thrashing that's more emotional and subjective than it is factual and objective
- frustration may cause group members to give up their quest for a solution and resort to voting or simply moving on to the next topic without closure

Helping groups make high-quality decisions is one of the most important functions of a facilitator.

To ensure that you're always facilitating high-quality decision processes, become aware of the traits of effective decision making:

- everyone is clear about the purpose of the decision-making conversation
- the group knows the extent of its power to make the decision in question
- the right people are present
- people understand the approach to be taken and are willing to follow it
- there is an objective and open atmosphere in which ideas are freely exchanged and considered
- people understand the approach to be taken and are willing to follow it
- all ideas are viewed as equally important and no individual or subgroup dominates
- if the decision process becomes deadlocked, group members stop and examine why they're stuck and seek ways of ending the impasse
- discussions end with a sense of closure and clear next steps

Know the Four Types of Conversations

Groups tend to share information. Teams do more planning, problem solving, and relationship building.

The first step in being able to support effective decision making is awareness that conversations fall into one of the following categories:

Information sharing—this includes giving update reports, sharing research, or brainstorming ideas for later ranking. Note that there is no decision making in these types of discussions. Information-sharing discussions are typically chaired, rather than facilitated, and result in little collaboration among participants.

Planning—these discussions feature activities such as visioning and creating goal statements, describing objectives and expected results, assessing needs, identifying priorities, and creating detailed action steps. Budget planning and program planning discussions fall into this category. Managed change initiatives are also planning activities. Lots of decisions are made during planning conversations, thus they require structure and active facilitation to ensure input from members.

Problem solving—encompasses activities that engage participants in identifying and resolving issues together.The core activities involve gathering data, identifying problems, analyzing the current situation, using criteria to sort potential solutions, and planning for action. Customer service initiatives and process improvement projects fall into this category. Because these types of discussions result in actions that create change, problem solving needs to be carefully structured and systematically facilitated.

Relationship building—this includes activities that help people get to know each other and build cohesion. It inculdes activities such as icebreakers, norm development sessions, and conflict mediations. Structured team-building sessions are an example of relationship-building discussions. Important agreements are made during relationship-building discussions, so they also need to be carefully structured and assertively facilitated.

Always identify whether the purpose of a discussion is to make decisions or simply to share information.

At the start of each conversation, facilitators must determine which of the four discussion types is taking place and whether or not the group is making decisions:

If it's information sharing, list making, or brainstorming:

– no decisions will be made
– facilitation isn't critical
– synergy isn't important
– closure is not needed
– next steps optional

If it's planning, problem solving, or relationship building:

– decisions will be made
– a clear process is needed
– facilitation is important
– people need to build on each other's thoughts
– closure and clear next steps are needed

The Four Levels of Empowerment

For all decision-making conversations, it's very important to clarify the level of empowerment at which a decision is being made and communicate that information to group members at the start of any discussion.

It's essential to clarify empowerment levels.

Nothing causes greater confusion and distrust than a lack of clarity about empowerment levels. It's very unfortunate when a group assumes that it has final say in a decision, only to discover that management was merely asking for their opinions. Fortunately, empowerment doesn't have to be a confusing concept when you use the following four-level empowerment model.

The Empowerment Continuum

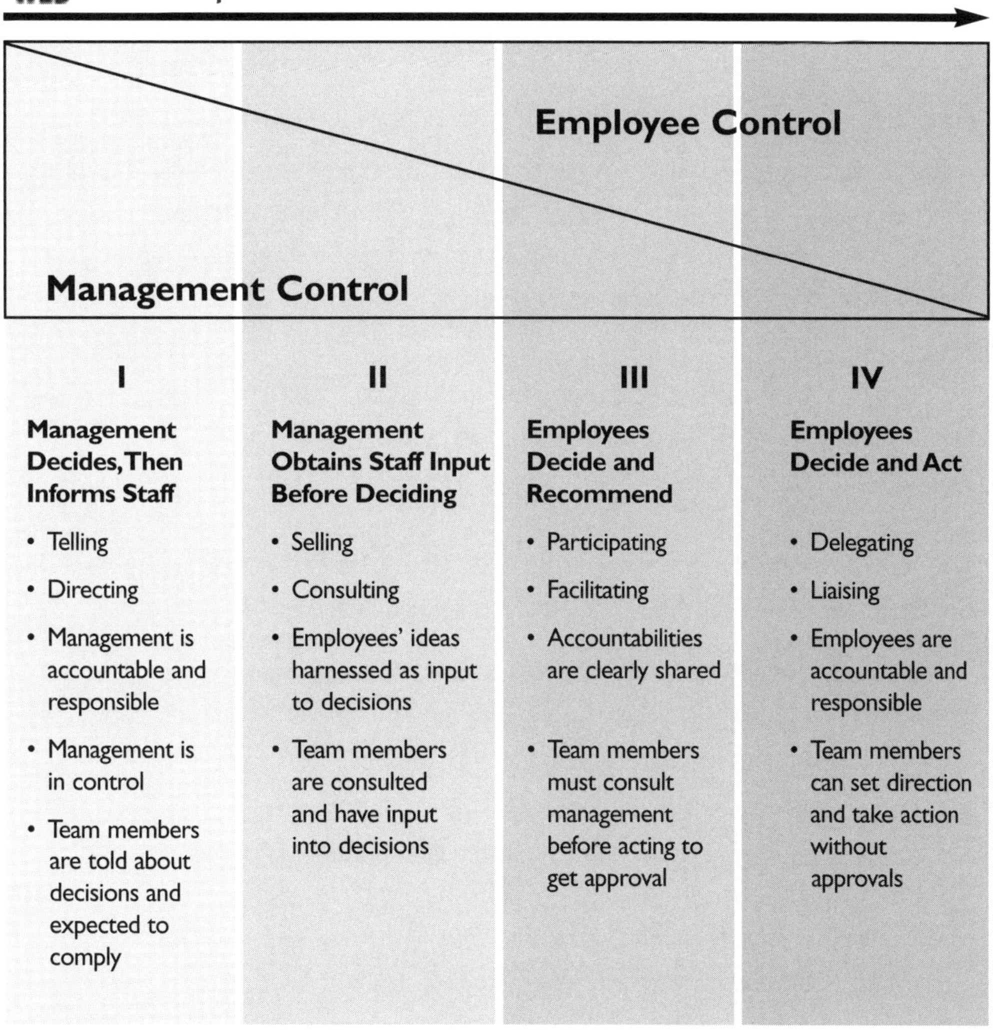

Share the empowerment chart with group members.

I	II	III	IV
Management Decides, Then Informs Staff	**Management Obtains Staff Input Before Deciding**	**Employees Decide and Recommend**	**Employees Decide and Act**
• Telling	• Selling	• Participating	• Delegating
• Directing	• Consulting	• Facilitating	• Liaising
• Management is accountable and responsible	• Employees' ideas harnessed as input to decisions	• Accountabilities are clearly shared	• Employees are accountable and responsible
• Management is in control	• Team members are consulted and have input into decisions	• Team members must consult management before acting to get approval	• Team members can set direction and take action without approvals
• Team members are told about decisions and expected to comply			

Clarifying the Four Empowerment Levels

Level I—This refers to any decision made by management without input from employees. Employees are informed of the decision and expected to comply.

Level II—This is a decision made by management after seeking input from employees. Employees are consulted but have no actual say in the final outcome and are expected to comply. An employee focus group is an example of a Level II decision-making process.

Level III—In this category of decision, employees discuss and recommend a course of action, but are unable to act without gaining final approval. Problem-solving workshops are often set up as Level III activities.

Help groups identify which level of empowerment is most effective in each decision area.

Level IV—In this level of decision, the group has been given full authority to make a decision and implement action plans without having to seek further approvals.

It's the role of the facilitator to help group members determine the extent of their empowerment in each decision-making activity. This should ideally be done during the assessment and design phases of the facilitation process, although empowerment is often clarified at the start of discussions. Clarification involves asking questions such as:

- *"Who's accountable for the outcomes of the decision?"*
- *"Who is best qualified to make the decision in terms of expertise?"*
- *"To what extent is it important that there be high levels of buy-in to the decision?"*
- *"To what extent is it advantageous to have group members actively engaged in every step of making the decision and implementing actions?"*

If you're testing a group's assumptions about the empowerment level related to a specific topic, you can ask questions such as:

- *"Is the decision being made elsewhere?"* (Level I)
- *"Are you being asked for your recommendations?"* (Level II)
- *"Are you making recommendations that require approval before you can act?"* (Level III)
- *"Are you fully able to go ahead and implement whatever decision is made by the group?"* (Level IV)

Adjusting Empowerment Levels

If a group feels that a decision is being made at the wrong level, facilitate a discussion about the empowerment level the members think they need. While this is often about gaining more empowerment, there are situations in which groups feel the need to reduce their level of accountability for a decision.

To *raise* empowerment, facilitate a discussion that asks:

- *"What empowerment level is appropriate for this activity?"*
- *"Why does the group need these powers?"*
- *"What are the risks of the group having these powers?"*
- *"What concerns is management likely to have?"*
- *"What checks and balances could be put into place to encourage management to empower you more?"*
- *"What accountabilities are group members prepared to assume individually and as a group to gain more power?"*

Encouraging Groups to Accept Greater Empowerment

Groups are often reluctant to take on empowerment.

There are instances in which group members may feel that they're being asked to assume too much power. This can have a number of root causes:

- there may be a feeling that the actions planned by the group aren't within their job description
- some people are unused to being empowered and are afraid to take risks
- many people may already be overcommitted
- there may be a lack of confidence or skill on the part of some participants
- there may be a lack of true buy-in to the action plans that were created
- there may be a justified lack of trust that the organization is going to support the group's initiatives

To explore the need to reduce empowerment, facilitate a discussion that asks:

- *"What power and authority are appropriate for this activity?"*
- *"Why should the empowerment level be lower?"*
- *"What accountabilities are group members unprepared to assume?"*
- *"What risks should management be made aware of?"*

It's important to note that there are situations in which group members shy away from assuming greater responsibility when they shouldn't. A common example is groups in which members enjoy analyzing a problem and brainstorming solutions, but back away from taking responsibility for action.

Unlike managers, who may have the authority to "order" reluctant employees to take on new tasks, facilitators have to rely on their process skills to encourage people to overcome resistance. If you encounter unjustified resistance to empowerment, the following line of questioning can be useful:

1. ***Acknowledge the resistance***—don't ignore or deny it:

   "I can tell by your reaction that you don't want to take on responsibility for this decision/program."

2. ***Invite members to verbalize their reticence***—allow people to vent their fears and concerns:

   "Why do you think responsibility should rest elsewhere?"

3. ***Empathize with their situation***—sympathize without agreeing:

   "I can understand that you're concerned about taking on more responsibility at this time."

4. ***Engage members in identifying strategies***—ask them to identify conditions for overcoming their resistance:

   "Under what conditions would you consider assuming more responsibility?"
   "What assurances, training, or support would make you feel you'd be willing to give it a try?"

5. ***Paraphrase and summarize their statements***—encourage them to agree to greater empowerment by ratifying their suggestions:

   "So you're saying that you'd be willing to take this on with some training and coaching."

Facilitators may need to help groups work through their resistance to increased empowerment.

In most situations, group members will identify feasible and realistic things that can be done to encourage them to buy in further. If, on the other hand, group members state unreasonable conditions, such as having their pay doubled, don't react. Record all unreasonable ideas along with the others until the list of conditions is complete. Then ask the group to help review the list of conditions to identify which are feasible and which are unrealistic. In most cases, other group members will edit out the more outrageous demands of their peers.

Does this approach always work? The truth is that nothing works in every situation. It is, however, the only process tool available given the facilitator's lack of true power over the group. If this approach fails to work, you will have to refer the problem of group reluctance to assume accountability to the leader, who will decide whether ordering increased empowerment is the best course of action.

Be aware that bringing in leaders to order members to take on more empowerment will result in reduced buy-in and may also regress the group's maturity. To avoid these negatives, always try to engage members in conversations aimed at overcoming their resistance first.

Shifting Decision-Making Paradigms

All facilitators need to be aware that when organizations start involving groups to make decisions that were formerly made soley by management, this may represent a major shift in the cultural values of the organization.

Many managers are used to listening to input and then making important decisions themselves. Such patterns are a reality that all facilitators have to understand. When staff input into decision making represents a major change to traditional power arrangements, you must help leaders and members appreciate the value of participative decisions and create the right setting in which people can be encouraged to express their ideas freely.

Help leaders become comfortable with group decisions.

When working with a group you don't know, never assume that participative decision making is understood or practiced by either the group or the leader. Instead, check by asking questions that probe how the organization normally makes decisions. Ask things like:

- *"How are decisions of this nature typically made in this organization?"*
- *"To what extent are employees used to making these types of decisions?"*
- *"Are member decisions often overturned by leaders?"*

In addition, leaders who are accustomed to a directive style may have concerns about relinquishing control. These leaders often need time to buy into the idea of participation in decision making. They also need to understand how this greater employee involvement benefits them. Some points that may be helpful in encouraging a leader to accept increased group decision making include:

Raising empowerment levels and sharing decision-making authority can create a paradigm shift for the organization.

- group decision making has the benefit of generating more ideas, building commitment, and encouraging members to take greater responsibility.
- group decision making relieves the leader of many tasks and frees him or her to play more strategic roles in the organization.
- decisions that involve a degree of risk can managed at empowerment Level III to ensure that the leader approves member decisions before they are implemented.
- decisions that group members are fully empowered to make at Level IV can be given clear parameters to ensure they meet key success criteria, such as compliance with budgetary guidelines, support of the overall strategic plan, etc.

While facilitators often lead decision-making sessions at Level II, it should always be made clear to leaders that this isn't the full use of a group's powers. Years of experience has shown that decision making at Levels III and IV more fully taps into the talents and resources of group members and creates a more fully engaged organization.

Consensus building creates participation and buy-in to the generated solutions.

Multi-voting is a good tool if there are a lot of options or a lot of people involved.

The Decision-Making Options

When helping a group make a decision, five distinct decision-making methods are available. Each of these represents a different approach. Each has pros and cons associated with it. The decision option should always be chosen carefully to be sure it's the most appropriate method. These options are as follows:

Consensus Building

Consensus building involves everyone clearly understanding the situation or problem to be decided, analyzing all of the relevant facts together, and then jointly developing solutions that represent the whole group's best thinking about the optimal decision. It's characterized by a lot of listening, healthy debate, and testing of options. Consensus generates a decision about which everyone says, *"I can live with it."*

Pros—it's a collaborative effort that unites the group. It demands high involvement. It's systematic, objective, and fact-driven. It builds buy-in and high commitment to the outcome.

Cons—it's time-consuming and produces low-quality decisions if done without proper data collection or if members have poor interpersonal skills.

Uses—when decisions will impact the entire group; when buy-in and ideas from all members are essential; when the importance of the decision being made is worth the time it will take to complete the consensus process properly.

Steps—Name the issue, topic, or problem. Share all of the known facts to create a shared understanding of the current situation. Generate potential courses of action/solutions. Generate criteria for sorting the courses of action/solutions. Use the criteria to sort the ideas (a decision grid, vote, or multi-vote). Make a clear statement of the decision. Ratify that all can live with the solution.

Multi-Voting

This is a priority-setting tool that is useful for making decisions when the group has a lengthy set of options and rank ordering the options, based on a set of criteria, will clarify the best course of action. (Refer to page 186.)

Pros—it's systematic, objective, democratic, non-competitive, and participative. Everyone wins somewhat, and feelings of loss are minimal. It's a fast way of sorting out a complex set of options. Often feels consensual.

Cons—it's often associated with limited discussion, hence, limited understanding of the options. This may force choices on people that may not be satisfactory to them, because the real priorities do not rise to the surface or people are swayed by each other if the voting is done out in the open, rather than electronically or by ballot.

Uses—when there's a long list of alternatives or items to choose from.

Steps—After the group has generated a wide range of solutions, clarify the criteria that define the votes (most important, easiest, least expensive, greatest impact, etc.). If using stickers, hand out strips of dots. If using markers, tell people how many marks to make. If using points, clarify how many points people can distribute (10/100, etc.). Allow people to mill as they affix their votes.

Compromise

A negotiated approach is applicable when there are two or more distinct options and members are strongly polarized (neither side is willing to accept the solution/position put forth by the other side). A middle position is then created that incorporates ideas from both sides. Throughout the process of negotiation, everyone wins a few favorite points, but also loses a few items he or she liked. The outcome is, therefore, something that no one is totally satisfied with. In compromises, no one feels he or she received what he or she originally wanted, so the emotional reaction is often, *"It's not really what I wanted, but I'm going to have to live with it."*

A compromise creates feelings of both winning and losing.

Pros—it generates lots of discussion and does result in a solution.

Cons—negotiating when people are pushing a favored point of view tends to be adversarial, hence this approach divides the group. In the end, everyone wins, but everyone also loses.

Uses—when two opposing solutions are proposed, neither of which is acceptable to everyone, or when the group is strongly polarized and compromise is the only alternative.

Steps—Invite the parties to describe the solution or course of action that they favor. Ask the other party to make notes and then give a short summary of the solution or position favored by the other group. Engage the entire group in identifying the strengths and weaknesses of each proposed approach. Bring forward the strengths of both approaches. Create a third option or hybrid that builds on all of the strengths. Ask each group to willingly give up some aspects of their original approach in order to arrive at decisions that represents a middle ground. Clarify, summarize, and ratify the middle-ground approach.

Majority Voting

This involves asking people to choose the option they favor, once clear choices have been identified. Usual methods are a show of hands or secret ballot. The quality of voting is always enhanced if there's good discussion to share ideas before the vote is taken.

The quality of any voting exercise increases dramatically if it's preceded by a thorough discussion.

Pros—it's fast and decisions can be of higher quality if the vote is preceded by a thorough analysis.

Cons—it can be too fast and low in quality if people vote based on their personal feelings without the benefit of hearing each other's thoughts or facts. It creates winners and losers, hence dividing the group. The show of hands method may put pressure on people to conform.

Uses—when there are two distinct options and one or the other must be chosen; when decisions must be made quickly and a division in the group is acceptable; when consensus has been attempted and cannot be reached.

Steps—Ask members to describe both options in some detail to build a shared understanding. Identify criteria for deciding which is more effective (timeliness, cost, impact, etc.). Once everyone understands both options and the criteria for deciding, use a show of hands or paper vote to identify which option to implement.

One Person Decides

Many groups ignore the fact that many decisions are best made by one person.

This is a decision that the group decides to refer to one person to make on behalf of the group. A common misconception among teams is that every decision needs to be made by the whole group. In fact, a one-person decision is often a faster and more efficient way to reach resolution. The quality of any one person's decision can be raised considerably if the person making the decision receives advice and input from other group members before deciding.

Pros—it's fast and accountability is clear. Can result in commitment and buy-in if people feel their ideas are represented.

Cons—it can divide the group if the person deciding doesn't consult with others, or makes a decision that others can't live with. A one-person decision typically lacks in both the buy-in and synergy that come from a group decision-making process.

Uses—when the issue is unimportant or small; or when there's a clear expert in the group; or when only one person has the information needed to make the decision and can't share it; or when one person is solely accountable for the outcome.

Steps—Identify the expert who is best qualified to make the decision. To build buy-in, conduct a consultation during which group members tell the expert about their needs and concerns regarding the item to be decided. Gain agreement that everyone will accept the decision of the expert.

Decision Options Chart

Option	Pros	Cons	Uses
Consensus Building	• collaborative • systematic • participative • discussion-oriented • encourages commitment	• takes time • requires data and member skills	• important issues • when total buy-in matters
Multi-Voting	• systematic • objective • participative • feels like a win	• limits dialogue • influenced choices • real priorities may not surface	• to sort or prioritize a long list of options
Compromise	• discussion • creates a solution	• adversarial • win/lose • divides the group	• when positions are polarized; consensus improbable
Majority Voting	• fast • high quality with dialogue • clear outcome	• may be too fast • winners and losers • no dialogue • influenced choices	• trivial matter • when there are clear options • if division of group is acceptable
One Person Decides	• can be fast • clear accountability	• lack of input • low buy-in • no synergy	• when one person is the expert • individual willing to take sole responsibility

Be aware of the impact of each method on group unity.

The Divergence/Convergence Model

Beware of letting groups tackle overly broad issues, since topics get bigger during divergence.

Regardless of which decision tool is used, a general pattern that facilitators need to understand is the Divergence/Convergence Model shown below. This model shows that the level of detail diverges or increases in the early stages of most decision-making processes and does not converge or reduce until the later stages. This happens because in the early stages of analyzing the current situation, collecting data, uncovering root causes, and brainstorming, a broad range of ideas all tend to place more information on the table. The convergence stage does not occur until later when all the data that has been amassed and sorted down into actionable items.

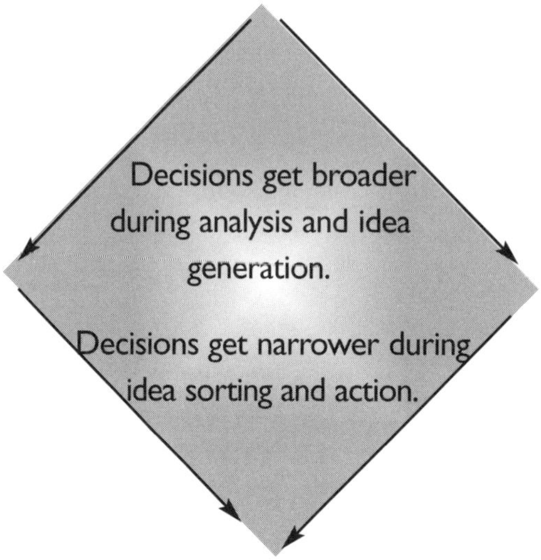

This model provides a warning. If the topic or issue being discussed is extremely broad to begin with, there is a strong likelihood that it will become even broader during the divergence phase. If, for example, group members identify more than one solution for each piece of data shared in the analysis phase, the amount of information before the group could double or triple.

Understanding this model helps facilitators plan their agendas. Divergent conversations are detailed and typically take longer than divergent ones. Also, facilitators must be alert to the fact that if they allow a group to tackle an issue that is too vague or generic, it may expand in the diverge phase to a point at which it is impossible to manage.

The Importance of Building Consensus

The crucial importance of building consensus simply cannot be overstated and must be fully understood by all facilitators. In fact, facilitation and consensus building are based on the same set of core values and beliefs.

Besides being the number 1 choice for making all important decisions, facilitators always seek to build consensus with everything they do. The following are all examples of consensus activities:

- summarizing a complex set of ideas to the satisfaction of group members
- gaining buy-in from all members as to the purpose or goal of a session
- obtaining everyone's input about a clear goal and objectives
- linking thoughts together so people can formulate a common idea
- making notes on a flip chart in such a way that each member feels he or she has been heard and is satisfied with what's been recorded

Because all facilitation activities must strive to be collaborative, participative, synergistic, and unifying, they are essentially consensus building in nature!

Consensus building is at the heart of facilitation.

Hallmarks of the Consensus Process

Regardless of whether a multi-step process is being used to build a decision or the facilitator is only synthesizing group thoughts into a consensus statement, the same hallmarks of the process are always present:

- lots of ideas are being shared
- everyone's ideas are heard
- there's active listening and paraphrasing to clarify ideas
- people build on each other's ideas
- no one's trying to push a pre-determined solution; instead, there's an open and objective quest for new options
- the final solution is based on sound information
- when the final solution is reached, people feel satisfied that they were part of the decision
- all feel so consulted and involved that even though the final solution isn't the one they would have chosen working on their own, they can readily "live with it"

Some decisions are so important that only consensus will do.

There are many situations in which the decisions to be made are so important that consensus is the only acceptable method. Defaulting to voting or any other technique that creates division within the group allows dissenters to absolve themselves of responsibility for important group outcomes. In these cases, the group must agree to keep discussing the issue until everyone indicates that he or she can live with the outcome.

It is also important never to end a consensus exercise by asking whether everyone is happy or everyone agrees with the outcome. Consensus is not about either happiness of total agreement. At the end of even a great consensus process, people have usually made concessions and are usually not getting everything they wanted.

Don't ask: *"Do we all agree?"* or *"Is everyone happy?"*
Instead ask: *"Do we have a well-thought-through outcome that we can all feel committed to implementing and that everyone can live with?"*

A consensus decision is one that everyone can live with.

One of the major contributions of any facilitator is in helping a group overcome the temptation to "pressure" dissenters into agreement. By openly accepting and discussing differences, facilitators help members reach decisions that have been objectively explored and tested.

Consensus isn't designed to make people happy or leave them in 100 percent agreement. Its goal is to create an outcome that represents the best feasible course of action, given the circumstances.

Overcoming Blocks to Consensus

It's very common that some group members may be reluctant to support a particular decision. In these cases never yield to the temptation to pressure dissenters to give in. To do so would be to court "group think."

Instead, reframe dissenters as people who may potentially have an important idea overlooked by the group. This involves acknowledging and accepting the dissent, then harnessing it to improve the decision. This is done by allowing the dissenters to express their concerns in really concrete terms and then making them accountable for finding solutions to the issues that they raise.

This sounds something like this:

- *"I'm noticing that we have some differing views."*
- *"Differing points of view always have the potential to improve the quality of a decision, so please let's listen carefully for ideas that may have been missed."*
- *"Tell us the specific issue that you have with the group's decision. What do you see as the flaws in this decision? What's been overlooked?"*
- *"What changes do you propose could be made to the group's solution that would make it acceptable to you? What are the solutions to the problems that you raise?*

Things to Watch for in Decision Making

__ Be clear up-front on the process to be used. Explain any tools or techniques that will be used.

__ Ask people what assumptions they're operating under, either about the issue or the organizational constraints. Note these and test them with the rest of the group.

__ Conflict is a natural part of many decision-making discussions. Always confront differences assertively and collaboratively. Don't strive to avoid conflict or accommodate by asking people to be nice and get along.

__ Urge people not to fold or just give in if they feel they have important ideas. When everyone agrees just to make things run smoothly, the result is "group think." This creates poor decisions made just to get it over with and ensure that everyone stays friends.

__ If the group has chosen to go for consensus because the issue is important, stick with it, even if the going gets tough. Beware of the tendency to start voting, coin tossing, and bargaining to make things easier.

__ Be very particular about achieving closure on any items that are decided. Test for consensus and make sure things are final before letting the group move on to other topics.

__ Stop the action if things start "spinning" or behaviors are ineffective. Ask: *"What are we doing well? What aren't we doing so well?"* and *"What do we need to do about it?"* Then act on all suggestions.

Sharing this chart may help encourage group effectiveness.

Effective Decision-Making Behaviors

To make any decision process work, group members need to behave in specific ways. These behaviors can be suggested to the group or generated as norms in advance of any decision-making session.

Sharing this chart may help encourage group effectiveness.

BEHAVIORS THAT HELP	BEHAVIORS THAT HINDER
Listening to others' ideas politely, even when you don't agree	Interrupting people in mid-sentence
Paraphrasing the main points made by another person, especially if you're about to contradict the person's ideas	Not acknowledging the ideas that others have put on the table
Praising others' ideas	Criticizing others' ideas, as opposed to giving them useful feedback
Building on others' ideas	Pushing your own ideas while ignoring others' input
Asking others to critique your ideas, and accepting the feedback	Getting defensive when your ideas are assessed
Being open to accepting alternative courses of action	Sticking only to your ideas and blocking suggestions for alternatives
Dealing with facts	Basing arguments on feelings
Staying calm and friendly toward colleagues	Getting overly emotional; showing hostility in the face of any disagreement

Symptoms, Causes, and Cures of Poor Decisions

When groups make poor-quality decisions, one or more of the following symptoms may be in evidence:

Symptom 1: Aimless drifting and random discussions. The same topic is kicked around meeting after meeting without resolution. Feels like the group is spinning its wheels.

Cause: No plan or process for approaching the decision. Group members simply launch into the discussion without any thought to which tools to use. Without a systematic approach, people start proposing solutions before there has been a thorough analysis of the situation. There is a lack of proper information. Everyone puts his or her favorite solution on the table. No one takes notes. No solution is definitively agreed to. Detailed action plans aren't written down.

Cure: The group needs a structured approach to decision making that uses the right decision-making tool and is assertively facilitated.

Symptom 2: The group uses voting on important items where total buy-in is important, then uses consensus to decide trivia.

Cause: A lack of understanding of decision-making options. The group doesn't understand the six key decision-making options and when to use each of them.

Cure: The group needs to become familiar with the six main decision-making options and consciously decide which to use before launching into any decision-making discussion.

Symptom 3: The group always seems to run out of time just when the important decisions are on the table.

Cause: Poor time management. Time isn't budgeted or monitored. There's no detailed agenda that sets aside sufficient time to deal with important items. Hence, time is wasted discussing less important aspects. Meetings often start late or run over.

Cure: The group needs to create a detailed agenda before each meeting. During discussions, the facilitator must be assertive about keeping the group on track and on time.

Symptom 4: When an important item is on the table, people grow heated and argumentative. No one really listens to the opposing viewpoints. Everyone pushes his or her point in an attempt to "win." Some members dominate, unconcerned that others are silent.

Cause: Poorly developed group interaction skills. People have become positional and competitive. No one is listening to the points other people are making, just pushing his or her own. Facilitation is nonexistent or weak. As a result, there's an absence of the synergy that exists when people build on each other's ideas. This confrontational style strains relationships, which only makes things worse.

Cure: The members need training in group effectiveness skills so that they can exhibit more listening, supporting, and idea building. If a facilitator is present, he or she should stop the conversation and explain active listening and paraphrasing. When conversation resumes, the facilitator should assure that people are acknowledging each other's points.

Symptom 5: After a lengthy discussion, it becomes clear that everyone is operating on slightly different assumptions about what the problem is and what the constraints or possibilities are.

Cause: Failure to check assumptions. Everyone has a different view of the situation and is basing his or her input on that view. Assumptions are never put on the table for sharing or testing.

Cure: Use probing questions to uncover the assumptions underlying statements made by the members. These questions can be related to the situation, the organization, or the people involved. Once assumptions are clarified and validated, members will be operating in the same framework.

Symptom 6: In spite of the fact that the discussion has been going in circles for some time, no one takes action to get things back on track.

Cause: No process checking. Even when things are going nowhere and frustration levels are running high, no one knows to call time-out to take stock and regroup. This, once again, reflects the absence of facilitation.

Cure: Stopping the discussion periodically to ask how things are going, whether the pace is right, whether people feel progress is being made, whether people feel the right approach is being taken. (Refer to the discussion of process checking on page 20.)

WEB

Decision Effectiveness Survey

Anonymously provide your feedback about your team's decision process.

1. How thoroughly did people do their homework?

1	2	3	4	5
Poor	Fair	Satisfactory	Good	Excellent

2. Was there clarity about their assumptions surrounding the topic?

1	2	3	4	5
Poor	Fair	Satisfactory	Good	Excellent

3. How clear was the goal of the decision process?

1	2	3	4	5
Poor	Fair	Satisfactory	Good	Excellent

4. Did we exhibit effective behaviors in dealing with contentious items?

1	2	3	4	5
Poor	Fair	Satisfactory	Good	Excellent

5. How thorough was our analysis of the current situation?

1	2	3	4	5
Poor	Fair	Satisfactory	Good	Excellent

6. How creative and innovative were the ideas that we generated?

1	2	3	4	5
Poor	Fair	Satisfactory	Good	Excellent

7. How objective and balanced was our evaluation of options?

1	2	3	4	5
Poor	Fair	Satisfactory	Good	Excellent

8. How satisfied are you that the final solution was one that everyone can live with?

1	2	3	4	5
Poor	Fair	Satisfactory	Good	Excellent

9. Were the potential blocks and barriers to action adequately anticipated?

1	2	3	4	5
Poor	Fair	Satisfactory	Good	Excellent

10. Rate your overall assessment of the quality of the decision process.

1	2	3	4	5
Poor	Fair	Satisfactory	Good	Excellent

What would you do to improve our next decision-making session?

____

____

Notes

Chapter Seven
Facilitating Conflict

Dealing with conflict is a fact of every facilitator's life. Consider the following scenario: you're facilitating an important meeting. Everything is going along great until you hit the third agenda item. Suddenly two members start arguing. Listening goes out the window, as each person pushes his or her ideas. The rest of the group becomes uncomfortable as the two combatants become ever more emotional. The discussion spins in circles. What do you do now?

For starters remember that differences of opinion are a normal part of any human interaction, so relax. The fact that people are arguing does not mean that you're doing a poor job. It is, however, a call to action. As facilitators, we need to intervene to restore group effectiveness. Standing on the sidelines and watching people fight is simply not an option.

Accept that differences of opinion are normal and that you need to play an active role to restore group effectiveness!

Comparing Arguments and Debates

All facilitators need to be attuned to the differences between a debate and an argument. Healthy debate is essential. If a group doesn't express differences of opinion, then it's basically incapable of making effective decisions. Dysfunctional arguments, on the other hand, lead to disaster. Facilitators don't want to limit debate, they just want to make sure that it doesn't become dysfunctional. Differing points of view are essential for making good decisions.

IN HEALTHY DEBATES	IN DYSFUNCTIONAL ARGUMENTS
→ People are open to hearing others' ideas.	→ People assume they're right.
→ People listen and respond to ideas even if they don't agree with them.	→ People wait until others have finished talking, then state their ideas without responding to ideas of the other person.
→ Everyone tries to understand the views of the other person.	→ No one is interested in how the other person sees the situation
→ People stay objective and focus on the facts.	→ People are attacked and blamed.
→ There's a systematic approach to analyzing the situation and looking for solutions.	→ Hot topics get thrashed out in an unstructured way.

TECHNIQUES THAT CREATE HEALTHY DEBATE	TECHNIQUES THAT ALLOW DYSFUNCTIONAL ARGUMENTS
→ stay totally neutral	→ join the argument
→ point out differences so they can be understood	→ ignore differences—just pray that they will go away
→ insist that people listen politely—have rules and use them	→ let people be rude—set no norms
→ make people paraphrase each other's ideas	→ ignore the fact that no one is really hearing anyone else
→ ask for concerns	→ sidestep hot issues
→ make people focus on facts	→ let people get personal
→ problem solve concerns	→ get defensive
→ invite and face feedback	→ squash dissent
→ facilitate assertively	→ stand by passively
→ get closure and move on	→ let it drag on and on

Your actions can determine whether people debate or argue.

Here's an important tip: Even though we write about conflict, never say the actual word "*conflict*" in a group setting, even if that word accurately describes what's going on. The word conflict is loaded with meaning. It also makes differences seem more serious and could make matters worse.

Instead of talking about conflict, talk about differing views.

Instead, use language that downplays what's going on. Instead of saying: *"It seems that you two are having a conflict,"* substitute *"It seems that there are differing views on this subject. Let's stop and make sure these points of view are heard and understood."* This less inflammatory language helps make differences look like a normal exchange.

Steps in Managing Conflict

One of the most helpful things to know about managing conflict is that it needs to be handled in two separate and distinct steps. Mixing the two or jumping into the second step without having completed the first step is a common mistake and one to be avoided. Here are the steps for managing conflict.

Step 1: Venting—This involves listening to people so that they feel heard and so that their built-up emotions are diffused. People are rarely ready to move on to solutions until they have had the opportunity to fully vent their feelings.

Step 2: Resolving the issue—When it appears that feelings have been expressed and all differing views have been heard and acknowledged, help members resolve the issues. This involves taking a structured approach to help group members reach solutions. Resolution can come through a collaborative problem-solving activity, helping members create an acceptable compromise, or supporting some members in accommodating or consciously avoiding the topic temporarily to allow time for emotions to further cool. Let's look at these steps in detail.

Step 1: Venting Emotions

Facilitators need to vent emotions when the following are in evidence:

- people are pushing their points of view without being at all receptive to the ideas of others
- people are becoming angry, defensive, and personal with each other
- there's negative body language, such as glaring and finger pointing
- sarcastic or dismissive remarks are made
- people "yeah but" and criticize each other's ideas
- some people shut down and withdraw
- there's extreme anger

When negative emotions are in evidence, facilitators need to act quickly so that these feelings don't poison the dynamics of the group. To vent conflict:

In conflicts you need to facilitate calmly, yet assertively!

- ***Slow things down***—Get the attention of group members by stopping the action and asking people to slow down. You can use the excuse that you can't take notes as quickly as people are talking. Ask speakers to start over and repeat their key ideas.
- **Stay totally neutral**—Never take sides or allow your body language to hint that you favor one idea or one person over another.
- ***Watch your language***—Don't use loaded words like *"arguing," "conflict,"* or even *"anger."* These can make things worse.
- ***Stay calm***—Maintain your composure and do not raise your own voice. Speak slowly with an even tone. Avoid using emotional body language.
- ***Emphasize listening***—Paraphrase key points and ask people to tell the group what they are hearing others say.
- ***Revisit the norms***—Point out the existing norms and remind people of their prior agreements. Ask people to tell you the difference between a healthy debate and an argument. Ask them which they are interested in having. Have them tell you the rules that will make a healthy debate possible. Add these new norms to the existing norm set.
- ***Be assertive***—Move into referee mode. Insist that people speak one at a time. Stop people who are interrupting. Don't stand by passively while people become emotional.
- ***Make interventions***—Don't ignore ineffective or dysfunctional behaviors. Refer to the Making Interventions section later in this chapter for the appropriate wording for making interventions that redirect behavior.
- ***Record key ideas***—Make notes about key points so they aren't lost and to stop group members from repeating points. Read these notes back to the group whenever you want to regain control.
- ***Seek permission to move on***—Ask members whether they feel that their points of view have been heard and acknowledged. Also ask whether they are ready to move on to resolve the matter.

When dealing with a group that is deeply locked in conflict, it may be helpful to hand out a sheet that features the LECSR model that follows.

Use this handout if people need reminders about how to act.

Listen-Empathize-Clarify-Seek Permission-Resolve

1. ***Listen***—Instead of arguing when you hear a point you disagree with, listen attentively to the other person's main points. Let people share their views without interruption. Look interested and say things like:
   - *"Tell me more. That's interesting. Uh-huh."*
   - *"I'm not sure I understand. Could you go over that again?"*
2. ***Empathize***—Accept the views of the other person even if you don't agree with them. Let people know you understand their feelings. Say:
   - *"I don't blame you for feeling that way. I see what you mean."*
   - *"I understand how you feel. I'm sure I'd feel the same way if. . . ."*
3. ***Clarify***—Delve deeper to ensure that you have a clear understanding of what the other person is saying to you. Say:
   - *"Let me see if I have it straight; what you're saying is. . . ."*
   - *"Is it possible that . . . ? The idea you're proposing is. . . ."*
4. ***Seek Permission***—Tell your side after the other person has expressed all of his or her concerns and feels clearly understood. Say:
   - *"Now that I understand your views, can I explain mine?"*
   - *"It seems that this would be a good time to bring up a few points you haven't mentioned."*
5. ***Resolve the Issue***—Once you have both heard each other, this is the time to start dealing with the problem together.

Step 2: Resolving Issues

Once emotions have been vented and acknowledged, there are five basic approaches that can be used to address the underlying issue:

Avoid	Offer members the option of placing the issue in the parking lot to be addressed later. Avoiding does not solve anything.
Accommodate	Ask both parties whether either one of them can simply accept the other's ideas and give in.
Compromise	Help members create a middle position that combines elements from each of the original positions. This is a form of resolution that asks each person to give up some of what he or she originally wanted in order to receive other things.
Compete	This is a form of conflict resolution in which people debate until one party wins. Results in a win/lose.
Collaborate	Both parties explore the issue or challenge together. Both take part in analyzing the facts and proposing solutions. They jointly identify the criteria for sorting solutions and agree to support the implementation actions. This results in a solution that all can live with and provides a feeling of win/win.

The Five Conflict Options: Pros and Cons

Each of the aforementioned approaches can work in specific situations. Facilitators need to understand each one and choose the one that suits the situation.

Avoiding—When conflict is avoided, nothing is resolved. Yet this is the right approach to use if the issue at stake is very trivial, can't be solved, or will result in a total lose/lose situation for the group. Avoiding is sometimes a wise interim strategy to give people a chance to calm down before addressing issues.

The main consequence of avoiding is that issues aren't resolved and there's no creativity applied toward finding a solution. The problem remains to fester and can crop up later. While avoiding has its place, groups become ineffective if they avoid too many issues.

When people are emotional, avoiding can be a wise interim strategy.

Accommodating—This is a social response aimed more at keeping the peace than solving the problem. This approach can involve asking everyone to just get along or asking one party in a dispute to give in to the other party.

Accommodating is the appropriate approach in situations in which one person is only slightly interested in the issue, while the other party cares deeply. It's also the right approach to take when exploration of the issue reveals that one party is wrong. This style is most applicable to family and other social gatherings in which tolerance and civility may be of greater importance than finding the right answer.

The consequence of accommodating is that the underlying issues are often left unexplored in the interest of keeping the peace.

In some situations, one party might be willing to give in.

Compromising—This is a mediated approach to managing conflict that is used when two people or two groups have formulated strong positions. Neither party feels he or she can accept the position of the other, so a neutral middle option needs to be developed.

The good thing about compromising is that it does yield a solution. The problem is that both parties must give up some things they want in order to get others. The process of compromise also tends to be adversarial. People know what they want so they feel dissatisfied when they have to give up parts of their proposals.

At the end of a compromise, people feel that they've both won and lost. They may also harbor negative feelings toward the other party because there often is some resentment over giving up key elements of a proposal. Compromise leaves people feeling like: *"I'm going to have to live with it!"*

Compromising can be adversarial and can leave people divided.

Competing—This is a strategy of defending oneself and debating one's point of view in order to score a win over another person. Competing has its place in those situations that are clearly defined as competitive, such as sports and war. In these situations, the winner doesn't worry about the feelings of the loser. Since competing is combative and adversarial, facilitators never use this approach to settle issues.

Competing is a combative and hence unacceptable approach.

Collaborating—In this approach the group strives to build consensus. It involves naming the issue and then engaging group members in analyzing the facts of the current situation, generating creative ideas, objectively sorting through potential solutions, and agreeing on a course of action.

Collaborating means helping people work together to explore the issue and develop a solution that is the result of ideas for everyone. People listen actively and build on each other's points. Solutions are generated through the use of non-competitive processes such as brainstorming. The best course of action is determined by applying a set of criteria to the choices available.

At the end of a collaboration, everyone feels that he or she was heard and that the final strategy reflects his or her thinking. While the final outcome may not be exactly what someone would have decided on his or her own, all members feel that they have had a say. Because collaboration emphasizes working together for a win/win, it creates a consensus. At the end of a conflict resolved through collaboration, people's feelings about the solution are: *"I can live with it!"*

Collaborating promotes a win/win outcome.

The main drawback to collaboration is that it requires a great deal of time and thus may result in a waste of energy if used on an insignificant issue.

The Five Options in Action

Consider the following conflict situation:

Fred and Bill are becoming very heated talking about whether or not to conduct classroom computer training for the new software about to be introduced.
Fred thinks that hands-on help, while people work with the system, is the way to go.
He thinks the proposed two days of classroom time is costly and takes people off the job for too long.
Bill is arguing that the new system is too complex for people to learn on the job and that too many mistakes will be made if people learn through trial and error.

Now consider possible facilitator responses using each of the five conflict options. Which work? Which don't? Why?

The facilitator uses avoidance

"You two seem quite deadlocked. Let's move on and discuss something else during our remaining time."

The facilitator encourages accommodation

"Look, Bill, Fred is pretty adamant that his people can't be off the job for any length of time. Since most of the staff are in his department, could you forget the idea of training classes?"

The facilitator fosters competing

"Why don't you keep debating until it's obvious one of you is right."

The facilitator suggests compromise

" Is there an option that is a hybrid of both approaches?"

The facilitator uses a collaborative technique

"Let's put all of the facts on the table. What are the details of our work and time pressures? Which skills do people need? What are all the possible options for training people? What are the characteristics of the best options? Which of our options looks like it meets those criteria? What is the best course of action?"

In the previously mentioned five scenarios, you will have noticed:

Avoiding doesn't deal with the issue.	→ Use it in those 10 percent of situations when issues can't be resolved.
Accommodating just smoothes things over.	→ Use it only in those 5 percent of situations when keeping the peace is of more importance than finding a solution.
Competing divides groups and creates win/lose.	→ Facilitators should never let people compete! 0 percent applicability.
Compromise seeks to find the middle ground.	→ Use it in those 20 percent of situations when faced with polarized choices.
Collaboration gets people working together to find the best solution for everyone.	→ This is the number 1 preferred approach for all facilitators. Use it in 65 percent of all conflict situations.

Collaboration is the optimal approach for settling important disputes.

Collaboration encourages people to work together to objectively seek solutions that everyone can live with. Because it's consensual, it unites and generates solutions that everyone feels committed to implementing.
It is the superior conflict management option for facilitators.

Assumptions Underlying Collaboration

Collaboration is a superior way of solving a problem during a meeting; however, a number of conditions should be in place to ensure a successful outcome. Members must:

__ have sufficient trust among themselves to open up and be supportive of each other when necessary
__ have a positive intent to work toward a win/win solution
__ have relevant information on hand to make a sound decision
__ have the time to make this decision
__ believe the topic is important enough to warrant spending the time it will take

Conflict Management Norms

Any time you anticipate that a session has the potential to become contentious or if the group has had stormy meetings in the past, it's important to create new norms specially targeted for conflict situations. As with all other norms, these are best when created by the members. These norms can be set at the start of the session or they can be established during the interviews in the assessment phase. The following questions can be used to trigger the discussion:

- *"What behaviors and rules should we adhere to if we find ourselves getting into serious disagreements?"*
- *"What can we do to ensure that we have a healthy debate instead of a heated argument?"*

Norms are your best tool for heading off potential conflict.

Some sample norms targeted at conflict situations include:

- only one speaker at a time
- look at each other when speaking
- always acknowledge valid points made by the other person
- build on others' ideas
- don't dismiss any idea without really exploring it
- make sure everyone is heard, not just a few people
- don't be emotional, argumentative, or personal
- never engage in personal attacks
- call a time-out to stop and look at how things are being done when things are heated
- take a systematic approach to resolving issues rather than just pushing personal points of view
- be willing to accommodate in the interest of group progress

Giving and Receiving Feedback

Every facilitator encounters situations that require feedback: perhaps the meeting is dragging, maybe people need a break, perhaps the group needs to confront the tone the meeting has taken on. Managing feedback is an important facilitator responsibility. Feedback involves stopping the group's discussions to ask them to assess how it's going. Feedback can be about:

- how the meeting is going
- how members are conducting themselves
- whether or not the goal is being achieved
- how decisions are being made
- how the facilitator is doing

Every facilitator needs to know the core model for giving feedback.

General Principles of Good Feedback

Feedback is always meant to be constructive. The goal is to improve the current situation or performance, never to criticize or offend. The structure of giving feedback is a reflection of this positive intent. No matter what form feedback takes, the following general principles always apply:

Be descriptive rather than evaluative—Tell the other person what you notice or what has happened. Avoid all comments about him or her as a person.

Be specific instead of general—Describe exactly what happened so that facts, not impressions, form the basis of the feedback.

Solicit feedback rather than impose it—Ask the other person whether you can give him or her feedback. If the person says no, respect that this may not be a good time. Collaborate to determine a more convenient time.

Time it—Feedback should be given as soon as possible after the situation being described.

Focus on what can be changed—Make suggestions for improvements that the person is capable of implementing.

Check the feedback—Make sure your understanding is accurate and fair. Check with the person, or even with others, to avoid misjudging the situation.

Demonstrate caring—Offer feedback with the positive intent of helping the other person.

Feedback Formats

Feedback can take a number of forms. You'll find sample formats throughout this book, but here are a few to get you started. You can:

- Hand out a survey for members to complete at a break, then share results with the group for their analysis and action planning.

- Post selected questions and ask members to rate each item, then discuss the results and look for solutions to any items that received low ratings.
- Ask group members to give each other written feedback in response to questions such as: *"What things are you doing well?"* and/or, *"What could you do to become even more effective?"*
- Use force-field analysis to surface what is and is not going well. The group then creates remedies for all of the things that aren't going well.
- Simply ask members to offer concrete suggestions about what could be done differently.

The Eight-Step Feedback Process

WEB

Imagine you're at a meeting at which no one is putting the real issues on the table. Everyone is being polite and the problems of the group aren't being resolved. In this situation, the facilitator must stop the action and give feedback so the participants can resolve their problems and move on. It's never easy giving direct feedback, so use the right language and follow the steps outlined below:

Every facilitator needs to know the core model for giving feedback.

Step 1: Ask Permission to Offer Feedback

Asking permission lets people tell you if this is a bad time to hear feedback, and ensures that they're ready to pay careful attention. Asking permission is a way of signaling that you intend to give feedback.

- *"I'm going to stop this meeting now and give you some input that I think you need to hear. Is that okay?"*

Step 2: Describe Specifically What You Are Observing

Give a clear and specific description of what you observed. Avoid generalizing, exaggerating, or offering emotional accounts.

- *"During the interviews I held with more than half of you, the issue of some people not pulling their weight was mentioned by everyone as the most serious problem facing this team. We have been talking about team problems for two hours and yet no one has mentioned this issue."*

Step 3: Tell People About the Impact of Their Actions

Describe the impact on individuals, the program, or the department. Keep it very objective and don't get personal. Avoid blaming. Deal with the facts of the current situation.

- *"Since the issue of people not pulling their weight has not been mentioned, there's a good chance that these discussions are not going to resolve your most serious team problem."*

Step 4: Give the Person(s) an Opportunity to Explain

Listen actively, using attentive body language and paraphrasing key points.

- *"You're telling me that this problem isn't being discussed because it's too sensitive and people are concerned about offending each other."*

Step 5: Draw Out Ideas from Others

Frame the whole thing as a problem to be solved. Urge people to offer their ideas. Remember that people are most likely to implement their own ideas. The more they self-prescribe, the better. Support their efforts at self-correction.

- *"What do you think we could do to make it feel safe enough so that this issue can be discussed? What guidelines will create the comfort we need?"*

Step 6: Offer Specific Suggestions for Improvement

Make suggestions that will improve the situation. Wherever possible, build on the ideas suggested by others.

- *"I think the guidelines you have come up with are excellent. I'd like to add a few ideas about how we can tackle this with sensitivity. Would this be okay?"*

Step 7: Summarize and Express Your Support

Demoralizing people does not set the stage for improved performance, whereas offering encouragement and ending on an optimistic note does.

- *"I want to thank you for being willing to tackle this tough subject."*

Step 8: Follow Up

Make sure you end the feedback discussion with clear action steps. This ensures that the whole exercise doesn't need to be repeated later on.

- *"I'm going to stop the action in about an hour and check with you to see whether we're now tackling our real problems and if the guidelines we set are working."*

The Language of Feedback

Here is some feedback language that you can add to your tool kit:

Openers to Feedback

- *"I'd like to give you input about . . . "*
- *"I have a concern about . . . "*
- *"I have information that I think you might be interested in."*
- *"I'd like to make a suggestion, if you're interested."*

Facilitators use specific language to share their observations.

Examples of Feedback Statements

- *"Instead of . . . , it would be better if you would . . . ."*
- *"I know that you have a lot on your plate but I need . . . ."*
- *"When you . . . , I sense that you are/are not . . . ."*
- *"I'd like to propose that we try . . . rather than trying to . . . ."*

Avoid "usually" or "always," as these words may offer more emphasis than you intended or evoke a negative reaction. Never use judgmental labels that describe personal traits, such as "lazy," "thoughtless," and "sloppy." Instead, offer specific details about what the person did and when, like missing a deadline, not consulting on a decision, or leaving a room untidy. Also avoid using the word "should" when redirecting behavior. Instead, try phrasing like *"how about," "please try,"* or *"I need you to."*

Tips for Receiving Feedback

If you've ever been involved in a feedback exercise, you know how difficult it can be, especially for the person on the receiving end. To make it easier, teach participants how to receive feedback in a non-defensive manner. Share the following tips:

Always encourage people to be open and non-defensive.

Listen Actively

- Make eye contact with the speaker. Ask probing questions to make sure you understand what's being said.

Don't Become Emotional

- Breathe deeply. Sit back. Adopt a relaxed body posture. Lower your voice. Speak slowly.

Don't Be Defensive

- This isn't aimed at you personally. Understand the other person's perspective before presenting your side of the story. Ask for more details on points you don't agree with.

Accept the Input

- Even when you don't agree with everything being said, there will be some good ideas, so accept these. This shows respect for the other person's perspective.

Work to Improve

- Devote your energy to finding improvements rather than disputing observations. Do not put all of the burden for finding solutions on the other person. Offer ideas of your own.

Making Interventions

During any workshop or meeting, there may be occasions when the facilitator will need to make an intervention. The definition of an intervention is "any action or set of actions deliberately taken to improve the functioning of the group." This may be necessary in situations in which:

- two people are having a side conversation
- people are interrupting and not listening to each other's points
- people become overly emotional
- the discussion is stuck or off track

Interventions are needed in a wide variety of situations.

Intervening is like holding up a mirror to the participants so that they can see what they're doing and take steps to correct the problem. Regardless of its length and complexity, an intervention is always an interruption. You're stopping the discussion about the task to draw member attention to an aspect of the process. Since this constitutes an interruption in the flow of discussion, it should be done as quickly as possible so that members can return to the task.

The need to intervene may arise because of one individual, two people, or the whole group. Groups commonly experience problems that involve all of the members, such as when everyone is looking at a handheld device and not paying attention to the discussion or when people become tired and zone out.

Facilitators need to be cautious about whether or not to intervene. If you intervened every single time there was a problem, you could be interrupting too frequently. Instead, keep a watchful eye for repetitive, inappropriate behaviors that aren't resolving themselves. Those are the ones that deserve an intervention.

Deciding Whether or Not to Intervene

Below are questions to ask when deciding whether an intervention is advisable:

__ Is the problem serious?
__ Might it go away by itself?
__ How much time will intervening take? Do we have that time?
__ How much of a disruption will intervening cause?
__ How will it impact relationships, the flow of the meeting?
__ Can the intervention hurt the climate or damage anyone's self-esteem?
__ What's the chance that the intervention will work or fail?
__ Do I know these people well enough to do this?
__ Do I have enough credibility to do this?
__ Is it appropriate given their level of openness and trust?

Facilitators don't intervene at the smallest sign of trouble, but failing to make an intervention when one is needed is a mistake.

Finally, ask yourself what would happen if you did nothing. If the answer is that the group's effectiveness would decline, you're obligated to take action.

Wording an Intervention

WEB

Interventions are always risky because they have the potential to make the situation worse. For this reason, interventions need to be carefully worded. There are generally three distinct wording components to an intervention:

"I'm noticing..."

Statement 1: *Describe what you see*. This is non-judgmental and doesn't attribute motive. It's based solely on observations of actual events. Example: *"I'm noticing that we're now on a topic that's not on our agenda."*

"I'm concerned..."

***Statement 2: Make an impact statement*.** Tell members how their actions are impacting you, the process, or other people. Base this on actual observations. Example: *"I'm concerned that you aren't going to get to your other topics."*

"I need you to...." or "What should be done is ...."

Statement 3: *Redirect inneffective behavior(s)*. This can be done by (a) Asking members for their suggestions. Example: *"What do we need to do to get back to our agenda?"* (b) Telling members what to do. Example: *"Would you please end this conversation so we can get back on track?"*

Statement 1: Takes a snapshot to create awareness of an ineffective situation. Statement 1 does not resolve the situation, but is important to set the stage for the rest of the intervention.

Statement 2: Expresses a concern that serves as a rationale for making the intervention. Impact statements are best when they express concern for the person to whom the intervention is aimed. Impact statements can be omitted from an intervention if they seem to lay blame or worsen the situation in any way. Like Statement 1, impact statements do not resolve the situation.

Statement 3: Redirects the situation and is the most important element in an intervention. Statement 3 resolves the situation. It can be in the form of tactfully telling people what to do or asking them for their suggestions to improve the situation.

An intervention can be made using all three statements or Statements 1 and 3 or Statements 2 and 3 or Statement 3 on it's own. The bottom line is that Statement 3, the redirect, is always there.

Choose the right language to intervene: don't assume or judge!

Telling Versus Asking

In some interventions, the facilitator tells people what to do, while in others they are asked. When making an intervention, remember the following rules:

- Asking is always better than telling because people are more likely to accept their own interventions.
- The more a group acts maturely and responsibly, the more effective it is to ask, rather than tell.
- A directive or telling intervention is appropriate if individuals are exhibiting dysfunctional or low maturity behavior. With these people, asking will not elicit an effective response.

Wording for Specific Situations

The key to intervening effectively is to use extremely tactful language that doesn't sound critical or put anyone down. The examples below are all very tactfully worded to sound supportive rather than punitive. Don't be overwhelmed by this technique. It may seem difficult, but there are really only about twenty dysfunctions that routinely occur. Simply write out the likely situations and create the three sentences that you will use and memorize them. Then you will be ready to react at a moment's notice!

Make your intervention feel supportive of the people being addressed.

When two people are side-chatting: *"Alan. Sue. I see you having a discussion. I'm concerned that we're no longer benefitting from your ideas. We need you back."*

When people run in and out of a meeting: *"I've noticed several people coming and going. I'm concerned this may be disrupting the flow. What should we do?"*

When one person dominates the discussion: *"Joe, I'm noticing that you've already shared a lot of ideas. I'm concerned that you're not going to get to hear anyone else's report. Please wrap up with a summary of the most important ideas that you have shared so far."*

When two people are arguing and not listening to each other: *"I'm noticing that you are each repeating your points. I'm concerned that you may not be hearing each other's ideas. I'm going to ask you both to first paraphrase what the other has said before you make your own comment."*

Members are disregarding their own norms: *"I'm noticing that you're ignoring some of your rules. So let's stop and look at the norms we set last week. What do we need to do to ensure they're being followed?"*

When the meeting has totally digressed: *"I'd like to point out that you're now discussing a topic that isn't on the agenda. I'm concerned that you aren't going to get to your other topics. Do you want to continue discussing this topic or should we park it?"*

When someone is being sarcastic: *"Ellen, I'm concerned that your ideas aren't being heard because of the tone of voice you're using. Please make your point again, only in a more neutral way."*

When one person is putting down the ideas of another: *"Joe, you've been listing the cons of Carol's ideas. I'm concerned that we haven't tapped into your expertise. Please tell Carol what you think the pros of her idea are or offer her some suggestions to improve her idea."*

When someone has hurled a personal slur at someone else: *"Jim, rather than characterizing Sally as being sloppy, please tell her specifically about the state of the meeting room after her session, so that she can address the situation."*

When the meeting has stalled: *"I'm noticing that I haven't written anything for a while. I'm concerned the meeting may be stalled. What can we do to get things going again?"*

When the whole group looks exhausted: *"I'm noticing that people are slumped in their seats and that we're not making much progress. Tell me what this means, and what should we do about it?"*

Norm-Based Interventions

One of the reasons for creating a set of norms is that these can be used to manage ineffective behaviors. When group members break one of the rules that they set themselves, the norm can be used as the basis for the intervention. Here are some examples:

When people run in and out: *"I'm noticing that several people have left the meeting this hour. I'm concerned that you're breaking a rule you set earlier. Please remember your commitment not to come and go during the meeting."*

When people talk over each other: *"I'm concerned that you're breaking your own rule about only one conversation at a time. Please remember that you agreed to listen actively and not interrupt while others were speaking."*

When people get out their laptops and handhelds: *"I'm noticing that several people are texting. I'm concerned that you are ignoring the rule you set earlier about this. Please hold off until the break."*

Intervening is difficult, but allowing conflict to rage is not effective.

Body Language Interventions

People constantly communicate nonverbally. They will do things like fold their arms, roll their eyes, or look puzzled. Facilitators intervene about nonverbal communication to help people express what they're projecting.

Body language interventions follow a formula that is a variation of the three-step model already described. Here is that variation:

Step 1. Describe what you see.
Step 2. Ask what it means and offer options.

Here are some examples:

- *"I see a frown. What does that mean? Have we missed a point or is there something you don't agree with?"*
- *"I'm noticing some yawns. Tell me what that means. Do we need a break or should we pick up the pace?"*
- *"I see a puzzled look. Tell me what that means. Are you clear about what is being discussed or has someone made a point you need to hear more about?"*

Making interventions is not easy, but it is essential! Facilitators simply cannot stand by while ineffective behaviors rage. The key is to master the language of interventions so your comments are supportive and helpful rather than critical or punitive!

Making Interventions in Private

Intervening with someone in front of others can be risky, especially if that person is a senior manager or somewhat emotionally fragile. In some instances it is definitely better to pull the person aside to share feedback. Unfortunately, it's just not possible to call a break every time there's a need to help someone back to effectiveness.

For this reason, every facilitator has to master the art of making tactfully worded interventions. In fact, the three-step model, with its focus on stating a concern for the person being spoken to, has been designed precisely to avoid damaging the climate.

Another important thing to note is that, even when an intervention is made off side, it should still be done using the three-step language discussed earlier. Using this model will help to keep the atmosphere positive whether you are intervening in public or in private.

It may be advantageous to make some interventions in private, but you can't call a break every time you need to intervene!

Using Silence

One technique that has to be mentioned when discussing conflict management is the use of silence. When mediating differing views, it is sometimes very powerful to allow some silence in the room. This can be introduced after two parties have shared their points of view. In this instance the facilitator can say something like: *"Now that you've heard all of the major points, let's have a couple of minutes while each of you reflects about what has been said."*

Then look down and perhaps turn away from the group. Let the thoughtful silence sit there for at least a minute and maybe two. Look back only when the time is up and you are ready to offer a process for moving forward.

Silence is a helpful technique in conflict situations since it calms the air. People can catch their breath and think. It also signals to the group that you are in charge of the situation and have a plan. This instills their confidence in you.

Break the silence with a specific and constructive proposal. This would be something like engaging members in identifying the criteria useful for sorting out which course of action might be best.

Silence is okay. Use it to break the tempo of a conflict and to give people a chance to catch their breath.

Dealing with Resistance

It is a fact of life in today's busy workplace that people may be stressed by demanding workloads. In these situations they may resist the idea of taking part in any activities that could add to their workloads. Facilitators always have to be aware of this and be prepared with a strategy for dealing with both open and hidden resistance.

Always be on the alert for signs of resistance.

Groups can resist your facilitation efforts for a number of reasons:

- the timing or location of the meeting might be poor
- participants may have received insufficient notice of the meeting
- the topic of the meeting may not reflect the participants' needs
- people may worry that the session will result in additional work
- they may suspect that nothing will happen as a result of the meeting
- they may fear that the organization won't support their ideas

Sometimes this resistance comes out in the open when an outspoken member speaks up and vents a concern. At other times it remains hidden, expressed only in people's negative body language or lack of participation.

There's a right and a wrong way to deal with resistance. Using the wrong way will make the resistance grow. Choosing the right approach will make it manageable.

To help you become attuned to dealing with resistance, read the following scenarios and see whether you can identify what makes one response better than the other:

Resistance Scenario 1

Someone says: "*The last time we had a two-day retreat nothing happened afterwards. All the promises made were forgotten. People's projects went unsupported. These things are a waste of time!*"

Wrong thing to say: "*Well, we're here now and you've each been handpicked to do this project. Senior management is expecting you to do this. You have to accept that organizations are tough places to get things done. This is no time to turn back.*"

Right approach for handling resistance:

A. ***You ask:*** *"Why do you feel this way? What happened in the past? How did it impact you?"*

B. ***You listen and paraphrase the key points. Then you ask:*** *"What would make you a willing participant this time? Under what circumstances or with what assurances would you consider moving forward with the agenda?"*

Resistance Scenario 2

Someone says: "*This meeting is a waste of time. We all have tons of work to do back at the office. I suggest we adjourn right now!*"

Wrong thing to say: "*We're here now and some good progress has already been made. We booked the room. It will take months for all of us to coordinate our schedules again. We've even ordered lunch!*"

Right approach for handling resistance:

A. *"I want to hear why you think this meeting is a waste of time. What's gone on so far that's caused this frustration?"*

B. *"What changes can we make to the day to eliminate your main concerns? Under which circumstances would you consider staying?"*

Assertively making interventions does not violate facilitator neutrality since behavior is a process element.

Resistance Scenario 3

Someone says to you: "*Nothing personal, but we don't know you. What makes you think you can run this meeting?*"

Wrong thing to say: *"I have a master's degree in organization development, and this is exactly the sort of work I've been doing for ten years. Besides, I've been hired by the director of this division to run this meeting."*

Right approach for handling resistance:

A. You say: *"I can understand that you might have reservations about my role today, since you don't know me. Can you elaborate a bit on what those specific concerns might be?"*

B. You listen and paraphrase, and then you say: *"I want to be an effective facilitator at this meeting. What would make you change your mind about me? What would you need to see me doing at this session?"*

Did you notice that in the wrong approach, the facilitator became defensive and started telling and selling? In the wrong approach, the facilitator pushed back. Now let's look at what went on in the right approach.

Remember to never become defensive. When you are defenseless you are invincible!

The Right Approach

In reading the three scenarios, you may have noticed that when using the correct approach, the facilitator adhered to a consistent process. The correct approach for dealing with resistance consists of two steps:

Step 1: Venting the concerns. You invite the resistor to express his or her resistance while you listen actively, paraphrase, and offer empathy. No matter what he says or how he says it, you stay calm and act totally supportive of the resistor. You say things like:

- *"Tell me why you feel this way."*
- *"What happened last time?*
- *"What went wrong?"*
- *"Why did it happen?"*
- *"How did you feel?"*
- *"What were the consequences for you?"*

Step 2: Resolving blocks and barriers. After all the concerns have been acknowledged, you ask questions to prompt the resistor to suggest solutions to the barriers. This questioning is intentionally detailed and complex so that the resistors have to stop and think. It centers on questions like:

- *"What circumstances would make you willing to stay?"*
- *"What assurances would eliminate your concerns?"*
- *"What supports would enable you to continue?"*
- *"What can we do to make this work for you?"*

Using telling or selling to deal with resistance never works when you have no power or control over the group.

Why This Approach Works

Taking a facilitative or questioning approach works because the resistor is allowed to vent his or her frustration and be heard. The person is then consulted about what to do next. Since people don't generally refuse to act on their own suggestions, most people will abandon their resistance and move forward.

Telling people they have to comply usually makes them more angry. Selling makes them feel manipulated and generally increases their resistance.

Every day, meeting leaders handle resistance incorrectly by telling people they have no choice and to "just get on with it." The problem with using this kind of force to blast through resistance is that it erodes people's commitment. They'll comply, but they won't give it their best effort or most creative ideas. That's why the two-step facilitative approach is always superior to the directive telling approach when dealing with resistance. Another important reason for using the two-step approach is that facilitators don't usually have any power over the groups they're working with. When you have no control over people, ordering them to do something they don't want to do usually doesn't work.

Common Conflict Dilemmas

Regardless of how well a session is prepared, there are always things that can go wrong. The following are common facilitation dilemmas and strategies that can help.

Scenario 1: The Group Resists Facilitation. The group desperately needs structure for its discussions, but doesn't like following a step-by-step process. They insist they don't want a facilitator. Members say it feels too formal. Sometimes there's a controlling chairperson present and he or she rejects the idea of having a formal facilitator.

Strategy: Offer to facilitate. If rejected, don't hesitate to offer the group methods for tackling the discussion. Facilitate informally: monitor time, ask questions, paraphrase, and synthesize ideas, just as you would from the front of the room. Make notes and offer your summaries when they're appropriate.

Potential facilitator mistake: Accepting that the group doesn't want process help and letting it flounder. While it's always best to be able to "officially" facilitate, it's possible to help a group by covertly playing the process role. Some attention to process is better than none.

Scenario 2: Early in the Meeting It Appears the Original Agenda Is Wrong. In spite of data gathering and planning, it becomes clear that the entire premise for the meeting is wrong. The group legitimately needs to discuss something else.

Strategy: Stop the meeting and verify your assessment that the existing agenda is now moot. Take time to do agenda building. Ask members what they want to achieve at this session. Prioritize the issues and assign times. Take a short break to regroup and create a new process design. Ratify the new agenda with the members. Be flexible and stay focused on the needs of the group.

Potential facilitator mistake: Force the group to follow the original agenda because of the energy and preparation that went into creating the design.

Scenario 3: The Meeting Goes Hopelessly Off Track. Members are usually good at staying focused but have now gone totally off track and refuse to return to the planned agenda.

Strategy: Stop the off-topic discussion and determine whether members are aware that they're off topic and if they're comfortable with this. If they decide they want to stay with this new topic, help them structure their discussion. Ask:

> *"How long do you want to devote to this?" "What's the goal of this new discussion?" "What tools or methods should we use?"* etc.

Facilitate the new discussion. If members decide to return to the original agenda, "park" the current discussion and return to it at the end of the meeting.

Potential facilitator mistake: Stepping down from the facilitator role because the group isn't following the planned agenda or allowing the group to have a lengthy off-topic discussion without deliberately deciding that this is what they want to do. Trying to force a group back on topic when members feel a pressing need to discuss something else creates unnecessary conflict.

Scenario 4: Group Members Ignore the Process They Originally Agreed On. There's a clear process for the session, but the members simply ignore it. When you attempt to get people to follow the agreed-on method, they revert to random discussion.

Strategy: Let them go on this way for a while, then ask: *"How's this going? Are we getting anywhere?"* Once a group has recognized that it isn't making progress, members are often ready to accept a more structured approach.

Potential facilitator mistake: Give up and stop watching for an opening to step back in and offer structure. Take an "I told you so" attitude if members admit frustration with their approach.

Scenario 5: The Group Ignores Its Own Norms. Members have set clear behavioral norms, but start acting in ways that break these rules.

Strategy: Allow them to be dysfunctional for a while, then ask: *"How do you feel this meeting is going in terms of the rules you set?" "Which rules are being broken and why?" "What can you do to adhere to these rules?"*

Implement member suggestions. If they don't suggest anything, recommend that one or two group members be in charge of calling the group's attention to the rules any time they're being ignored or broken. This puts the onus on members to police themselves.

Potential facilitator mistake: Make verbal interventions without using the power of peer pressure to manage behavior.

Scenario 6: People Use the Session to Unload Emotional Baggage. The agenda is swept off the table as people start venting their frustrations about their jobs, other people, or the organization.

Strategy: Often groups can't focus on the task at hand because of pent-up feelings. In these cases, it's healthy to encourage participants to express their views. The key is to structure this venting so that it can be managed and feelings can be channeled into actions. Useful venting questions include:

- *"How important is it that you share these feelings now?"*
- *"Do we need to have any rules about how we do this?"*
- *"How long should this go on?"*

Potential facilitator mistake: Trying to suppress the venting process or letting it happen without time limits or a plan that leads to action steps.

Scenario 7: No Matter What Techniques Are Used, No Decision Is Reached. The group has been discussing options for hours and no clear decision is emerging. The discussion is spinning in circles and precious time is being wasted.

Strategy: Stop the action and look at the decision method that's being used. There are many decisions that simply can't be made through consensus or voting. Consider using another method like using a decision grid that allows for a more objective rating of individual aspects of competing options.

Another approach is to analyze the blocks to making a final decision by asking the group to identify what's keeping them from making a decision. Record the barriers and spend time removing the key ones.

Potential facilitator mistake: Letting the group spin around for the entire meeting without checking the decision method and/or examining the decision barriers.

Scenario 8: Members Refuse to Report Back Their Discussions. After a small group discussion, no one is willing to come forward and present the subgroup's ideas back to the larger group. There's a real concern that one or several of the ideas are too sensitive and that there might be repercussions.

Strategies: Divide the presentation and have two to three members from each group share the spotlight. If there's a lot of material, the whole team can present portions back to the larger group. Also set the stage with the larger group by asking them to listen with an open mind and not react negatively to the presentation before having explored its potential.

Potential facilitator mistake: Taking the burden from the members and speaking for them. This shifts responsibility for the recommendations from members to yourself and can result in members taking little responsibility for follow-up actions.

Scenario 9: Members Balk at Assuming Responsibility for Action Plans. People love discussing problems and brainstorming ideas, but when it comes to action planning, everyone is suddenly too busy or unsure about his or her ability to complete the task.

Strategy: Make it clear from the start that any problem-solving exercise includes action planning and that members will be expected to assume major responsibility for implementing their ideas.

Implementing action plans is often a growth activity if people can be given support and encouragement to stretch beyond their present capabilities. When people are concerned that they can't succeed, help them identify what materials, training, or other support they need in order to move forward.

If members have time barriers to participating in implementation, these need to be identified and problem solved. Organizations often ask the same hard-working people to be on every committee. If there's any control over who is going to be asked to work on an activity, considerable thought should be given to whether these individuals have the time needed to devote to the activity.

Potential facilitator mistake: Letting people "off the hook" too easily by not problem solving the blocks or letting the same people shoulder all of the work. The worst strategy of all is to take responsibility for the action steps yourself.

The Facilitative Conflict Management Process

The steps in managing differences of opinion collaboratively are essentially the same ones outlined in detail on pages 103 to 107 in Chapter Six on decision making. Once the emotions surrounding the situation have been vented, managing conflict collaboratively involves:

Step 1: Clarify the issue—create a clear statement of what the issue is. Ensure that everyone understands that statement.

Step 2: Make sure appropriate norms are in place—if things are likely to get emotional, make sure the team has the kind of rules needed to keep people safe and ensure effective behaviors.

Step 3: Set the time frame for the discussion—set limits so that people will know this will not drag on indefinitely.

Step 4: Explain the process to be used—the step-by-step approach that will be taken. Emphasize that tools will be used that ensure objectivity and thoroughness.

Step 5: Analyze the facts of the situation—help members gain a shared understanding of the situation. Make sure everyone is heard and that there's a full exploration of all relevant facts.

Step 6: Generate a range of possible solutions—use participative techniques like brainstorming or written brainstorming to create a wide range of potential solutions. Encourage people to build on each other's ideas to further dilute the idea that some ideas are the property of any one person.

Step 7: Evaluate the solutions—establish objective criteria for sorting through all the possible solutions. This can be multi-voting or a form of decision grid.

Step 8: Plan to implement the highest-ranked solutions—ensure that the what, how, who, and when are specified. Troubleshoot the action plan to make sure the steps are doable.

Use the following worksheet when you wish to provide detailed feedback to two people interacting during conflict.

Interpersonal Conflict Worksheet

Behaviors That Help	Person "A"	Person "B"
1. Leaning forward—listening actively		
2. Paraphrasing—"Is this what you're saying?"		
3. Questioning to clarify—"Let me understand this better."		
4. Showing respect to the other's opinion—valuing input		
5. Calmness—voice tone low, relaxed body posture		
6. Open and vulnerable—showing flexibility		
7. Clearly stating position—assertive stance		
8. Checking for agreement on what is to be resolved		
9. Laying out ground rules—"What will help us?"		
10. Showing empathy—checking perceptions		
11. "I" statements—disclosing feelings		
12. Using other person's name		
13. Body contact—if appropriate		
14. Problem solving—looking at alternatives		
15. Win/win attitude—concern for other person		
16. Congruence—between verbal and nonverbal behavior		
17. Concern for other person's goal		
18. Feedback—giving specific descriptive details		

Behaviors That Hinder	Person "A"	Person "B"
1. Interrupting		
2. Showing disrespect		
3. Entrapment questions		
4. Talking too much		
5. Pushing for solution		
6. Arguing about personal perception		
7. Aggressive manner		
8. Accusing, laying blame		
9. Smirking, getting personal		
10. "You made me" statements		
11. Non-receptive to suggestions		
12. Not identifying real feelings		
13. Ending before finishing		
14. Incongruity of words and actions		
15. Defensiveness		
16. Denying, not owning problems		
17. Blocking, talking off-topic—changing the subject		
18. Not giving specific feedback		

Use the following observation checklist to give feedback to a group about how members handle conflict.

Group Conflict Checklist

Throughout today's meeting pay special attention to the following ineffective behaviors:

- ❑ **No plan or process for approaching the task.** Group wanders from one topic to another because there's no format for discussion. No time is taken at the start of the meeting to establish a process.
- ❑ **Lack of active listening.** Instead of acknowledging each other's points before making their own, people push their own ideas without acknowledging each other.
- ❑ **Personal attacks.** People use a sarcastic tone, ignore each other, interrupt, or even attack each other. They don't focus on the facts.
- ❑ **Lack of process checking.** The group forges ahead without ever stopping to assess whether the process is working or requires modification.
- ❑ **Dominant members.** A few people do all the talking. No one notices or even cares that some people are left out.
- ❑ **Poor time management.** Time isn't budgeted or monitored. Time is wasted on the wrong things.
- ❑ **Folding.** People just give in when things get rough. They don't systematically follow through on issues.
- ❑ **Lack of skill.** There's no evidence that members possess decision-making tools. They also lack basic interpersonal skills.
- ❑ **Passive or nonexistent facilitation.** No one is providing order or policing the action. No notes are kept. Everyone is taking sides. If there's a facilitator, he or she is unwilling to offer procedural options or keep order.
- ❑ **Lack of closure.** The group moves from one topic to another without summarizing or identifying a course of action.

Use the following checklist while observing a facilitator handle conflict.

Conflict Observation Sheet

At today's meeting observe the facilitator's approach to conflict. Make note of as many specific incidents as possible to enrich the feedback.

Behaviors That Help	Behaviors That Hinder
__ letting people vent	__ arguing
__ asking for dissenting views	__ defensiveness
__ paraphrasing a lot	__ asking entrapping questions
__ showing respect for opposing views	__ letting a few people dominate
__ eye contact	__ favoring one side of any debate
__ effective body language	__ letting it get emotional or personal
__ calmness	__ ending before resolution
__ non-defensiveness	__ sidestepping the really hot issues
__ validating speakers	__ not using a process
__ redirecting sarcasm	__ not using the norms
__ confronting the facts	__ lack of empathy for member feelings
__ taking a problem-solving approach	__ letting it drag on
__ using norms for control	
__ showing concern for others' feelings	
__ making interventions	
__ checking on how people are doing	
__ disclosing personal feelings	
__ ensuring a good decision is made	
__ bringing proper closure	
__ mediating conflicts between two people	
__ making sure everyone stays involved	
__ evaluating how the team did during the conflict to learn from mistakes	

Implement the next survey to raise awareness of current patterns.

WEB

Conflict Effectiveness Survey

Read the following statements and rate how your group currently manages conflict. Be totally honest. Remember that this survey is anonymous. The results will be tabulated and fed back to the group for assessment.

1. Listening

1	2	3	4	5
People assume they're right.				People are open to hearing new ideas.

2. Acknowledging

1	2	3	4	5
People make points without acknowledging the points made by others.				People acknowledge each other's points even when they don't agree with them.

3. Objectivity

1	2	3	4	5
We tend to get emotional and argue for our favorite ideas.				We tend to stay calm and look objectively at the facts.

4. Building

1	2	3	4	5
We tend not to admit that anyone else's ideas are good.				We generally take the ideas of fellow members and try to build on them.

5. Norms

1	2	3	4	5
We don't have or use norms to manage conflict situations.				We have created a good set of norms that work well to help us manage conflicts.

6. Trust and Openness

1	2	3	4	5
People don't say what's really on their minds.				There is a lot of trust that you can say whatever you have on your mind.

7. Approach to Conflict

1	2	3	4	5
Most often we either avoid or argue vehemently.				We tend to collaborate to find solutions we can all live with.

Conflict Effectiveness Survey, cont'd

8. Interpersonal Behaviors

1	2	3	4	5

People often become emotional and make personal attacks. — We stay calm and stick to the facts. No one ever is personally attacked.

9. Structure

1	2	3	4	5

We never take a systematic approach. Mostly we just speak our minds. — There is always a clearly defined process for discussions.

10. Closure

1	2	3	4	5

Most of our conflict sessions end without resolution. — We are excellent at getting to solutions and clear action steps.

11. Process Checking

1	2	3	4	5

Once an argument starts we never call time-out and correct ourselves. — We always stop to look at how we're managing our conflicts so we can improve.

12. Time Management

1	2	3	4	5

When things get heated, we lose all track of time and our agenda goes out the window. — We carefully monitor time to make sure we aren't wasting it.

13. Aftermath

1	2	3	4	5

People are usually angry for a long time afterward. — We work at clearing the air of hurt feelings.

Use the survey feedback process to debrief the results.

Notes

Chapter Eight
Meeting Management

One of the key facilitator roles is to know how to design and manage effective meetings. First, sensitize yourself to the ingredients of an ineffective meeting:

- — lack of clarity about the meeting goal
- — a vague or nonexistent agenda
- — no time limits on discussions
- — no discernible process for working on important issues
- — no one facilitating discussions
- — people haven't done their homework
- — discussions that go off track or spin in circles
- — lack of closure to discussions before moving on
- — people vehemently arguing points of view rather than debating ideas
- — a few people dominating while others sit passively
- — meetings that end without detailed action plans for agreed next steps
- — absence of any process checking of the meeting as it unfolds
- — no evaluation at the end

Meetings are ineffective for a wide range of reasons.

Meetings That Work

By contrast, here are the ingredients shared by all effective meetings:

- — a detailed agenda that spells out what will be discussed, the goal of the discussion, who is bringing that item forward, and an estimate of how long each item will take
- — clear process notes that describe the tools and techniques that will be used
- — assigned roles such as facilitator, chairperson, minute taker, and timekeeper
- — a set of group norms created by the members and posted in the meeting room
- — clarity about decision-making options to be used
- — effective member behaviors
- — periodic process checks
- — clear conflict-management strategies
- — a process that creates true closure
- — detailed and clear minutes
- — specific follow-up plans
- — a post-meeting evaluation

Our Meetings Are Terrible!

Below are some of the symptoms of dysfunctional meetings and prescriptions for their cure. These are, of course, easier to identify than to fix, but if you can help team members become aware of their patterns, they can begin to resolve them.

Know the signs and symptoms of ineffective meetings.

SYMPTOMS	CURES
As each person finishes speaking, the next person starts a new topic. There is no building on ideas, thus no continuity of discussion.	Have each person acknowledge the comments of the last speaker. Make it a rule to finish a point before moving forward.
People argue their views, trying to convince others that they're right rather than understanding either the issue or anyone else's input. There is no listening.	Train members to paraphrase what is said in response to their points. Use the flip chart to record all sides of an issue. Get everyone to understand these differing views.
As soon as a problem is mentioned, someone announces that he or she understands the problem. A solution is very quickly proposed and the discussion moves to another topic.	Use a systematic approach to bring structure to discussions. Become thorough in solving problems. Avoid jumping to obvious solutions.
Whenever someone disagrees with a group decision, the dissenting view is ignored.	Develop an ear for dissenting views and make sure they are heard. Have someone else paraphrase the dissenting opinion.
The group uses brainstorming and voting to make most decisions.	Pre-plan meeting processes so other tools are on hand, and then use them.
Conversations often go nowhere for extended periods. In frustration the group moves on to a new topic without closure.	Set time limits on each discussion and periodically evaluate how it's going. Use summaries to achieve closure.
People often speak in an emotional tone of voice. Sometimes they even say things to others that are quite personal.	Have people stop and rephrase their comments so there are no distracting personal innuendoes.
People use side-chats to share their thoughts.	Encourage honesty by valuing all input. Draw side-chatterers back to group conversation.
Group members don't notice they've become sidetracked on an issue until they've been off topic for quite a while.	Call "time out" or have some other signal to flag off-track conversations. Decide whether you want to digress or park the particular issue.
The extroverts, or those with power, do most of the talking. Some people say little at most meetings.	Use round-robins to obtain input. Call on members by name. Use idea slips to get written comments from everyone.
No one pays attention to body language or notices that some people have tuned out or even seem agitated.	Make perception checks and ask people to express their feelings.
There is no closure to most topics. Little action takes place between meetings.	Stress closure. Reach a clear decision and record it. Have an action planning form handy. Bring actions forward at the next meeting.
There is no after-meeting evaluation. People debrief in their offices.	Do a meeting evaluation and discuss the results before the next meeting. Post any new rules or improvement ideas.

The Fundamentals of Meeting Management

1. Create and Use a Detailed Agenda

Each meeting must have an agenda that's been developed ahead of time and ratified by the members of the team. By having the agenda in advance of the meeting, members can do their homework and come prepared to make decisions.

Agendas should include:

__ the name of each topic, its purpose and expected outcome
__ time guidelines for each agenda item
__ the name of the person bringing each item forward
__ the details of the process to be used for each discussion

A clear agenda circulated in advance is a key ingredient to success.

If the agenda can't be designed in advance for whatever reason, then the first order of business at the meeting should be agenda building. In this facilitated discussion, members design the agenda for that day's session.

2. Develop Step-by-Step Process Notes

Most of the books that have been written on meetings do not mention "process notes," largely because these books are geared toward meetings that will be chaired rather than facilitated.

When a meeting is facilitated, there *must* be detailed process notes for each agenda item. These notes specify how the discussion will be facilitated. They specify the tools to be used and how participation will be managed.

In the following sample agenda, we've added process notes to illustrate their important role. While some facilitators keep these design notes to themselves, it's often a good idea to openly share the process notes with the group. (Examples of detailed process notes can be found in Chapter Ten.)

Facilitators always develop detailed process notes for each discussion.

Sample Agenda with Process Notes

Name of group: Customer Fulfillment Team
Members: Jane, Muhammed, Jacques, Elaine, Carl, Fred, Diane, Joe
Meeting details: Monday, June 12, 2005, 11:00 to 1:00 (Brown Bag Lunch), Conference Room C

WHAT AND WHY*	HOW (PROCESS NOTES)
Warm-up (10 min) → Joe; create focus	• Members share one recent customer contact story
Review agenda and norms (5 min) → Joe; set context	• Ratify the agenda and the norms through general discussion. Add any new items; make sure there is clarity about the overall goal of the meeting
Bring forward action items (25 min) → all members; implementation monitoring	• Brief report back by all members on action plans created at the last meeting; addition of any new plans

WHAT AND WHY*	HOW (PROCESS NOTES)
Focus group updates (20 min) → Jacques and Diane; identify areas for improvement	• Report on the outcomes of six customer focus groups • Use force-field analysis to distinguish between what we are doing well and what we are not
Prioritization of customer issues (20 min) → Joe; set priorities	• Establish criteria to evaluate customer concerns • Use criteria matrix to appraise each issue and identify priorities for action
Problem solving of priority issues (30 min) → entire group; create improvement plans	• Divide into two sub-teams to problem solve the two top-priority issues; create detailed action plans for the top issues; meet as a group to share and ratify ideas
Next-step planning and agenda building (10 min) → Joe; ensure closure and design next session	• Make sure people know what they're expected to work on; create agenda for next meeting
Exit survey (10 min) → Joe; check meeting effectiveness	• Have people evaluate the meeting on their way out the door • Identify items to be brought forward at the next meeting

****Note:*** Times given above are totally speculative and are only included for illustration purposes.

3. Clarify Roles and Responsibilities

Clarifying roles helps reduce overlaps and power struggles.

Effective meetings require people to play defined roles, such as those described below.

Chairperson: runs the meeting according to defined rules, but also offers opinions and engages in the discussion if he or she chooses. The chairperson has traditionally not been neutral. Most often, the chairperson of any meeting is the official leader, who plays an active role as both decision-maker and opinion leader.

Facilitator: designs the methodology for the meeting, manages participation, offers useful tools, helps the group determine its needs, keeps things on track, and periodically checks on how things are going. A facilitator doesn't influence *what* is being discussed, but instead focuses on *how* issues are being discussed. A facilitator is a procedural expert who is there to help and support the group's effectiveness.

Minute taker: takes brief, accurate notes of what's discussed and the decisions made. Also responsible for incorporating any notes on flip charts. Most often, minute-taking responsibilities are rotated among the regular members of a work group. However, for special meetings or if resources allow, this role can be assigned to a neutral outsider.

Timekeeper: a rotating role in which someone keeps track of the time and reminds the group about milestones periodically. Not a license to be autocratic or shut down important discussions if they're running over. The use of an automatic timer will allow the timekeeper to participate in the discussion.

Scribe: a group member who volunteers to help the facilitator by recording group comments on a flip chart. Some facilitators are more comfortable asking others to make notes on the flip chart while they facilitate. This has the benefit of freeing the facilitator from the distraction of writing, but adds its own complications. The scribe may start facilitating or may not take accurate notes. Since having a scribe takes an additional person out of the discussion, it is an impractical strategy for small groups. It is a standard practice for facilitators to make their own notes. If a scribe is used, clarifying questions should always be channeled through the facilitator, instead of the scribe interacting directly with the members.

Balancing the Roles of Chairperson and Facilitator

Chairing and facilitating are two distinct meeting management roles. Each has its purpose and place.

Chairing is most useful at the start of a meeting in order to review past minutes, share information, and manage a round-robin report-back by members.

Chairing traditionally relies on the use of pre-published rules of order.

Since chairs are not neutral, their major drawback is that they tend to influence decisions and concentrate power. It's not uncommon for a strong chairperson to make final decisions on important items.

A consequence of this decision mode is that the chair "owns" the outcome. There's also little emphasis on using process tools by traditional chairpersons.

Facilitating is designed to foster the full and equal participation of all members for items on which their input is needed. Because facilitators are neutral, they empower members. They rely on consensus and collaboration to reach important decisions. This results in decisions for which the whole group feels it has ownership.

Facilitation creates rules from within the group, rather than imposing rules from a book. Facilitation is also associated with a rich array of tools and techniques designed to create synergy and obtain better ideas.

A very common role arrangement is to have a meeting leader who uses a chairperson approach to start the meeting and review the agenda, take care of the housekeeping and information-sharing portions of the session, and then switch to facilitation in order to obtain input on specific topics.

Effective chairpersons know when to switch roles in order to facilitate.

All good facilitators should know when and how to act as effective chairpersons. Conversely, it would be ideal if all chairpersons were also skilled facilitators, who could switch roles whenever it was desirable to get participation and ownership.

With advance planning, these roles don't need to conflict. The keys are to remember that each has its place and to be clear about which approach is being used in which situations.

In Summary

Chair when you want to:	Facilitate when you want to:
• review past minutes and agenda items	• gain participation and shift ownership
• hear members report back or exchange information	• engage people in planning, problem solving, or relationship building
• remain accountable for decisions	• help members to make decisions

Always ensure that norms are posted and accurately used.

4. Set Clear Meeting Norms

Make sure that the group has clear norms for behavior and that those norms are created by the group. Help the group tailor its norms to meet the demands of particular meetings by engaging members in setting targeted norms if they are needed. (Refer to the conflict management norms on page 124.)

5. Manage Participation

Make sure that everyone is part of the discussion, that structure exists for each item, that there's effective use of decision-making tools, and that closure is achieved for all items.

Facilitators are responsible for ensuring that members know and exhibit effective group behaviors. If members lack group skills, facilitators need to conduct simple training exercises, such as those, suggested on page 82.

6. Make Periodic Process Checks

Process checking is a technique to use during meetings to keep things on track. This involves stopping the discussion periodically to redirect member attention to how the meeting is going.The purpose of this shift in focus is to engage members in a quick review in order to identify needed improvements.

There are four elements in process checking:

1. Check the purpose: Ask members whether they're still clear about the focus of the meeting, to make sure everyone is still on the same page.

When to check the purpose: If the conversation seems to be stuck, or if people seem to be confused; at least once per session.

2. Check the process: Ask members whether the tool or approach being used is working or needs to be changed. *"Is progress being made?"* Ask for or offer suggestions for another approach.

When to check the process: When the process tool being used isn't yielding results, or it's evident that the process isn't being followed as originally designed.

3. Check the pace: Ask whether things are moving too quickly or too slowly. Implement suggestions for improving the pace.

When to check the pace: When things seem to be dragging or moving too fast; any time people look frustrated; at least once per session/meeting.

4. Check the people: Ask members how they're feeling. Are they energized? Tired? Do they feel satisfied or frustrated? Ask for their suggestions about how to change energy levels.

When to check the people: Any time people look distracted, frustrated, or tired; at least once during each session.

Regularly check the process.

One of the most common challenges in meetings is when the wheels start spinning and the discussion gets stuck. Getting stuck is a cue to conduct a process check. This intervention goes something like this:

- *"I'm noticing that points are being repeated but nothing is being decided."*
- *"Are you stuck? Why is this happening?"*
- *"Is anyone confused about the topic under discussion?"*
- *"Is the approach being used working or do we need to try something else?"*
- *"Are we moving too fast, too slow?"*
- *"How are people feeling? What can we do to start moving again?"*

Although process checks are usually done verbally, they can also be conducted in the form of a survey posted on a flip chart. Members are invited to anonymously rate how the meeting is going, usually as they leave the room for a break. When members return, they are asked to interpret the survey results and brainstorm ideas for improving the remainder of the session. All practical suggestions are implemented.

Meetings need to end with true closure.

Sample Process Check Survey

Tell us how it's going so far.

Purpose: *To what extent are you clear about our goals?*

1	2	3	4	5
Poor	Fair	Satisfactory	Good	Excellent

Progress: *To what extent are we achieving our goals?*

1	2	3	4	5
Poor	Fair	Satisfactory	Good	Excellent

Pace: *How does the pace feel?*

1	2	3	4	5
Far too slow	Slow	Just right	Fast	Far too fast

Pulse: *How are you feeling about the session?*

1	2	3	4	5
Totally frustrated	Exhausted	Satisfied	Pleased	Energized

7. Determine Next Steps

Never let a group leave a meeting without clear next steps in place. This means defining what will be done, by whom, and when. These action plans need to be brought forward at all subsequent meetings to make sure that the group is following through on commitments.

8. Evaluate the Meeting

Effective groups make it a habit of routinely evaluating meeting effectiveness.

There are three basic ways to evaluate a meeting:

1. Conduct a Force-Field Analysis—this involves asking:

"What were the strengths of today's meeting?" **(+)**

"What were the weaknesses?" **(–)**

"What should we do to correct the weaknesses?" **(Rx)**

2. Post an Exit Survey—three to four questions are written on a sheet of flip-chart paper and posted near an exit. Members fill it out upon leaving the meeting. The results are brought forward and discussed at the start of the next meeting. On the next page you'll find a sample of exit survey elements.

3. Implement a Written Survey—create a survey and distribute it to members to complete anonymously. After tabulation, the results are discussed at a subsequent meeting. This is an appropriate exercise to be done three or four times a year for any ongoing group or team. A sample written Meeting Effectiveness Survey is provided on page 156 of this chapter. The survey feedback process is described on page 191 of Chapter Nine of this book.

Sample Exit Survey

Output—To what extent did we achieve what we needed to?

1	2	3	4	5
Poor	Fair	Satisfactory	Good	Excellent

Organization—How effective was the meeting structure?

1	2	3	4	5
Poor	Fair	Satisfactory	Good	Excellent

Use of Time—How well did we use our time?

1	2	3	4	5
Poor	Fair	Satisfactory	Good	Excellent

Participation—How well did we do on making sure everyone was involved equally?

1	2	3	4	5
Poor	Fair	Satisfactory	Good	Excellent

Decision Making—How well-thought-out were our decisions?

1	2	3	4	5
Poor	Fair	Satisfactory	Good	Excellent

Action Plans—How clear and doable are our action plans?

1	2	3	4	5
Poor	Fair	Satisfactory	Good	Excellent

Implement the next survey to create impetus for improving meetings.

Limit exit surveys to five or six questions.

Implement this survey to create impetus for improving meetings.

Meeting Effectiveness Survey

Rate the characteristics of your meetings by circling the appropriate number on each scale to represent your evaluation. Remain anonymous. Return the survey to your group facilitator for review at a future meeting.

1. Preparation

Does everyone come prepared and ready to make decisions?

1	2	3	4	5
We are often unprepared				We are always well prepared

2. Communication

Are agendas circulated to all members in advance of the meeting?

1	2	3	4	5
Agendas are rarely circulated in advance				Agendas are always circulated in advance

3. Setting

Is there a quiet place for the meeting, with ample space and support materials?

1	2	3	4	5
The meeting place is not well suited				The meeting place is excellent

4. Meeting Objectives

Are objectives and expected outcomes clearly set out for each agenda item?

1	2	3	4	5
Objectives and outcomes are never clear				Objectives and outcomes are always clear

5. Start Times/End Times

Do meetings start/end on time?

1	2	3	4	5
Meetings hardly ever start/end on time				Meetings always start/end on time

6. Time Limits

Are time limits set for each agenda item?

1	2	3	4	5
We do not set time limits				Time limits are always set for each item

7. Role Clarity

Are roles such as timekeeper, scribe, and facilitator clearly defined?

1	2	3	4	5
Roles are not clarified				Roles are always clearly defined

Meeting Effectiveness Survey, cont'd

8. Past Meeting Review

Are action items from the previous meeting(s) brought forward?

1	2	3	4	5

Items are seldom brought forward — Previous items are always brought forward

9. Process

Is there clarity before each topic as to how that item will be managed?

1	2	3	4	5

There is rarely any structured process — There is always a structured process

10. Interruptions

Are meetings being disrupted due to people leaving, pagers, phones, etc.?

1	2	3	4	5

There are constant interruptions — We control interruptions

11. Participation

Are all members fully engaged and taking responsibility for follow-up?

1	2	3	4	5

People hold back and don't take ownership — Everyone offers ideas and takes action

12. Listening

Do members practice active listening?

1	2	3	4	5

We don't listen closely to each other — Members listen actively

13. Conflict Management

Are differences of opinion suppressed, or is conflict effectively used?

1	2	3	4	5

We tend to argue emotionally — We debate objectively

14. Decision-Making Quality

Does the group generally make high-quality decisions?

1	2	3	4	5

We tend to make low-quality decisions — We tend to make high-quality decisions

15. Leadership

Does one person make all the decisions, or is there a sharing of authority?

1	2	3	4	5

A few people make most decisions — Decision making is shared

Meeting Effectiveness Survey, cont'd

16. Pace

How would you rate the pace of your meetings?

1	2	3	4	5
Poor				Excellent

17. Tracking

Do meetings stay on track and follow the agenda?

1	2	3	4	5
Meetings usually stray off track				Meetings usually stay on track

18. Record Keeping

Are quality minutes kept and circulated?

1	2	3	4	5
No, they're not				Yes, they are

19. Consensus

Do we work hard to make collaborative decisions that we can all live with?

1	2	3	4	5
We abandon consensus too easily				We work hard to reach consensus

20. Closure

Do we effectively end topics before moving on to new ones?

1	2	3	4	5
We move on without closure				We close each topic before moving on

21. Follow-Up

Is there timely, effective follow-up to commitments made at meetings?

1	2	3	4	5
We tend not to follow up				There is consistent follow-up

Note: Use the survey-feedback process described in Chapter Nine to engage participants in assessing the results of the Meeting Effectiveness Survey in order to identify meeting improvement strategies.

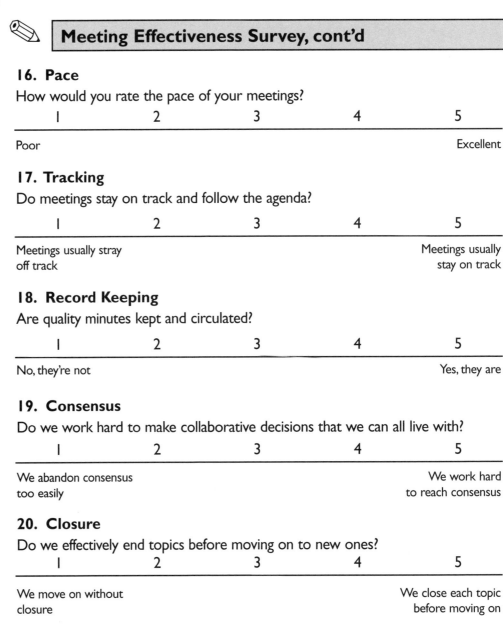

Facilitating Virtual Meetings

There is an ever-growing trend toward meetings that take place over the phone or the Internet. In the next few years this trend is going to increase as more and more new kinds of technology become available. Hopefully, more of these virtual meetings will feature a visual component to make them feel less disconnected and more interactive.

First, let's look at some of the special challenges of virtual meetings:

- people can't see each other, so the meetings tend to feel impersonal and disconnected
- because people can't see each other, interaction tends to be stilted and conversations tend toward one-way information sharing
- since people have to wait for a chance to talk, meetings can drag on far too long
- sometimes people sit in silence for long stretches listening to conversations that have nothing to do with them
- it's impossible to read body language to pick up on the nonverbal clues that identify how people are feeling or whether they're fully engaged as the meeting progresses
- if differences of opinion crop up, it's very difficult to manage the conflict effectively, bring other people into the conversation, or help the parties arrive at a mutually agreeable solution
- while minutes are usually sent out afterward, there are no flip-chart notes being taken during conversations to keep everyone focused and to help the conversation move forward
- meeting participants could be doing any number of other tasks during the session like reading, eating, working on their computers, or sorting out their desks, rather than paying attention
- it's easy for people to walk in and out of a virtual meeting without detection by the other participants
- if materials weren't sent out ahead of time, it's impossible to hand out new information

One of the most important guidelines for all virtual meeting is to design them to include only those things that need real-time interaction. Too many hours of valuable work time are wasted if people are reporting in and sharing updates that could have been posted before the call on a shared Internet bulletin board.

Use calls to become acquainted, discuss problems, jointly search for solutions, make decisions, ratify action plans, clarify work assignments, etc.

Don't waste call time on reviewing notices, reading each other's reports and sharing routine updates, or anything else that can be done before the virtual meeting via email or on a shared site.

This means that the facilitator needs to send out pre-work and any notices that people need to read to prepare for the call. The call host also needs to clarify what needs to be done before the session and what will be handled at the session.

Virtual meetings improve when they're given more structure.

As with any face-to-face meeting, virtual meetings need an agenda that is circulated ahead of time and that specifically describes the objectives and expected outcomes of the meeting. The guidelines for developing an effective meeting agenda complete with process notes can be found earlier in this chapter.

While facilitation was created for face-to-face meetings, many key elements can be borrowed from the facilitator tool kit to help make distance meetings more effective.

The facilitation techniques that most improve virtual meetings are many of the same ones that work in a face-to-face meeting: providing a clear purpose, describing the process, conducting a warm-up exercise, making interventions, calling on people by name, conducting periodic process checks, paraphrasing key ideas, offering periodic summaries, ensuring that key items have closure, and providing clear action steps. Here is how you can use these strategies to improve any virtual meeting:

Before the Meeting

- Contact participants by phone or email to seek their input to the agenda.
- Create a detailed agenda, with process notes, that identifies the various types of conversations that will be held (information sharing, planning, problem solving, relationship building).
- Identify who needs to be involved and for which segments of the call, plus the information that each participant needs to prepare.
- Distribute the agenda to the participants so they can do their homework and dial in to the call at the time they'll be needed.

At the Start of the Virtual Meeting

- Conduct a roll call to establish that people are engaged and ready to proceed. If applicable, invite each person to state what he or she wants to get out of the meeting. Record these personal goals and refer to them throughout the meeting to help keep people engaged and let them know you have them in mind.
- Create a name map on a blank sheet of paper in front of you. Beside each name, write down the person's stated goal for the session. As the meeting progresses, make a check mark beside people's names every time they speak. This will remind you of who is on the line and what each of them needs from the session. It will also help you identify the people who need to be brought into the conversation.
- Review the agenda to clarify the overall purpose of the call, the purpose and process for individual segments, and the time associated with each segment. Also be clear about who needs to be part of which conversations.

- Clarify the rules of the meeting. This can be a facilitated conversation, or you can propose a core set of rules that participants can amend and ratify. The following rules are provided as an example of norms that will help improve the quality of any virtual meeting.

Norms for Virtual Meetings

To ensure that this call is productive, we will all:

- be as clear and concise as possible
- try to engage others by asking questions and offering our opinions
- ask for clarification if it's needed
- freely express concerns and opinions
- speak up if we notice we've been silent for too long or if a particular conversation needs to wrap up
- strive to stay focused: avoid doing other tasks
- ask for a summary any time we need to refocus
- announce when we are leaving the call

Virtual meetings require their own targeted norms.

During the Virtual Meeting

- At the start of each topic, review the purpose, process, and time frame for each item.
- Call on people by name, both to present and to comment on what others have said. Keep track of who is getting airtime.
- Periodically make process checks to ensure that things are still on track.

The Virtual Meeting Process Check

- Is the purpose still clear?
- Is our approach working? Are we making progress?
- Is the pace okay? . . . too fast? . . . too slow?
- Have we lost anyone?

- To bring closure to a topic, offer a summary of the key points that were made. If it was a decision-making discussion, turn the summary into a decision statement, then conduct a roll call to ask them to accept the final decision.
- Help the group create action plans for any topics that need them. Encourage people to take responsibility for follow-through.

Virtual meetings need closure just like any other meeting.

At the End of the Virtual Meeting

- Review the summaries for each topic and the action steps that have been identified.
- Invite each person to say whether his or her goal for the meeting has been achieved or to make a statement of what he or she takes from the meeting.
- Conduct a brief post-meeting evaluation by asking people to identify what worked or did not work and ideas to improve future sessions. If this is impractical, create an evaluation form online and deploy it through email.
- Share details about when and how the minutes will be shared.
- Identify any future teleconferences.
- Express thanks for everyone's participation and sign off.

Chapter Nine
Process Tools for Facilitators

Imagine a carpenter trying to build a house without the proper tools. It would certainly be ineffective, if not altogether impossible! Fortunately for facilitators, there is a rich set of tools available to help them do their work.

Since scores of process tools exist, it would be impossible to explain them all. Only the most commonly used tools will be highlighted in this chapter. This set represents the basic processes that every facilitator should know how and when to use. You'll find a detailed description of the following tools in this chapter:

- Visioning
- Sequential Questioning
- S.W.O.T.
- S.O.A.R.
- Facilitative Listening
- Appreciative Review
- Brainstorming
- Written Brainstorming
- Affinity Diagrams
- Gap Analysis
- Needs and Offers Dialogue
- Force-Field Analysis
- Root-Cause Analysis
- The Five Whys
- Gallery Walk
- Multi-Voting
- Decision Grids
- Constructive Controversy
- Exit Surveys
- Survey Feedback
- Systematic Problem Solving
- Troubleshooting

It's important to know how to use a variety of process tools.

In addition to these tools, all facilitators should learn the techniques associated with quality improvement such as process mapping, story-boarding, histograms, scatter diagrams, and critical path charts.

Visioning

What is it? A highly participative approach to goal setting.

When to use it? When members need to clarify their own thoughts and then share those ideas with each other to create a shared statement of the desired future.

What's its purpose? Allows people to put forward their ideas. Makes sure everyone is involved and heard from. Creates energy. Helps people to align. Gives people an interactive method to identify a group goal.

What's the outcome? The visioning process is very participative and energizes everyone in the room. It also creates buy-in because the group's direction is coming from the members themselves. Everyone is involved at once. All ideas are heard. This is a great way to conduct goal-setting with a group.

How to Do Visioning

Step 1. Post a series of questions that relate to the task and ask how the final outcome ought to look at a future point in time. The vision questions will always be different, of course, depending on the situation.

> ***Sample Visioning Questions for a Customer Service Improvement Team***
> Imagine that it's exactly two years from today:
> - *Describe how you now serve customers.*
> - *What specific improvements have been made?*
> - *What are people saying about the team now?*
> - *What problems has the group solved?*
> - *What specific outcomes have been achieved?*
> - *How are people behaving differently?*

Step 2: Ask each person to write down his or her own responses to the questions. Allow at least five minutes. Give more time if needed. Ask people not to speak to each other during this writing phase.

Step 3: Ask everyone to find a partner. Ideally, this is the person he or she knows least. Allocate three to five minutes for the first partner to share his or her vision. Ask the other partner to facilitate. After three to five minutes, ask the partners to switch roles so that the second person can talk.

Step 4: When time is up, ask everyone to find a second partner. Repeat the process outlined in Step 3, only allow slightly less time per person. Encourage people to "steal" any good ideas they heard from their last partners and incorporate these into their own visions.

Step 5: Repeat the process again with new partners. This time, limit the exchange to one to three minutes per person in order to encourage people to prioritize and share key points.

You can stop after only a few rounds or continue until everyone has spoken to everyone else.

Step 6: Ask people to return to their original seats, and then begin facilitating a discussion to pull the ideas together. You'll find that ideas have become fairly homogenized by this point.

In a very large group, you can gather ideas by using the Gallery Walk method described later in this chapter.

Sequential Questioning

What is it? An assessment exercise in the form of a series of closed-ended questions, which are posed to the whole group at the start of a workshop.

When to use it? To uncover important information about the group, their issues, or their activities. To test and probe in a challenging manner. To raise issues and create awareness of shared needs.

What is its purpose? Yields information, lets you test assumptions, and engages people. Allows people to safely surface complex issues. Vents negative feelings and creates an obvious need to take action. Helps the facilitator anticipate the issues that might come up throughout the day. When done well, this technique creates a shared desire for change. It also acts as a group warm-up.

What's the outcome? Sequential questioning is a challenging technique that creates sparks. It raises issues and starts people talking about the barriers. It raises people's consciousness about what the important problems are. It sets the stage for problem solving and solution development.

Since there is potential for disagreement, if you plan to use sequential questioning, you have to be prepared to make interventions and manage differing opinions.

How to Do Sequential Questioning

Step 1: Analyze the overall topic and create five to ten questions working from macro to micro issues. Build questions around issues people identified in pre-workshop interviews. Pose the questions as closed-ended questions or items to be rated on a scale. Choose someone to answer yes or no to each item. Each question should probe the situation in a challenging way so that the ensuing discussion reveals honest information that is important to the issue at hand.

Step 2: Write each question at the top of a separate sheet of flip-chart paper. Use the rest of the sheet to record reactions. Don't let people see the questions until you pose them. As you turn over each sheet, read the question, pause, then ask one person in the group to respond. Record that person's response.

Then, invite others to add their thoughts. Discuss people's reasons until you have recorded all comments. It's not always necessary to get agreement, but strive to create a summary statement that expresses key ideas.

Sample questions are offered on the next page, but remember that questions always have to be created to fit the particular situation.

A Sample of Sequential Questions

Topic: Business Improvement

Answer ***yes*** or ***no,*** then explain your response.

yes or ***no***	The overall business environment for the next five years is going to be advantageous for our business.
Rationale➤	
yes or ***no***	We are fully prepared to handle all the opportunities that will occur in the next five years.
Rationale➤	
yes or ***no***	Our current business development strategy is dynamic and flexible enough to respond to constant changes in the business environment.
Rationale➤	
yes or ***no***	Our business strategy should be developed by people at the higher levels.
Rationale➤	
yes or ***no***	Our staff are ready and motivated to overcome barriers.
Rationale➤	
yes or ***no***	We completely understand our customers' needs and wants.
Rationale➤	
yes or ***no***	We have an early warning and performance measurement system that lets us track our progress and make timely corrections.
Rationale➤	
yes or ***no***	There is a high level of harmony and cooperation that ensures synergy and teamwork inside our organization.
Rationale➤	
yes or ***no***	We have the best products on the market. We own the market in our field.
Rationale➤	
yes or ***no***	We have a fairly flawless delivery system for getting our product to our customers.
Rationale➤	
yes or ***no***	We often have creative business development discussions during our regular meetings. Better customer service is a topic we discuss all the time.
Rationale➤	

S.W.O.T.

What is it? A fundamental analysis tool useful at the start of strategic conversations. The letters stand for Strengths, Weaknesses, Opportunities, and Threats.

When to use it? To provide a framework at the start of a strategic planning activity. To gather data about the environment.

What's its purpose? To create a balanced picture of both the positives and negatives that need to be taken into consideration during the planning process.

What's the outcome? S.W.O.T. fosters a constructive, growth-oriented and possibility-focused understanding of the organization's potential.

How to Do a S.W.O.T. Analysis

Step 1: Circulate the questions associated with the four categories of inquiry to allow participants time to reflect and prepare.

Step 2: For groups of fewer than twelve individuals, facilitate a group discussion in which the questions are explored and discussed in depth. Record key ideas. In a large group, create small groups of three or four people. Allow fifteen to twenty minutes for discussion of the questions in all four categories.

Step 3: Create areas around the room where people can gather in small groups to share and record their ideas. Use the steps described in this chapter for the Gallery Walk process to encourage dialogue and to gather ideas.

A Sample S.W.O.T. Analysis

STRENGTHS

- What are we doing really well?
- What are our greatest assets?
- What are we most proud of accomplishing?
- What makes us unique?
- What do our strengths tell us about our skills?
- How do we use our strengths to get results?

WEAKNESSES

- What aren't we doing well?
- What are our greatest liabilities?
- In what areas have we underperformed?
- What are our limitations in the areas of resources, staff, technology, etc.?
- What do our weaknesses tell us about ourselves?
- What are some of the reasons that we have not yet overcome our weaknesses?

Opportunities

- What are the most profound changes shaping our environment?
- What innovation out there inspires us to change?
- How can we make a difference for the organization and its stakeholders?
- What are the top three opportunities on which we should focus our efforts?
- How can we reframe weaknesses or threats so they become opportunities?
- What are our customers asking us to do?
- What synergies can we create with other groups?

Threats

- Who or what is our biggest competitor or danger?
- What is the competition doing that could harm us?
- What would be the worst thing that we could do?
- What threat have we underestimated or failed to consider?
- What threats do our weaknesses expose us to?

S.O.A.R.

What is it? A strength-based analysis tool useful at the start of strategic conversations. A more positive version of the well-known S.W.O.T. Analysis. The letters stand for Strengths, Opportunities, Aspirations, and Results.

When to use it? To set a positive tone for planning conversations. At the start of strategic retreats. To reframe the current situation in positive terms in situations where issues of low morale need to be addressed.

What's its purpose? To create an upward spiral of thought, action, and behavior. To encourage creativity and out-of-the-box thinking. To guide strategic thinking toward the possible, without being hampered by the negatives.

What's the outcome? S.O.A.R. fosters a constructive, growth-oriented, and possibility-focused understanding of the organization's potential.

How to Do a S.O.A.R. .

Step 1: Circulate the questions associated with the four categories of inquiry to allow participants time to reflect and prepare.

Step 2: For groups of fewer than twelve, facilitate a group discussion in which the questions are explored and discussed in depth. Record key ideas. In a large group, create small groups of three or four people. Allow fifteen to twenty minutes for discussion of the questions in all four categories.

Step 3: Create areas around the room where people can gather in small groups to share and record their ideas. Use the steps described in this chapter for the Gallery Walk process to encourage dialogue and to gather ideas.

A S.O.A.R. Sample

Strengths

- What are we doing really well?
- What are our greatest assets?
- What are we most proud of accomplishing?
- What makes us unique?
- What do our strengths tell us about our skills?
- How do we use our strengths to get results?

Opportunities

- How do we collectively understand outside threats?
- What are the top three opportunities on which we should focus our efforts?
- How can we reframe them to see opportunities?
- What is the organization asking us to do?
- How can we best partner with our customers?
- What synergies can we create with other groups?

Aspirations

- When we explore our values and aspirations, what are we deeply passionate about?
- What's our most compelling aspiration? Who should we become?
- How do we allow our values to drive our vision?
- How can we make a difference for the organization and its stakeholders?

Results

- Considering our strengths, opportunities, and aspirations, what meaningful measures would indicate that we are on track for achieving our goals?
- What do we want to be known for?
- How do we tangibly translate our strengths, opportunities, and aspirations?

Facilitative Listening

What is it? A technique for getting people to listen to each other and really hear each other's ideas. A way of teaching people effective listening skills.

When to use it? To ensure that people really understand each other in situations in which there are opposing ideas and people have a history of not hearing each other's views. As a key first step in mediating a conflict.

What does it do? Allows everyone to receive a fair hearing and feel understood by the "opposing side." Circumnavigates conflicts by placing people in pairs and limiting their interactions to either presenting views or listening to understand.

What's the outcome? This structured approach to listening ensures that people listen to, comprehend, and acknowledge the opposing views of others. Because counter-arguments are not allowed, people have an opportunity to hear each other's views. Feeling heard relieves tension and sets a positive tone for tackling issues together.

How to Do Facilitative Listening

Step 1: Announce that you will be asking participants to take part in facilitative listening. Tell group members that they will be selecting partners. Review the following rules:

- One person will be speaking and expressing his or her thoughts about the subject at hand.
- The second person will not be expressing any thoughts on the subject, but only doing the following things:
    - *Staying neutral* no matter how he or she feels about what the other person is saying.
    - *Listening actively* by maintaining eye contact and using attentive and open body language.
    - *Asking probing questions* after each point made by the other person, to encourage the person to dig deeper.
    - *Paraphrasing* what the first person is saying to help him or her clarify his or her thoughts.
    - *Summarizing* what the other person has said to let the other person know that his or her ideas have been understood.

Step 2: Clarify the topic to be addressed. Then ask everyone to find a partner. It's important that people select a partner from the "opposing" group. Ask the partner pairs to spread out around the room so that they feel they have some privacy.

Step 3: Determine how much time is appropriate for the particular topic. Set a timer and have the pairs begin their conversations. After about ten to fifteen minutes, stop the action and have partners switch roles and repeat their conversations. This will allow each person a chance to speak as well as a turn being the facilitator.

Step 4: After both people have had turns to speak, ask everyone to find a second partner. Tell people to take what they learned from the first discussion and share it in the second session. Set the timer for the second session. When finished, you can ask group members to repeat with another partner if desired.

Step 5: If you are working with two individuals, ask each to make a short presentation back to the other person, summarizing his or her new understanding of the situation. Make sure these summaries are acceptable to both parties.

Step 6: If you're working with a group, gather up the comments by either facilitating a discussion (in groups under twenty) or use the Gallery Walk process (for groups over twenty), described next.

Appreciative Review

What is it? A positive discussion about the past in which group members answer questions about recent events to explore all of the good things that have happened.

When to use it? When the morale of a group has sagged. Very useful during the mid-point check meeting of any project. When it supports the effectiveness of the team to remember all of the positive things that they have accomplished and to appreciate each other. Great at the start of a strategic planning meeting before looking forward. Should be part of any discussion to help restart a team that has fizzled out.

What does it do? It encourages group members to reflect on all that they have accomplished and all of the positive things that they have going for them. Also gives individual group members a feeling that they have contributed and are valued by others.

What's the outcome? Group members have an opportunity to reflect on the good things that have taken place. They also receive public recognition for their contributions. This lifts the spirits of the members and reenergizes them for the work ahead.

How to Use Appreciative Review

Step 1: Create a series of questions similar to the ones below:

- *"Looking back over the last few months, what have we accomplished?"*
- *"What has been our greatest achievement? What makes us most proud?"*
- *"What outside factors helped us achieve those successes?"*
- *"What role did each of us play to achieve that?"*
- *"What lessons did we learn during our recent work?"*
- *"What excites us about the opportunities ahead?"*

Step 2: If the group has fewer than six members, facilitate a discussion of all of the questions in the total group. If the group is larger, break the group into subgroups of three or four members. Ask these subgroups to answer the first three questions and make notes so they can share their answers with the larger group.

Step 3: Bring the members back together and ask each subgroup to share what they discussed while you record answers on a flip chart or electronic board.

Step 4: Pose the question about what each person contributed to the whole group. Allow a minute or two for quiet reflection. Invite each person to speak about his or her contribution to the success of the group. If someone is downplaying his or her role, invite others to point out what they've seen that person contribute. It's not necessary to record this conversation. What matters is that it takes place publicly.

Step 5: Ask group members to form new subgroups so that they get to talk to others in the group. Pose the remaining two questions. Ask someone in each subgroup to take notes.

Step 6: Bring the members back together again to share their answers to the last two questions. Record all comments at the front of the room.

Brainstorming

What is it? A synergistic technique that frees people to think creatively and generate innovative ideas.

When to use it? When it's advantageous to generate a free flow of creative ideas that are not bound by the usual barriers. To involve everyone. To create energy. To generate a wide range of potential ideas.

What's its purpose? Allows people to explore new ideas and challenge traditional thinking. Lets people put ideas on the table without fear of being corrected or challenged. It separates the creation of ideas from the evaluation activity.

What's the outcome? A wide range of creative ideas. Because brainstorming frees people from practical considerations, it encourages them to think creatively. It's also an energizing process that helps move people to take action. Because it's highly participative, brainstorming makes everyone feel that he or she is an important part of the solution.

How to Do Brainstorming

Step 1: Announce that you will be using brainstorming. Review the rules:

- Let ideas flow
- There are no bad ideas
- Be creative
- Think in new ways
- Build on others' ideas
- Break out of old patterns
- Keep discussion moving
- No evaluation until later

Step 2: Clarify the topic being brainstormed, then allow some quiet time while people think about solutions.

Step 3: Ask members to let their ideas flow. While you can brainstorm by going round-robin around the group, brainstorming is best done spontaneously with members offering ideas as they come to mind.

Step 4: Record ideas as they're generated. Do not discuss or elaborate on them. Keep it moving.

Step 5: When people have run out of ideas, generate additional ideas by asking probing questions such as:

"What if money were no object?"
"What would our competitors wish we would do?"
"What's the opposite of something already suggested?"

Step 6: When the flow of ideas has stopped, explore each brainstormed idea in detail so that it's fully developed and clearly understood. Combine like ideas that are simply worded differently.

Step 7: Use a decision grid, affinity diagram, or multi-voting to sort the ideas.

Written Brainstorming

What is it? A private and individual idea-generation technique in which people write down their ideas, then pass them to other group members, who build on them.

When to use it? When people are reluctant to speak in front of others, or when there are outspoken members who might dominate a traditional brainstorming session. Also useful if the issue or topic is sensitive, since the initial idea-generation step is anonymous and private.

What's its purpose? The anonymity of this tool provides the freedom to encourage people to express their ideas.

What's the outcome? A lot of ideas are generated in a short time. It also allows people to to learn others' ideas in an anonymous setting.

How to Do Written Brainstorming

Step 1: Clarify the topic or issue for which ideas will be generated. Explain the process to members.

Step 2: Give each person small slips of sticky paper. Ask members to work alone to they think of ideas that relate to the topic being discussed. Allow anywhere from three to ten minutes for the idea-generation step.

Step 3: Ask members to fold their idea slips and toss them onto the center of the table. (Slips should not have names on them.)

Step 4: Mix the slips and ask each person to take back as many as he or she tossed in. If anyone pulls out his or her own slip, that person can toss it back or exchange it with a neighbor.

Step 5: Each person now has three to five minutes to think of additional ideas based on the thoughts stimulated by reading the ideas picked from the pile. These new slips should be thrown into the middle of the table and then tossed and also distributed.

Step 6: Once all ideas have been distributed, ask members to read aloud all the ideas on the slips they drew from the pile.

Step 7: Discuss each idea so that it is fully understood. Do not try to find out who suggested each idea. Stick all the slips on a wall or on flip charts.

Step 8: Use a decision grid (page 188) or multi-voting (page 186) to sort the most effective ideas to fit the situation.

Affinity Diagrams

What is it? A tool for organizing ideas into common themes. A visual tool for organizing a large amount of information into themes so that the ideas are more manageable.

When to use it? When there are a lot of ideas being generated. This can be during problem analysis as a way of sorting all of the contributing factors. It can also be used to sort ideas after a brainstorming session.

What's its purpose? To draw out common themes from a large amount of information. To discover previously unseen connections between various ideas or information.

What's the outcome? Turns random ideas into coherent themes. Allows the best ideas to emerge naturally.

How to Use Affinity Diagrams

Step 1: Help the group write a clear statement of the topic or problem situation being discussed and the purpose of the discussion. Clarify whether the group is analyzing a problem, generating solutions, or simply listing the elements of an event or project.

Step 2: Set up a large wall space with flip-chart paper or divide the surface of a whiteboard into sections. Hand out sticky note pads and markers. Have large sticky pads on hand to create headings.

Step 3: Allow quiet time while group members write ideas on their sticky notes. Go around the group and invite members to read their ideas. After all ideas are read aloud, allow more quiet time during which people can write the additional ideas that occurred to them while they were listening to the suggestions of colleagues.

Step 4: Help group members identify the headings or categories that will fit the ideas generated. Some examples of header cards are human resources, training, budgeting, policies, culture, resources, etc. Write the headings on the larger sticky notes and post these header cards on the wall or the electronic board.

Step 5: Invite group member to place each idea card in the category it most closely fits. Clarify the placement of any ideas that may be unclear or seem to fit in two places.

TRAINING SOLUTIONS	TECHNOLOGY SOLUTIONS	PERSONAL SOLUTIONS
☐	☐	☐
☐	☐	☐
☐	☐	☐
	☐	

Step 6: Review and ratify the organization of ideas. Stick duplicate ideas over one another. Allow people to add any new ideas that come to mind. Facilitate a discussion to see whether any obvious themes are emerging. Which categories have the most ideas? What does that indicate?

Step 7: Rank ideas within each topic area. Hand out markers or multi-voting dots and allow members to select the three to five best ideas for implementation in each topic area. Review these ranking and ratify the results. Organize members to create action plans for the top-rated items.

Gap Analysis

What is it? A planning tool that lets groups identify the steps they need to take in order to achieve a goal.

When to use it? When a group needs to understand the gap between where they currently are and where they ultimately want to be.

What's its purpose? Gap analysis encourages a realistic review of the present and helps identify the things that need to be done to arrive at the desired future.

What's the outcome? Gap analysis creates a shared view of what needs to be done to eliminate the gap between the present state and the desired future.

How to Do Gap Analysis

Step 1: Identify the future state. Use a tool like visioning or any other approach that generates a picture of where the group wants to be at a specific time. The description of the future must be detailed. Post the information on the right-hand side of a large blank wall.

Step 2: Identify the present state. Describe the same components featured in the future state, only do so in present terms. Again, be very detailed. Post the ideas generated on the left-hand side of the wall work space.

Step 3: Ask members to work with partners to identify the gap between the present and the future. Ask questions such as:

> *"What are the gaps between the present and the future?"*
> *"What are the barriers or obstacles to achieving the future?"*

Step 4: Once partners have finished their deliberations, share ideas as a total group and post the gaps between the "present" and the "future."

PRESENT STATE		GAP		DESIRED FUTURE
Teams operate without leaders for months because there aren't enough people trained	→	No team-leader training program	←	A trained cadre of leaders who can be deployed to support any team

Step 5: Once there's consensus on the gaps, divide the large group into subgroups. Give each subgroup one or more of the gap items to problem solve or action plan.

Step 6: Reassemble the whole group to hear recommendations and action plans. Ask members to ratify the plans, then create a follow-up mechanism.

Needs and Offers Dialogue

What is it? A constructive dialogue between two parties to identify action steps they can take to improve their relationship. A positive and constructive dialogue that lets people express past and present concerns about the relationship in totally constructive terms.

When to use it? To encourage dialogue between parties to either resolve a conflict or improve relations proactively before problems occur.

What's its purpose? To vent concerns and resolve interpersonal issues in a low-risk manner. To negotiate a new, more positive relationship.

What's the outcome? An improved understanding of each other's views and feelings. Mutually agree to action plans that will enhance relations.

How to Do Needs and Offers Dialogue

Step 1: Clarify who will be the focus of the exercise. This can be a team and its leader, two subgroups of the same team, a team and management, or two individuals.

Step 2: Set a positive climate for the exercise by talking about the value of giving and receiving feedback. Make sure that the appropriate norms are in place to encourage members to speak freely and honestly.

Step 3: Explain the rules of the exercise. The two parties will be separated for a period of twenty to thirty minutes. During that time, each party will identify what he or she needs from the other party in order to be effective. This process is identical whether the parties are two individuals or a team and its leader.

Step 4: When each party has written its "needs list," bring them back together to share their thoughts, one at a time. While one party is sharing his or her needs, the other must listen actively, then provide a summary of the other party's needs.

Step 5: Once parties have heard and acknowledged each other's needs, separate them again for twenty or thirty minutes while they consider what they're prepared to offer to the other party.

Step 6: Bring the parties back together and have them take turns sharing their offers. Allow for discussions or clarification. End the conversation by having members ratify what they have heard and make commitments to follow through.

Force-Field Analysis

What is it? Force-field analysis is a structured method of looking at the two opposing forces acting on a situation.

When to use it? When you need to surface all of the factors at play in a situation, so that barriers and problems can be identified. To encourage members to make a balanced assessment of a situation.

What's its purpose? Clarifies the resources available and also the barriers or obstacles. Helps the group to gain an understanding of the forces acting on their work.

What's the outcome? Force-field analysis is a valuable tool for analyzing situations and identifying problems that need to be solved. It helps groups make more effective decisions because it lets members look at both positive and negative forces at play.

How to Do Force-Field Analysis

Step 1: Identify a topic, situation, or project, for example: computer training.

Step 2: Help the group state the goal of the discussion: *"All staff to receive training in the new operating system in three weeks."*

Step 3: Draw a line down the center of a flip-chart sheet. Use one side to identify all of the forces (resources, skills, attitudes) that will help reach the goal. On the other side, identify all the forces that could hinder reaching the goal (barriers, problems, deficiencies, etc.).

A Sample Force-Field Analysis

Goal: train all staff in the new operating system in three weeks	
Forces That Help Us Resources in Place →	← ***Forces That Hinder Us Problems and Deficiencies***
• staff eager for improved software • state of the art software • computer-literate stuff • four great training rooms • 80 percent of staff at a central location • six qualified instructors	• disruptions to work schedules • software complexity • high need for ongoing coaching • lacking at least six training rooms • 20 percent of staff geographically scattered • costly external instructors • bad time of year for training

Step 4: Once all the help and hinder elements have been identified, use multi-voting or a decision matrix to determine which of the hindrances or barriers are a priority for immediate problem solving.

Step 5: Address the priority barriers using the Systematic Problem-Solving Model (page 193).

Variations of Force-Field Analysis

Force-field analysis has a number of variations. Each is used in approximately the same way as previously described.

These variations include:

- ✓ Pros ←——→ ✗ Cons
- ✓ Things we are doing well ←——→ ✗ Things we could do better
- ✓ Hopes ←——→ ✗ Fears
- ✓ Best case scenario ←——→ ✗ Worst case scenario
- ✓ Assets ←——→ ✗ Liabilities
- ✓ Strengths ←——→ ✗ Weaknesses
- ✓ Positives ←——→ ✗ Negatives
- ✓ Opportunities ←——→ ✗ Obstacles

Root-Cause Analysis

What is it? A systematic analysis of an issue to identify the root causes rather than the symptoms.

When to use it? When you need to delve below surface symptoms and uncover the underlying causes of problems.

What's its purpose? Leads to more complete and final solutions.

What's the outcome? Root-cause analysis enables groups to look more deeply at problems and to deal with the underlying causes. This often means that problems are more likely to be definitively resolved.

How to Do Root-Cause Analysis

Step 1: Explain the difference between "causes" and their "effects" to group members. For example, you can ask whether a noisy muffler is a cause or an effect. Once people have identified that it's an effect, ask them to list all of the causes. Point out that effects can't be solved, but underlying causes can.

Step 2: Use either of the two basic methods for identifying root causes: Cause and Effect Charting or Fishbone Diagrams.

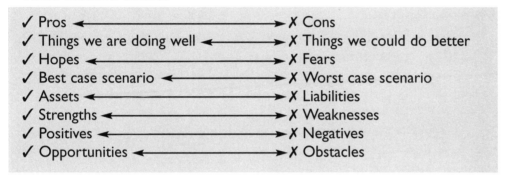

Cause and Effect Charting

1. To use this method, divide a flip-chart sheet in half and write "Effect" on the left side and "Causes" on the right.

   Example: Noisy Muffler.
   Effect: Noise and smoke when accelerating
   Causes: Corrosion, loose clamp, puncture

2. Whenever anyone offers a point of analysis, ask whether it's a cause or an effect. Write each item in its appropriate column. Uncover underlying causes by asking "Why? Why? Why?" about each effect. Continue until all causes have been identified. Use a tool like multi-voting to rank causes.

Fishbone Diagrams

A fishbone diagram is a visual tool to identify and then sort all of the contributing causes for the situation being analyzed. The cause categories within fishbone charts vary, but usually include people, machinery/equipment, methods, materials, policies, environment, and measurement. The number of categories will vary by subject.

Start by placing the observed effect at the "head" of the fishbone. Determine the major cause categories, then ask members to brainstorm all of the possible causes to link to each "rib" of the fish.

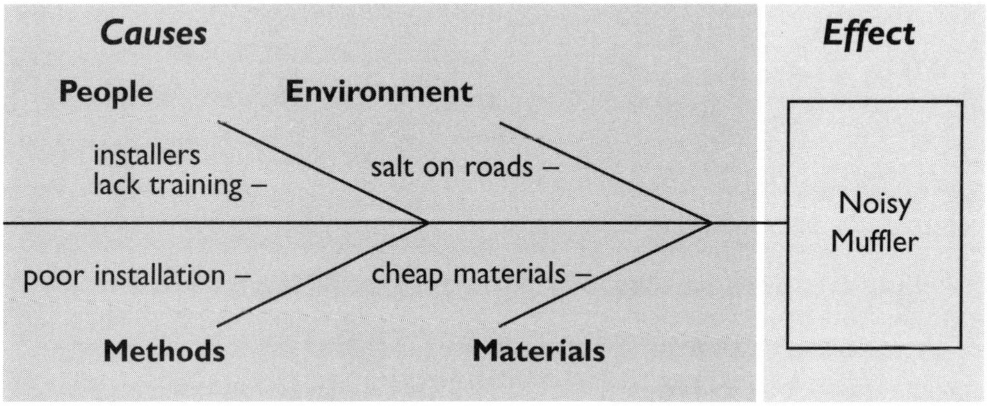

Step 3: Regardless of which approach is used, once all of the root causes have been identified, apply multi-voting to identify which causes are the highest priority for resolution.

The Five Whys

What is it? A simple technique for getting to the root of a problem.

When to use it? During the analysis step of problem solving.

What's its purpose? To uncover root causes layer by layer.

What's the outcome? Gets past symptoms to the deeper, underlying issues.

How to Do the Five Whys

Step 1: Clarify the symptom that's being explored to ensure that everyone is clear about what's being discussed.

Step 2: Ask the group: *"Why is this happening?"* Record all responses.

Step 3: Ask: *"Why is this happening?"* about either the original topic or about the newly recorded information.

Step 4: Repeat the last step three more times, each time recording all comments.

Step 5: Stop to review the notes. Ask members if they think the information generated reflects the root cause of the original issue. If there are multiple root causes identified, you can hand out voting dots and allow members to mark the three to five most significant root causes identified.

A Five Whys Example

My car will not start (problem/symptom)

Why?	The battery is dead.
Why?	The alternator is not functioning.
Why?	The alternator belt has broken.
Why?	The alternator belt was worn out and has never been replaced.
Why?	I don't maintain records of when parts need to be replaced.

Gallery Walk

What is it? A safe and participative means of engaging a large number of people in productive conversations about specific issues. A way of using the walls in a room to gain a lot of input from a large group in a short time.

When to use it? When you want to explore a wide range of topics with a large number of people and have little time to do it. To energize a group and bring everyone into the conversation. When there is a topic that people may not want to talk about in open conversation. When a large open space with useable walls is available and you have a group of at least twenty people.

What does it do? Creates a relatively safe and anonymous setting for conversation. Provides an alternative means of generating group synergy because people read and then build on each other's ideas.

What's the outcome? A large number of issues are explored. Group ideas are developed. Everyone participates and their ideas are added into the mix.

How to Do a Gallery Walk

Step 1: Set up the room by posting blank sheets of flip-chart paper in separate locations around the room. Electronic boards can also be used.

Step 2: Clarify the topic or series of topics to be discussed. Then divide the topic into segments or subtopics.

Step 3: Post one topic segment or subtopic at the top of its own flip-chart sheet.

Step 4: Instruct people to wander the room and gather at a flip chart that features a topic about which they have knowledge. Be clear that there must always be no fewer than three and no more than five people at each flip-chart. Once there, the participants discuss the topic and record their collective thoughts for a specified period, typically in the range of five minutes.

Step 5: At the end of five minutes invite everyone to wander to another flip-chart station, read what the first group has written, and confer with whomever else wandered there in order to add more comments to the sheet. This process can be repeated until all of the flip-chart sheets are filled. It is not necessary that each person visit each station.

Gallery Walk Variations and Applications

In planning exercises, the flip-chart topics can coincide with various key questions in the planning process, such as: What are the key consumer trends? What competitive forces do we face? What are our manufacturing strengths? What are our manufacturing weaknesses? What are the next technological innovations we need to prepare to adopt? and so forth.

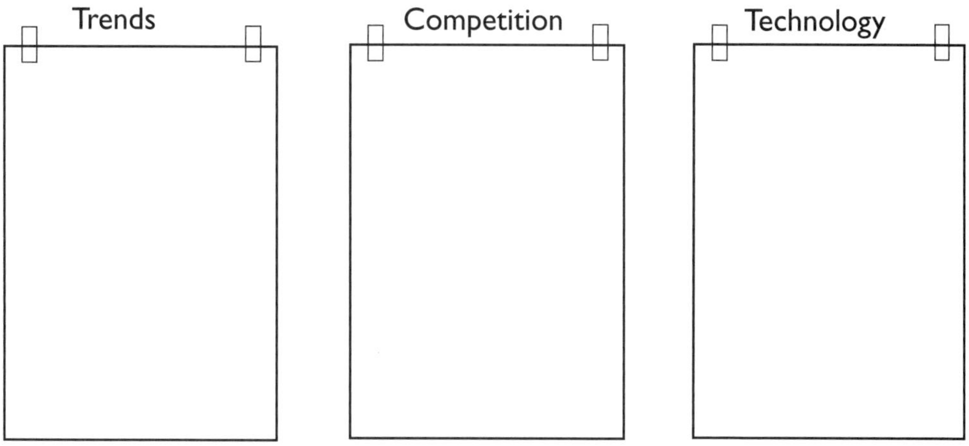

In a problem-solving exercise, it's possible to solve solve a large number of problems by posting each in a different area and then having participants wander to first analyze each problem. When all of the problems have been analyzed by at least three sets of wandering visitors, have people retrace their steps to read the completed analysis sheets and then begin to brainstorm solutions. After everyone has wandered to at least three stations to add solutions, give everyone a colored marker and invite the participants to tour all of the sheets of brainstormed solutions to check off the three ideas they think should be implemented.

Inadequate Phone System **Lack of Volunteers**

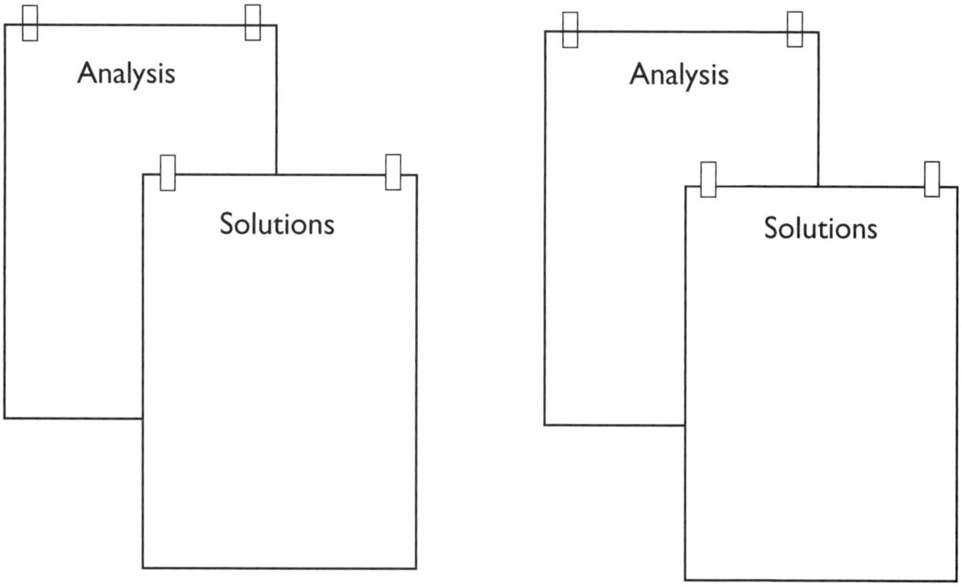

Multi-Voting

What is it? A priority ranking tool that enables a group to quickly sort through a long list of ideas.

When to use it? After any idea-generating discussion.

What's its purpose? Rapidly establishes priorities in a participative manner. Allows a group to sort a great number of ideas without having to discuss and compare them.

What's the outcome? Multi-voting is democratic and participative. Since most members will see several items they favored near the top of the priority list, multi-voting tends to result in a sense of *"I can live with it."*

How to Do Multi-Voting

Step 1: Clarify the items being prioritized. This may be a list of barriers from a force-field analysis or a list of ideas from a brainstorming session. Have members discuss each item to ensure everyone understands the choices.

Step 2: Identify the voting criteria to ensure that everyone votes with the same criteria in mind. Many situations benefit from voting several times, applying different criteria to each vote. Examples of criteria include:

- the most important items
- the lowest cost items
- the easiest items to complete
- the first items in a logical sequence
- the most innovative items
- the most significant given the strategic direction
- the most important to our customers

Step 3: Once the criteria are clear, there are various methods for conducting a multi-vote.

Voting with Sticker Dots

- Purchase sheets of file folder dots from an office supply store. Cut the sheets into strips.
- Distribute strips of from four to seven dots to each person. Use slightly fewer dots than half the items to be sorted to force people to make choices (for example, give out four dots to sort ten items).
- Ask members to place their stickers on their top four choices. Ensure that no one puts more than one sticker on any one item.
- When everyone has voted, tally the dots in order to arrive at the priorities.

Distributing Points

- Give each person points to distribute among the items to be sorted. The number of points is typically either 10 or 100.
- Members then write their points beside the items they favor. It's wise not to allow anyone to place more than 50% of their points on any single item.
- When everyone has voted, add the scores to arrive at the priorities.

Weighted Multi-Voting

In some prioritizing activities it's advantageous to assign weights to the voting dots. these weights could be as simple as numbering the dots from one to four. A more advantageous approach is to give some dots an even greater weighting. This results in a more clear dfferentaition of the ranked items.

- An example of simple weighting:

1 2 3 4

- An example of differentiated weighting:

10 7 4 1

Note: To avoid having people influence each other in how they are voting, consider asking people to mark their dots with the item they will be placing it beside before they approach the flip chart. This will cause all votes to be locked in and will eliminate what is known as "herding."

Decision Grids

What is it? A matrix that uses criteria to assess a set of ideas in order to determine which are most likely to be effective.

When to use it? To bring more objectivity and thoroughness to a decision-making process.

What's its purpose? To provide a structured decision-making process for dealing with a complex issue involving multiple elements. Transforms a random debate into one in which solutions are judged against an objective set of criteria.

What's the outcome? Clear, sorted ideas emerge from a mass of random inputs. Grids also make the sorting process more systematic. Since everyone casts votes or expresses opinions, the use of grids is participative.

How to Use Decision Grids

Two types of decision grids are illustrated below: Impact/Effort Grids and Criteria-Based Grids.

Impact/Effort Grids

Step 1: Re-create the chart on a flip-chart paper or electronic board.

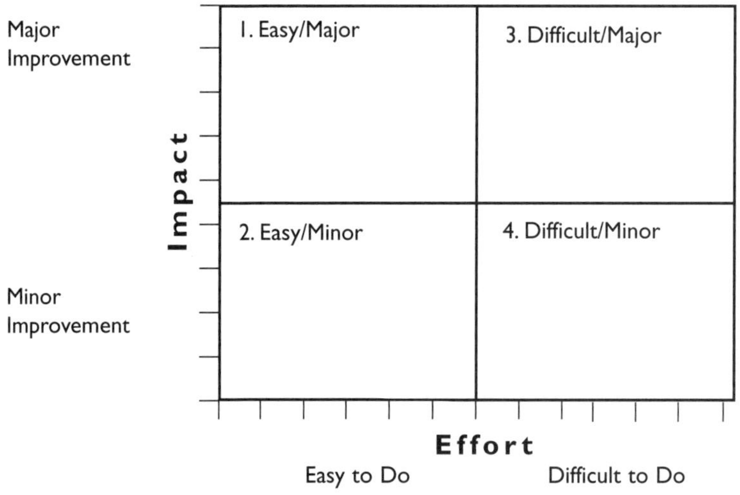

Step 2: Discuss the various choices, then place each in one of the four boxes:

1. Easy to do and yielding a big improvement for immediate implementation
2. Easy to do but yielding a small improvement for immediate implementation
3. Difficult to do and yielding a big improvement action as major projects
4. Difficult to do and yielding small improvement/discarded

Step 3: Once all ideas have been placed in one of the four boxes, help group members to develop action plans, starting with those ideas that were identified to be easy to do.

Impact/effort grids are somewhat simpler to use than criteria-based grids because the grid has already been designed and there's no need to create criteria.

The major difficulty in using an impact/effort grid lies in clarifying exactly what is meant by the terms "easy to do," "difficult to do," "small improvement," and "big improvement". Being clear about terminology at the start will avoid much heated debate.

Criteria-Based Grids

Step 1: Ask members to identify the criteria against which potential solutions will be judged. Examples are:

- saves time
- saves money
- reduces stress
- is timely
- is feasible
- is affordable
- supports the strategic plan
- is something we can control
- represents the right sequence
- doesn't disrupt our operation
- will get management support
- satisfies customer needs

Step 2: The relevant criteria are chosen from this list and placed along the top of a grid. The options being considered are placed down the left column. Note that some criteria may be more important than others, and hence given more weight. An example of weighted criteria uses the following scale:

(x 1) = does not meet the criteria
(x 2) = somewhat meets the criteria
(x 3) = good at meeting the criteria

Step 3: The choices are then evaluated as to the extent each meets the criteria. Scores are tallied to identify the best choice.

Example: Decision grid for assessing solutions to the challenge of training fifty people in new software in fourteen days.

	Criteria	**Cost-Effective (x 1)**	**Meets Customer Needs (x 3)**	**Speed (x 1)**	**Lack of Disruption (x 1)**	**Totals per Solution**
Choices	Shut down to give all staff two days' classroom training	1 2 1 1 ÷ 4 = 1.25	1 1 1 1 ÷ 4 = 1.00	3 3 3 3 ÷ 4 = 3.00	1 1 1 1 ÷ 4 = 1.00	**8.25**
	Have experts on site for two weeks to give one-to-one support	2 2 2 1 ÷ 4 = 1.75	2 3 2 2 ÷ 4 = 2.25	1 2 1 1 ÷ 4 = 1.25	3 3 3 3 ÷ 4 = 3.00	**12.75**
	Have only ten people off for two days at a time	2 2 3 3 ÷ 4 = 2.50	2 3 3 2 ÷ 4 = 2.50	2 2 2 2 ÷ 4 = 2.00	2 2 2 3 ÷ 4 = 2.25	**14.25**

Constructive Controversy

What is it? A technique for understanding a solution more fully or for improving it by arguing for and against the idea.

When to use it? For very important decisions that need careful deliberation. When there are two or more ideas on the table and group members have differing points of view about them. When exploration of those differences could yield important insights and a better decision.

What does it do? Helps ensure that all points of view have been considered and that the final choice is based on sound analysis. Encourages groups to draw conclusions based on evidence and well-structured reasoning.

What's the outcome? When opposing views are aired in a constructive environment, the result is a better-thought-out decision.

How to Use Constructive Controversy

Step 1: Develop a set of possible solutions or implementation ideas. Use a decision grid or multi-voting to identify the top two or three.

Step 2: Form advocacy teams around the selected ideas. Allow teams time for research into all the positives of the selected course of action. Encourage teams to create scenarios of what the selected idea would look like if implemented.

Step 3: Allow each team to present its case to the wider group. The objective is to help others understand the choice being presented. Listeners are encouraged to make notes and ask detailed questions to push the team to defend their positions.

Step 4: When all teams have presented their research, teams are then challenged to reverse their positions. They are given time to identify the points against the ideas they originally advocated. This exploration allows teams to deepen their understanding and gain new insights.

Step 5: Each team presents its newly discovered counterpoints to the wider group. Listeners are once again encouraged to ask probing questions.

Step 6: When all of the advocacy presentations are complete, take time to explore what insights people have gained from the exchange. Record these on a flip chart or electronic board for all to see.

Step 7: Ask group members to drop their advocacy roles to make a decision. Use a form of multi-voting to ensure member anonymity. Tally the votes and ratify the choice with the members.

Exit Surveys

What is it? An anonymous survey posted near the exit used to take the pulse of a group in order to find out how satisfied members are with overall progress.

When to use it? At the mid-point of a meeting or workshop. Whenever there's a need to uncover hidden issues and concerns.

What does it do? Provides data about the effectiveness of the meeting or event so that issues can be further explored and addressed. Allows for venting concerns.

What's the outcome? An exit survey acts as a safety valve for releasing anxieties or concerns. It channels concerns into solutions and in this way empowers the group to resolve its own issues.

How to Use Exit Surveys

Step 1: Identify two to four questions. Write these on a flip-chart sheet that can be brought forward when the meeting resumes. The following are typical examples of exit survey questions:

Please provide your response to the questions below:
1 = poor **2** = fair **3** = satisfactory **4** = good **5** = excellent

1. Did we achieve what we needed to at today's meeting?

1	2	3	4	5

2. Were everyone's ideas heard and taken into consideration?

1	2	3	4	5

3. Did we make well-thought-out and equitable decisions?

1	2	3	4	5

Step 2: Post the survey sheet on a wall near the exit so group members can mark it as they leave the room. To provide anonymity, place the survey on a flip-chart stand and turn it against the wall to protect the privacy of raters. Provide markers and ask people to rate each survey item.

Step 3: At the start of the next session with that group, review the exit survey sheet. Use the survey feedback process on the next page to address each item.

Step 4: At the end of the discussion, review improvement ideas. These will fall into two categories: action steps or new norms. The new norms should be added to the existing norms for this team. Conduct exit surveys periodically as a preventative means of keeping meetings running effectively.

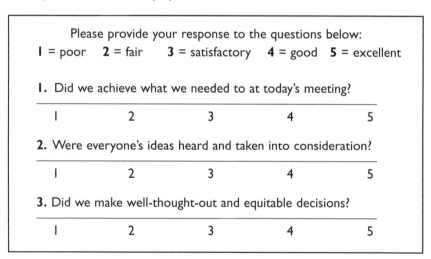

Survey Feedback

What is it? A process that involves gathering information and feeding it back to members so that they can interpret the data and identify action steps.

When to use it? When there's a problem that group members need to address, about which they lack information. Can be implemented when a problem has been identified. Can also be used periodically as a preventative measure.

What's its purpose? Provides the group with a means of assessing the efficiency and effectiveness of a meeting or activity. Also provides a method for generating actions to resolve any identified problems.

What's the outcome? Creates a sense of commitment and accountability among members for making improvements. Acts as a catalyst for making improvements.

How to Do Survey Feedback

Step 1: Design and conduct a survey. This can take an anonymous form or be an open process, such as an exit survey. The survey can be about:

- meeting effectiveness
- team/group effectiveness
- leader performance
- process effectiveness
- customer satisfaction
- a recent event or project

Step 2: After the surveys have been individually completed, they're returned to a designated member of the group. This person tabulates the survey results by combining all of the responses onto a blank survey form. The person doing the tabulation doesn't interpret the results; he or she only combines the ratings from the individual surveys.

Step 3: Tabulated survey results are fed back to the group. After members have had an opportunity to read the results, two categories of questions are posed:

1. *"What is the survey data telling us is going well? Which items received high ratings? Why did these items receive high ratings?"*
2. *"What is the survey data telling us are problems or issues? Which items received low ratings? Why did these items receive low ratings?"*

Step 4: Once members have identified the items that received sufficiently low ratings to be of concern, have them rank these in terms of priority to determine which should be addressed.

Step 5: Once the top priorities are clear, divide the members into subgroups of no fewer than four individuals. Give each subgroup one issue to work on for twenty to thirty minutes. Deal with as many issues as group size allows. In subgroups, members will answer two sets of questions about the item they have been given:

1. *"Why did this item get a low rating? What's wrong here? What is the nature of the problem?"* (Group members analyze the problem.)
2. *"What are possible solutions for this problem? What will remedy the situation?"* (Group members generate solutions.)

Step 6: Reassemble the total group and ask subgroups to share their recommendations. Encourage everyone to add their ideas and to ratify their final actions. Select the best ideas and implement them.

Step 7: Ask members to briefly return to their subgroups to complete any action plans that might be needed to ensure that improvements are implemented.

Systematic Problem Solving

What is it? A step-by-step approach for resolving a problem or issue.

When to use it? When members need to work together to solve a problem.

What's its purpose? Provides a structured and disciplined means for groups to explore and resolve an issue together. In-depth analysis ensures that groups understand the problem before jumping to solutions.

What's the outcome? Systematic problem solving results in doable action steps that members of the group take responsibility for implementing. Because the process is systematic, it discourages members from randomly suggesting ideas. Problem solving is at the heart of collaborative conflict resolution. It's also a key activity in any organization that is dedicated to improving its processes and service to customers.

How to Do Systematic Problem Solving

Step 1: Name the problem. Identify a problem that needs to be solved. Analyze it briefly to ensure that there's a common understanding of the issue. Then support the group in writing a one- or two-sentence description of the problem. This is called the problem statement.

Step 2: Identify the goal of the problem-solving exercise. Ask the group questions such as: *"If this problem were totally solved, how would you describe the ideal situation"* or *"How will things look if we solve this problem?"* Summarize this in a one- to two-sentence goal statement.

Step 3: Analyze the problem. If the problem is fairly technical, do a detailed analysis using a fishbone diagram (see page 182). Otherwise, ask a series of probing questions to help members think analytically about the problem. Categorize the observations as either "causes" or "effects." The goal is to get to underlying root causes of the problem.

Some useful questions during analysis could include:

- *Describe this problem to me in detail, step-by-step.*
- *What is it? How does it manifest itself?*
- *What are the noticeable signs of it?*
- *What makes this happen?*
- *How are people affected?*
- *What other problems does it cause?*
- *What are the most damaging aspects?*
- *What stops us from solving it?*
- *Who gets in the way of solving it?*
- *What are the root causes of each symptom?*

Step 4: Identify potential solutions. Use brainstorming (page 174) or written brainstorming (page 175) to generate potential solutions. When the ideas stop flowing, ask probing questions to encourage members to dig deeper. Some useful probing questions include:

- *What if money were no object?*
- *What if you owned this company?*
- *What would the customer suggest?*
- *What if we did the opposite of the ideas suggested so far?*
- *What is the most innovative thing we could do?*

Step 5: Evaluate solutions. Use multi-voting, a criterion-based decision grid, or an impact/effort grid to sift through the brainstormed ideas to determine which are most applicable to the situation.

Step 6: Create an action plan. Identify the specific steps needed to implement the chosen solutions. Specify how things will be done, when, and by whom. Each action step should also feature performance indicators that answer the question, *"How will we know we have been successful?"* This will help focus the action step and make it easier to measure results.

Step 7: Troubleshoot the plan. Use the Troubleshooting Worksheet to identify all of the things that could get in the way and then ensure that there are plans in place to deal with them.

Step 8: Monitor and evaluate. Identify how the action plans will be monitored and when and how the results will be reported on. Create and use a monitoring and report-back format.

Systematic Problem Solving Worksheet 1

Step 1. Name the Problem

Identify the problem that needs to be solved. Analyze it in just enough detail to create a common understanding. Use the space below to explore the general nature of the problem.

Now narrow in and select the specific aspect you wish to solve. Write a one- or two-sentence problem statement to define the problem clearly.

Problem statement:

Systematic Problem Solving Worksheet 2

Step 2. Identify the Goal of the Problem-Solving Exercise

Describe the desired outcome. Ask:

> *"What would things look like if the problem disappeared?"*
> *"How would things look if this problem were resolved?"*

Use the space below to record the ideas generated.

Now narrow in and write a one- or two-sentence goal statement.

Goal statement:

____

____

Systematic Problem Solving Worksheet 3

Step 3. Analyze the Problem

Dissect the problem thoroughly. Avoid coming up with solutions. Instead, concentrate on making sure that everyone is clear about the specific nature of the situation. Don't focus on symptoms, but delve behind each effect to determine the root causes.

Use a fishbone diagram if the problem is a complex technical issue that has many contributing factors. If it isn't a mechanical problem, use cause and effect charting by asking questions such as:

"How would we describe this problem to an outsider?"
"What is taking place? What are the signs and symptoms?"
"How are people affected? What makes this happen?"
"What are the root causes of each symptom?"
"What other problems does it cause?"
"What are the most damaging aspects?"
"What and who stops us from solving it?"
*"How do **we** contribute to the problem?"*

Systematic Problem Solving Worksheet 4

Step 4. Identify Potential Solutions

Use brainstorming or anonymous brainstorming to generate a range of potential solutions to the problem. When brainstorming, remember the rules:

- Let ideas flow: be creative, don't judge
- All ideas are good, even if they're way-out
- Build on the ideas of others

Probing questions to ask once the initial flow of ideas has stopped:

"What if money were no object?"
"What if I owned this company?"
"What would the customer suggest?"
"What's the opposite of something already suggested?"
"What is the most innovative thing we could do?"

Record brainstormed ideas here:

Systematic Problem Solving Worksheet 5

Step 5. Evaluate the Solutions

Use multi-voting, a criterion-based decision grid, or the impact/effort grid shown below to sort through the brainstormed ideas and identify a course of action.

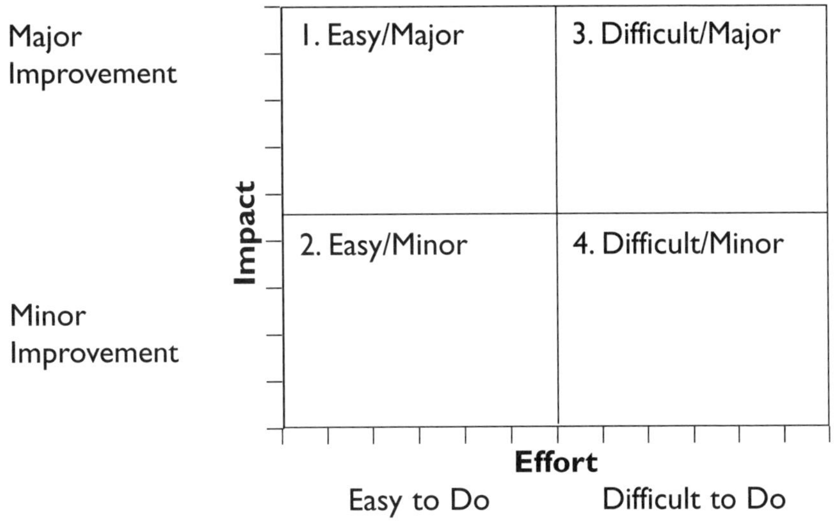

List all of the type 1 and 2 activities together for quick action	***List all of the type 3 activities here for development into action plans***

Systematic Problem Solving Worksheet 6

Step 6. Plan for Action

Create detailed action plans for items to be implemented. Ensure that action plans adhere to a logical sequence of steps. Provide details about what will be done, how, and by whom. Always include target dates for completion. Identify the performance indicator that answers the question: *"How will we know we did a good job?"*

What will be done and how?	*By whom?*	*When?*	*Performance Indicator*

Systematic Problem Solving Worksheet 7

Step 7. Troubleshoot the Action Plan

Identify the things that could get in the way of successful implementation of the action plan. Create anticipatory strategies to deal with each blockage.

Use the following questions to help identify trouble spots:

"What are the most difficult, complex, or sensitive aspects of our plan?"

"What sudden shifts could take place to change priorities or otherwise change the environment?"

"What organizational blocks and barriers could we run into?"

"What technical or materials-related problems could stop or delay us?"

"Should we be aware of any human resources issues? Which ones?"

"In which ways might members of this team not fulfill their commitments?"

What could go wrong, block us, or change suddenly?	***What actions do we need to take to overcome each block? (what, how, who, when, measure)***
→	
→	
→	
→	
→	

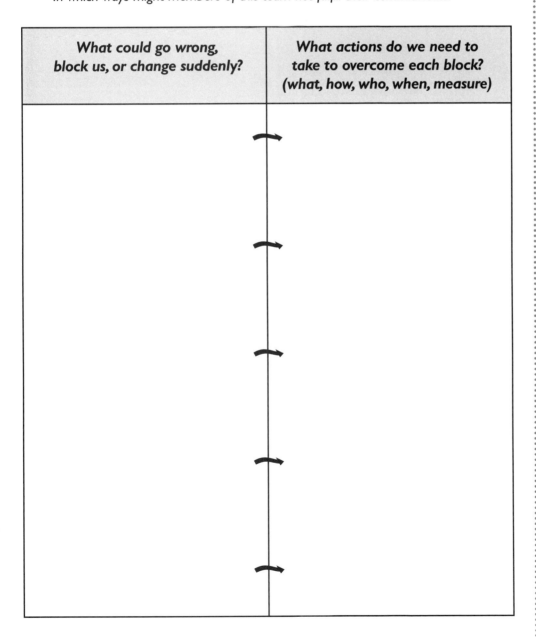

Systematic Problem Solving Worksheet 8

Step 8. Monitor and Evaluate

To ensure that action plans are actually implemented, identify:

How will progress be reported? Written ________ Verbal______________

When and how often will reports be made? ____________________________

Who needs to be informed? ____________________________________

How will results be monitored? ________________________________

Will there be a final report? __________________________________

Who will take responsibility for the above actions? ________________

____

____

Reporting on Results

- What activities have been implemented?
- What results have been achieved?
- Remaining items
- Expected dates for completion

Troubleshooting

What is it? A process for identifying potential blocks and barriers so that plans can be formulated to overcome them.

When to use it? When it's important to identify barriers to success and create action plans to deal with them. When the group has a history of poor follow-through on actions.

What's its purpose? Helps ensure that action plans are well thought out. To improve the likelihood of follow-through.

What's the outcome? Groups are less likely to be "surprised" by hidden circumstances, and hence, gain more control over their work.

How to Do Troubleshooting

Step 1: After a group has created action plans, ask members to consider a series of questions. These questions force a critical look at the circumstances that might impede the activity. For example:

> *"What are the difficult, complex, or sensitive aspects of our action plan?"*
> *"What shifts in the environment, like a change of priorities, should we keep our eye on?"*
> *"What organizational blocks or barriers could we encounter?"*
> *"What technical or materials-related problems could stop or delay us?"*
> *"What human resource issues should we anticipate?"*
> *"In what ways might members of this team not fulfill their commitments?"*

Step 2: Once potential barriers have been identified, ask members to identify strategies and action plans to overcome each one.

Step 3: Help the group write up its troubleshooting plans. Identify who will monitor follow-through. The following worksheet will help you lead this discussion.

Troubleshooting Worksheet

What could go wrong, block us, or change suddenly?	***What actions will overcome each block?*** *(what, how, by whom, when)*

Chapter Ten
Process Designs

Just as an architect wouldn't dream of showing up at a construction site without a well-thought-out design, facilitators need to create detailed blueprints for each discussion.

In fact, one of the most important contributions that facilitators make is to create meeting designs that address specific needs. Having the right process design is just as important to the success of any meeting as the ability to manage the interpersonal dynamics.

Facilitators create custom designs to fit specific situations.

On the following pages you'll find sample process designs. These illustrate the flow of specific types of meetings and show how individual tools and techniques might be used together. Since the times and sequences are *totally speculative*, it's unlikely that any of these samples will fit real-life situations well enough to be applied straight from the book. In fact, no design should ever be borrowed from somewhere else. Part of the challenge of facilitation is creating the right design to fit the situation.

Most designs are created through a rigorous process, which includes:

- conducting background research (for example, reading reports and making site visits)
- interviewing and/or surveying members to identify specific goals and needs
- creating a draft design
- obtaining ratification of the preliminary design by some or all members
- preparing a detailed agenda with step-by-step process notes
- communicating the agenda in advance of the meeting
- preparing needed worksheets, handouts, and overheads
- designing an appropriate evaluation form

A general rule of thumb worth noting is that professional facilitators charge as much time for research and design as they do for actually facilitating a session. This is an indication of the importance of rigorous preparation.

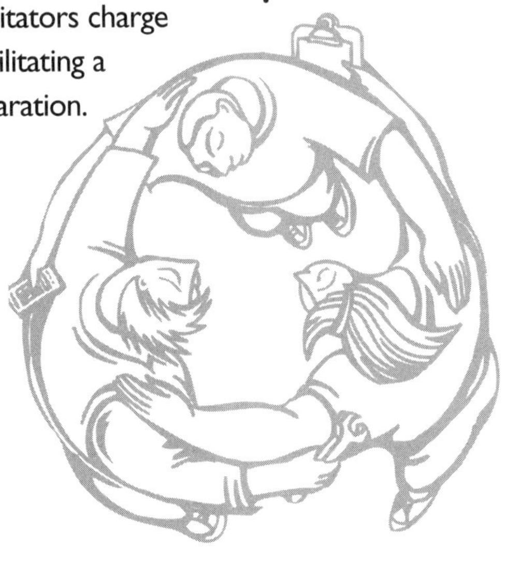

Introduction to the Sample Agendas

The sample agendas on the following pages are offered as an illustration of how various tools and techniques can be combined.

Each design is accompanied by a set of specifications and assumptions that explain the context for the activities chosen. All agenda items are accompanied by facilitator notes that describe the tools and techniques to be used. Handout materials, overheads, and other props are not included in this section, although most can be found elsewhere in this book.

Sample Design 1—Creating a Mission Statement and Objectives

Specifications: This is a new team coming together for the first time to create a clear, common goal and specific, measurable objectives. The eight members are passing acquaintances. Three hours have been set aside for this discussion.

Agenda	Process Design Notes
Welcome and agenda overview (5 minutes)	• Review the purpose of this meeting and how the three hours will be spent.
Introductions (25 minutes)	• Each person chooses a partner to interview; ask name, job, skills, family info, hobbies or interest, hopes and fears about being on this team. • Partners present each other to the group • Record hopes and fears.
Mission statement (60 minutes)	• Present the original rationale behind the team's formation and any other available parameters. • Ask members to work *alone* to answer key questions:

Sample Design 1 (cont'd)

Agenda	Process Design Notes
	What products and services are we responsible for? *What is our unique contribution that will help the organization achieve its goals?* *What must be noteworthy about our products and services?* *In summary, what is our mission?* • After members have written their responses, have each person sit with a partner and share his/her thoughts. • After two minutes per person, have everyone find a new partner with whom to share ideas. • After two rounds, share ideas with the whole group. Synthesize ideas together. • Create a one- or two-sentence mission statement. • Post the statement on the wall.
Team norms (10 minutes)	• Ask members: *What sorts of behaviors will make it a pleasure to be on the team? What rules should the team impose on itself to make sure that we build a positive team climate conducive to effective teamwork?* • Facilitate to pull together ideas from everyone. • Record ideas on flip chart and post on wall.
Team objectives (80 minutes)	• Divide members into pairs, and ask them to identify, without going into great detail, what the team needs to do to achieve the team's mission. • Have members share their lists with the whole group to ensure there is agreement about activities. • Provide input about how to create detailed objectives. • Ask members to work alone to write an objective for each of the identified activities. • Review and fine-tune the objectives; make sure they have been recorded for distribution.
Exit survey	• Give members a short survey to complete before they leave. Questions can include: On a scale of 1 to 5, rate: *How well-informed do you now feel about the team?* *How comfortable are you with the mission?* *How appropriate and realistic are the objectives?*
Adjourn	• Clarify the time, place, and agenda of the next meeting.

Sample Design 2—Work Planning, Roles, and Responsibilities

Specifications: This is a new team that has met once to create a mission statement and objectives, but has not started to work together in closely linked roles. Three hours have been set aside for this discussion. There are eight members.

Agenda	Process Design Notes
Welcome and agenda overview (5 minutes)	• Review the purpose of this meeting and how the three hours will be spent.
Review exit survey from last meeting (20 minutes)	• Post the tabulated exit survey results. • Divide the large group in half and let the subgroups talk for five minutes on each of the questions. *What are the issues raised by the results?* and *What can we do to remedy each of the issues?* • Reassemble as a large group and share ideas for improving the team; plan for action; record ideas.
Work planning (90 minutes)	• Make sure everyone has a copy of the team's objectives. Clear up any questions. Ensure members have information about items, such as budgets, at their fingertips when planning. • Ask members to identify the characteristics of a good work plan (for example, well balanced, allows people to try new skills, etc.). • For each objective, ask people to identify what needs to be done, how, and when. Allow time for individual work. • Ask individuals to write each objective and related work activities on flip-chart sheets. One objective per sheet. Post sheets around the room. • Hold a discussion of each item so that members can comment, share ideas, make changes.
Roles and responsibilities (60 minutes)	• For each objective and related activities, ask members to identify the time, skills, and other requirements of each activity. • Rank activities as high, medium, or low, based on the degree of complexity, difficulty, and time required for each. • Begin matching people with activities. Start by allowing each person to select his or her top item. Keep assigning tasks until all items are accounted for. Use the criteria to ensure that no one person has all the difficult tasks, while someone else has all the simple and low time demand tasks. • Check the work plan against the criteria set at the start; ratify it and then post.
Adjourn	• Clarify the time, place, and agenda of the next meeting.

Sample Design 3—Priority Setting/Cutback Planning

Specifications: This meeting is being held in response to a management directive to cut 20 percent from the budget. Some programs have to go to make the needed cuts. The members have worked together for years in the same department. There are eighteen members, plus a manager. A three-hour discussion is planned.

Agenda	Process Design Notes
Welcome by director (10 minutes)	• Information sharing about the purpose of the session. Encourages staff to accept the current challenge. Offers guidelines for the cutback exercise. Sets a positive tone. Q & A.
Agenda overview (5 minutes)	• Facilitator reviews the activities of the session. (director leaves)
Hopes, fears, and norms (20 minutes)	• Facilitator asks members to choose a partner. Partners interview each other: *Hopes:* *What's the best outcome we could hope for?* *Fears:* *What's the worst thing that could happen?* *Norms:* *What rules or guidelines do we need to impose on ourselves to make this exercise work?* • Have members share ideas and record outcome. Make sure there is a consensus on the norms. Post on a wall.
Activity review (45 minutes)	• On a large, empty wall, hang several sheets of flip-chart paper and draw a decision matrix chart. • Ask members to list each activity, program, or service currently being offered. • Share information about each activity so that everyone understands its purpose, customers, costs, benefits, difficulty, time demands, and any other vital factors. It's a good idea to have people prepare these activity profiles ahead of time to save time at the session. • Write the activities that will be subjected to cutbacks in the left column of the decision grid.
Establish criteria (20 minutes)	• Divide the members into subgroups of three or four members. Have the subgroups identify the criteria that ought to be used to rate the activities. Refer to the process tool section of this book for examples of criteria. • Facilitate a discussion to agree on the set of criteria to be used. Use multi-voting to sort the top five criteria if too many are initially proposed.

Sample Design 3 (cont'd)

Agenda	Process Design Notes
Rate the activities (20 minutes)	• Write the final criteria along the top of the decision grid. Clarify if any of the criteria should be given a greater significance than any others. Apply weights of 1x, 2x, or 3x to each criteria. • Explain the voting process. Let people work out their ratings on their own in their seats. When they're done, invite people to come up to the wall and record their ratings for each program.
Discuss the ratings (30 minutes)	• Once everyone has rated the activities, add all of the scores to arrive at totals for each activity. • Ask members: *What do the ratings tell us are our priority activities, programs, and services? Do we agree? Are there things we should consider eliminating or at least trimming back? Do we agree?*
Propose action steps (30 minutes)	• Subdivide the members into twos and threes. Assign them each one or more of the lower-rated activities. Ask people to discuss what sorts of alterations can and should be made to that program or service to help achieve the 20 percent reduction. • Reassemble the large group to share cutback ideas and get further input from the rest of the group. • Help the group make decisions and come to closure.
Adjourn	• Ensure that there are clear next steps in place. • Help members identify the time, place, and purpose of their next meeting.

Special Note: In many priority-setting sessions, the participative portion of the activity ends here. Management or a small subgroup takes the information from the ranking exercise and makes the final cutback decisions. This is often a wise course of action, as it may be unfair to ask people to suggest elimination of their own jobs or roles.

Sample Design 4—Inter-Group Negotiation

Specifications: This is a session with two teams who recently became embroiled in a dispute. They may be fighting over equipment, staff, customers, or budgets. The team leaders have tried to settle this, but the members continue to battle on. There are eight people on each team for a total of sixteen members, including the two team leaders. There are four hours for this intervention.

Agenda	Process Design Notes
Welcome, agenda overview (15 minutes)	• Information is shared about the purpose of the session and how it came about. Team leaders speak to the members about the need to cooperate and approach this with a collaborative mind-set. The details of each step in the negotiation are discussed.
Introductions (30 minutes)	• Create pairs, with one person from each team; ask people to interview each other to get information such as name, job or role, special interests or hobbies, and anything else that's relevant. • Members present their partners to the whole group.
Team presentations (20 minutes)	• Give teams ten minutes each to do a brief presentation about the team: what they do, their customers, their successes, etc.
Hopes, fears, norms (30 minutes)	• Everyone finds a new partner on the other team to discuss: *Hopes:* *What's the best outcome we could hope for today?* *Fears:* *What's the worst thing that could happen today?* *Norms:* *How should we conduct ourselves today to ensure that relations don't worsen?* • Have members share ideas and record the outcomes. Ask questions to set norms.
Perception sharing (40 minutes)	• Briefly explain the rules and language of giving feedback to ensure that everyone is clear on how feedback is different from criticism. • Give teams twenty minutes or so to create a point-form description of the current situation. They can describe exactly what happened, when, and what the impacts of those actions were. • Separate the group, preferably in different rooms, while they talk to construct their sides of the story. Have each team choose a spokesperson to present its side. • Reunite the two teams and explain that while one group talks, the other team members can't interrupt or use negative body language. They must listen to what the other team is saying even if they disagree totally. They can, however, ask clarifying questions.

Sample Design 4 (cont'd)

Agenda	Process Design Notes
Perception sharing, cont'd (40 minutes)	• Ask one side to tell the other their perception of what is causing tensions. When the team is finished, the spokesperson from the other team offers a summary of what's been said, paraphrasing only his or her understanding, not agreeing or disagreeing. This step is purely a listening/understanding exercise. • Repeat the process with the second team.
Needs and offers (30 minutes)	• Once each team indicates that the other team has accurately understood what each has presented, the teams are separated again. • Each team chooses a facilitator to discuss the following two items on which they will report back to the rest of the group: *"What do we need from the other team to resolve this situation?"* *"What are we prepared to do to resolve the situation?"* • The teams return to the large room and take turns presenting their wants and offers to each other. Again, the spokesperson for the listening team paraphrases what was said to make sure there are no misunderstandings.
Action planning (40 minutes)	• Once everyone has heard the wants and offers of the other team, the facilitator leads a discussion to negotiate final actions and help members create doable action plans that will help resolve the tensions. • Finalize the action plans and make sure there is a time and date set to meet with team spokespersons to follow up.
Adjourn	• Ensure that there are clear next steps in place. • Help members identify the time, place, and purpose of their next meeting.

Sample Design 5—Finding and Solving Problems

Specifications: This meeting is being held to identify and solve recurring problems being experienced by a department. The twenty members have been working together for some time. There are three hours for this activity.

Agenda	Process Design Notes
Welcome and agenda overview (5 minutes)	• Review the purpose of the meeting and how the three hours will be spent. • Review the group's norms. • Clarify any parameters or limits, like spending ceilings, that may impact the problem-solving activity. Also clarify the empowerment of members to solve this problem.
Clarify the focus (5 minutes)	• Have someone briefly describe the program, service, or activity that is being explored. • Make sure everyone is clear on what is being discussed.
Force-field analysis (20 minutes)	• Have members draw on their experience and any data gathered before the session to respond to the force-field questions: *"What are we doing really well, and what should we keep doing the same way?"* *"What aren't we doing well, and what needs to improve?"*
Multi-voting (20 minutes)	• Once the problems are listed and understood by all members, create criteria for identifying which blocks should be removed first. The voting criteria could be the biggest blocks, or the easiest to remove. • Hand out peel-off dots or distribute points; let members vote. • Tally the votes to reveal the ranking of the blocks.
Problem solving (90 minutes)	• Take the top three or four blocks and subdi vide the large group into subgroups to tackle one problem each. • Explain the steps in the Systematic Problem-Solving Model. Give out the worksheets. Have each subgroup appoint a facilitator. • Circulate among the groups to make sure they don't get stuck on any parts of the model.
Plenary (40 minutes)	• Bring groups together at the end to share their recommendations and action plans. Invite others in the group to add their ideas. • Have subgroups refine their plans and submit them to the minute taker. • Help the group plan its follow-up mechanism to ensure there are report-backs on progress made.
Adjourn	• Ensure that there are clear next steps in place. • Help members identify the time, place, and purpose of their next meeting.

Sample Design 6—Core Program Development

Specifications: This is a session for a long-established department or division within an organization that has lost its focus. The members now wish to review what they're doing and get back on track to achieve their main business. All of the members know each other. There are twenty-four people, and the session is planned to last from 8:30 a.m. to 4:30 p.m.

Agenda	Process Design Notes
Welcome and agenda overview (5 minutes)	• Review the purpose of the meeting and how the day will be managed.
Context setting (25 minutes)	• Senior manager puts the core program challenge into clear context, clarifies the empowerment of the group to make recommendations, and lays out his or her hopes and fears. • Question and answer session to get clarity on any issues members may have.
Hopes, fears, and norms (20 minutes)	• Facilitator asks everyone to choose a partner. Partners interview each other: *Hopes: "What would be the best outcome today?"* *Fears: "What's the worst thing that could happen?"* *Norms: "What rules or guidelines should we impose on ourselves to overcome the potential pitfalls of a core business discussion?"* • Partners report back information discussed. • Flip chart norms for setting group parameters.
Environmental scan (30 minutes)	• In the same room, divide members into subgroups of six people. Ask each group to choose a facilitator. Have them discuss: *"What is happening around us?" (in the marketplace/community/government, etc.)* *"What trends will have an impact on us?"* • Hold a brief plenary to share ideas between the subgroups. • Synthesize all ideas together on a flip chart. • Post summary on the wall.
Customer profile (30 minutes)	• The same subgroups choose a new facilitator and discuss: *"Who are our customers today?"* (describe) *"Who will our customers be tomorrow?"* *"Who are those customers—what do they want/need?"* • Hold a brief plenary to share ideas. • Post the customer profile.

Sample Design 6 (cont'd)

Agenda	Process Design Notes
Current focus (30 minutes)	• Ask subgroups to create a profile in response to these question: *"What business are we currently in?"* *"What are our current products and services?"* • When the products and services list is complete, pull together a complete list and write down the left-hand column of a Criteria-Based Decision Grid. • Post the grid, but don't develop it further at this time.
Strengths analysis (30 minutes)	• Have members return to subgroups and choose the next facilitator to discuss: *"What are our current strengths and capabilities? What are we especially skilled at?"* • Hold a brief plenary to share ideas between groups. Post strengths analysis.
Visioning (60 minutes)	• Reassemble entire group and give each person a blank piece of paper. Allow up to ten minutes for individuals to answer the following questions without talking to another member. *Imagine that today is exactly three years from now and we are hugely successful:* *"What business are we in? Describe our products and services. Who are our customers? What distinguishes us from the competition? What specific results have we achieved?"* • Once individuals indicate that they have answered the questions, have everyone find a partner and proceed as per the instructions for *Visioning.* • Facilitate a plenary discussion to synthesize ideas. Ensure there is clarity about the desired future of the organization. • Help members write a statement that describes what their core business needs to be. • Post the statement and key points on the wall.
Mid-point check	• Post a mid-point check survey on the wall and ask members to respond to the questions as they leave for lunch or a break. These can be about progress being made, the process, the pace, etc. • When the meeting resumes, review the ratings and make improvements.
Ranking products and services (45 minutes)	• Return to the decision grid. Down the left side add any future activities, products, or services that were agreed to in the visioning exercise.

Sample Design 6 (cont'd)

Agenda	Process Design Notes

Ranking products and services, cont'd (45 minutes)	• Facilitate a discussion to establish criteria to rank the items. Potential criteria can include:
	  • Supports the core business
	  • High profitability
	  • Builds on current strengths
	  • Meets a growing customer need, etc.
	• Write the criteria along the top of the decision grid, then other items. Assign weights of 1x, 2x, and 3x.
	• Have each person do his or her own ranking. Then ask members to write their rankings on the chart.

Ranking analysis (80 minutes)	• When all rankings are tabulated, ask subgroups to hold discussions to analyze the rankings:
	  "What do the rankings tell us we should be focusing on in support of our core business?"
	  "What do we need to start doing?"
	  "What do we need to keep on doing?"
	  "What do we need to stop doing?"
	• Facilitate a plenary to synthesize ideas and reach agreement on priorities for action.
	• Categorize activities/programs/services under three headings:
	  New activities that need to be developed;
	  Existing activities to be trimmed;
	  Existing activities to be eliminated.

Strategy development (90 minutes)	• Post the activities under the three headings and let members sort themselves according to their skills, interests, and knowledge. • Have subgroups take responsibility for developing action plans that develop new opportunities, reduce activity, or divest programs. The process for strategy development can center around the following questions: *"What's involved in starting/trimming/stopping this activity? List steps. Who's likely going to be affected? What are the implications? What's the likely cost/benefit? What are the next steps: what should be done, how, by whom, when, and with what result?"* • Hold a plenary to share ideas and have all action plans ratified by the whole group. • Help the group members identify how and when they will monitor and report on progress.
Evaluation (20 minutes)	• Evaluate member satisfaction by asking each person to comment on his or her feelings about the day. Compare these with hopes and fears set at the start.
Adjourn	• Ensure that there are clear next steps in place. • Help members identify the time, place, and purpose of their next meeting.

Sample Design 7—Survey Feedback/Issue Census

Specifications: A division or department within an organization wishes to identify its issues using a survey. This can be an employee satisfaction survey, a customer satisfaction survey, or a survey of the performance of a product or process. There are thirty-six people, who have been working together for some time, at this three-hour survey feedback meeting. The survey being discussed was conducted in the weeks preceding this meeting; results were tabulated and a copy of the final tally sheets was given, without interpretation, to all members.

Agenda	Process Design Notes
Welcome and agenda overview (5 minutes)	• Review the purpose of the session and the survey feedback method.
Review survey results (25 minutes)	• Lead the whole group through a review of each question. Discuss: *"Is this a high or low rating? Is everyone clear about what this question meant?"* • Without interpreting the results, sort the responses into three categories: Items scored as good or high; Items scored as poor or low; Borderline items.
Interpreting the results (60 minutes)	• Divide the members into subgroups of six members. • Ask each subgroup to appoint a facilitator. Give each group only one issue to work on. • Groups are to work through the following questions and steps in connection with their survey item: *"Why did these items get such low ratings?"* (analyze the situation) *"What are some actions that could improve these ratings?"* (brainstorm solutions) *"Which of our solutions do we think are most promising?"* (impact/effort grid or decision grid)
Plenary (60 minutes)	• Have members share their assessments in order to benefit from each other's comments and ratify the solutions being proposed.
Action planning (30 minutes)	• Have members return to their original subgroups to develop action plans for ideas ratified by the larger group.
Plenary (30 minutes)	• Ask subgroups to inform the rest of the members of their specific action plans for implementing the discussed improvements. • Make sure members have a plan for monitoring, reporting, and follow-up. • Evaluate the effectiveness of the session.
Adjourn	

Sample Design 8—New Leader Integration

Specifications: An established team or department, with a good track record, is about to receive a new leader. The organization is concerned that the new leader be integrated quickly. It's also hoped that the transition will be smooth. The new leader integration session is conducted in stages over a period of three hours. Any number of staff can attend. The first stage takes place the week before the leader joins the group.

Agenda	Process Design Notes
Stage 1 Welcome and agenda overview (10 minutes)	• At a preliminary planning session not attended by the leader, review the purpose of the new leader integration session and explain the process.
Profile preparation (90 minutes)	• Ask members to prepare a profile of the group. This profile will be given to the new leader in advance of a joint session. It should include: "*Who are we?*" (our purpose, products/services, staff/skills) *"What are we most proud of?"* *"What are we doing very well at this time?"* *"Why are we doing so well in this area?"* *"What aren't we doing that well? Why not?"* *"What are we doing to improve?"* *"What's ahead for us in six months, one year, three years?"* *"Under what leadership style do we work best? Why?"* *"How empowered have we been/should we be? For which activities?"* *"What do we need from our new leader?"* *"What are we offering our new leader?"* • The notes from this discussion should be recorded and typed for distribution.
Stage 2 Leader preparation	• The facilitator meets with the new leader and brings him/her the group profile. The leader is asked to read the profile, prepare one about him/herself along the same lines, and be ready to discuss his/her leadership style and philosophy of empowerment. • The leader is asked to be ready to discuss what he/she needs from the group and what he/she's prepared to offer.
Stage 3 Welcome and agenda overview (10 minutes)	• At the meeting of the members and the new leader, review the steps of the process.
Member presentation (60 minutes)	• Members are given the opportunity of speaking first to share their profile, needs, and offers.

Sample Design 8 (cont'd)

Agenda	Process Design Notes
Member presentation, cont'd (60 minutes)	• The leader is asked to listen and ask clarifying questions only.
Leader presentation (30 minutes)	• The leader is given the opportunity of presenting his/her profile, including leadership style, wants and offers, etc. Members are asked to listen and ask questions.
Discussions and negotiations (30 minutes)	• Once both parties have heard each other, the facilitator manages a discussion of any of the points where there appear to be differences or a need for further exploration. • If any item needs an action plan, the facilitator can help the group to identify its next steps.
Adjourn	• Have a coffee break planned to encourage social mixing.

Sample Design 9—Transition Planning

Specifications: A division or a department within an organization is about to undergo major change. Some staff will trade jobs. Others will trade territories. Some people will gain new titles. Others will need to acquire new skills. This planning exercise is being conducted to ensure that nothing slips between the cracks and that customer service levels remain high during the actual changeover period. Twenty-four people are involved. A full day has been set aside for the transition discussion.

Agenda	Process Design Notes
Welcome and agenda overview (5 minutes)	• Review the purpose of the meeting and how the session will be conducted.
Buy-in to the process (30 minutes)	• Have everyone find a partner to interview. • Pose the following questions for partners to ask each other: *"Why is it important that we have a transition plan?"* *"Why should we be the ones to create it?"* *"What would be the best possible outcome?"* *"What would be the worst outcome?"* *"What norms or rules should we impose on ourselves today to make sure that we create a fair plan everyone can live with?"* • Facilitate a discussion to gather up major thoughts and post these.
Information sharing (45 minutes)	• Presentations by those driving the change, detailing what needs to happen and when. • Question and answer session.
Identifying challenges (45 minutes)	• Divide the members by existing work groups if applicable, or create random subgroups of three to four members. • Ask them to use force-field analysis to identify: *"What aspects of the change are going to be relatively easy?"* *"What aspects of the change are going to be complicated/challenging?"* • Hold a plenary to create a common force field. • Use multi-voting to rank the challenges from most to least complicated/challenging.
Strategy development (120 minutes)	• Help the whole group identify the characteristics of an effective transition. This can include things such as, "doesn't disrupt customer service," or "allows people to get on-the-job coaching," etc. • Post these criteria. • Take the top four changes that were ranked to be most challenging or complicated and post these at four places around the room. • Ask members to go to the "change challenge" that involves them so that people who will be responsible for implementing each plan are in each group.

Sample Design 9 (cont'd)

Agenda	Process Design Notes
Strategy development, cont'd (120 minutes)	• Ask each subgroup to identify a facilitator and hold a strategy development discussion. • The following discussions make up this process: 1. Describe the old state—*What activities/products/services are involved? What skills, roles, and responsibilities are associated with each activity?* 2. Describe the new state—*What activities/products/services define the future state?* For each activity: *What are the skills, roles, and responsibilities? What are the implementation dates? What is negotiable versus non-negotiable? What can go wrong?* 3. Transition planning—*Given the time frames, is there a logical sequence of steps for implementing the change in stages? How many hand-offs are there? How can these be handled to ensure continuity? Given the new roles, who needs training/on-the-job coaching? What signals can be put in place to help us monitor the transition to ensure things don't go too far off track?*
Plenary (60 minutes) Insure that sensitive	• Have subgroups share their proposed transition plans. Encourage others to offer comments to fill in any gaps in the plans. Make sure the subgroup plans are linked together to form a coherent whole. • Check carefully for clarity and true consensus. Ensure that sensitive change issues are discussed and brought to proper closure.
Action planning (60 minutes)	• Have subgroups fill out action planning sheets that identify what will be done, how, by whom, and when. • Bring groups together one last time to hear each other's action plans. Ensure that notes are available for distribution soon after the meeting.
Communications planning (30 minutes)	• Ask members to identify who needs to be given information about the transition plan. • Record the communications strategy, specifying who needs to know what and when. • Ensure that clear responsibility is taken for communicating the details of the transition.
Monitoring (15 minutes)	• Help the group identify how it will monitor the plan and report on progress. • Set a date for the next meeting. • Go around the room and ask members how they felt about the day.
Adjourn	

Sample Design 10—Process Improvement

Specifications: A work group has received information that one of its key product/services/activities is problematic. The week before the session, a subgroup meets for three hours to prepare a process map showing each step of the current process. When the map is complete, key internal stakeholders and selected external customers are interviewed to gain their perspectives on how the process currently functions. Eighteen people, who know each other well, will be at the session; about three hours are available to find viable improvement ideas.

Agenda	Process Design Notes
Welcome and agenda overview (5 minutes)	• Review the purpose of the meeting and how the session will be conducted.
Buy-in and norms (15 minutes)	• Ask members to find partners to discuss two questions: *"Why is it important to improve this particular process?"* *"What rules should we set for ourselves today to make sure we reach consensus on improvements that will really make a difference?"* • Facilitate a plenary to synthesize the ideas of the partners. • Post key ideas and norms.
Map review (45 minutes)	• Ask the members who constructed the process map to explain all of the steps they identified. • Encourage the rest of the members to ask questions and add any missing details. • Ratify that the map is acceptable to all present. • Have members who did the interviews hand out copies of the data gathered and share highlights. Encourage questioning by others.
Force-field analysis (45 minutes)	• Facilitate the whole group in a force-field analysis exercise as they identify: *"What does the data tell us is working well? What is fine as it is?"* *"What does the data tell us isn't working well? What needs improvement?"* • Use multi-voting to identify the priority issues that need to be resolved by this group at this day's session.
Problem solving (60 minutes)	• Post the top three issues in different parts of the room. • Ask members to divide themselves into groups based on interest and knowledge to work on these issues. • Review the steps of the problem-solving model and ask subgroups to select one or more facilitators to manage the session. • Hold a plenary to share recommendations and ratify action plans.
Next steps (10 minutes)	• Ensure that a time and date have been set for the next meeting to follow up on the action plans. • Evaluate the session.

Sample Design 11—Project Retrospective

Specifications: A major project has ended. It is vitally important to learn from the venture. It is also important to gain input from a wide range of stakeholders. This meeting is for a large group of from twenty to thirty individuals. The large size of the group is a strategic decision to ensure anonymity of the members through the use of large group techniques. Before the meeting, a detailed top-down flowchart is created to show the stages and timeline of the project. This project map is distributed before the retrospective workshop.

Agenda	Process Design Notes
Welcome and agenda overview (5 minutes)	• Review the purpose of the meeting and how the session will be conducted.
Buy-in and norms (15 minutes)	• Ask members to find partners to discuss two questions: *"Why is it important to improve this particular process?"* *"What rules will make it safe for everyone to freely critique the project?"* • Facilitate a plenary to synthesize the ideas of the partners. • Post key ideas and norms. Ratify norms.
Map review (45 minutes)	• Ask team members who are present to give a brief overview of the project map and timelines. • Encourage the rest of the members to ask questions and add any missing details. • Ratify that the map is acceptable to all present. • Give each person a small human figure cut out of a piece of sticky note paper. Invite each person to approach the map and stick the figure on the map to signify the point at which he or she entered the project or was affected by it.
Positive elements (45 minutes)	• Give each person a sticky note pad and allow time for them to write down all the positive events that took pace in the project. This could be things that were done well, achievements, breakthroughs, good teamwork, etc. • Invite everyone to approach the map and post notes on the map at the point at which these events occurred. • Allow group members to reflect on the map. Facilitate a discussion about the strengths of the project, when these things happened, and who was involved.
Pitfalls (45 minutes)	• Give each person a sticky note pad of a different color and allow time for them to write down all the negative events that took place during the project. This could be things that were done poorly, mistakes, lack of teamwork, conflict, etc. • Invite everyone to approach the map and post their notes on the map at the point when these events occurred.

Sample Design 11 (cont'd)

Agenda	Process Design Notes
	• Allow group members to reflect on the map. Remind members about the norms that were set at the start of the session. Facilitate a discussion about the pitfalls of the project, when these things happened, and who was involved. • Record these on a flip chart or electronic board. • Use weighted multi-voting to identify the priority issues.
Problem solving and plenary (90 minutes)	• Post the top three issues in different parts of the room. • Ask members to divide themselves into groups based on interest and knowledge to work on these issues. • Review the steps of the problem-solving model and ask subgroups to select one or more small group facilitators to manage the breakout groups. • Have groups analyze the topic for fifteen minutes, then brainstorm solutions for fifteen minutes, then sort the solutions to identify the best ideas to improve future projects.
Summation (30 minutes)	• Have groups prioritize their proposed recommendations and learnings to bring only top-ranked ideas to the large group. • Hold a plenary to share recommendations. • Collect all notes for a final report. • Conduct an exit survey.

Sample Design 12—Team Adjournment

Specifications: A team has been together for some time and has completed its work. As was planned, the team will now cease to operate. To mark the end of the team's life together, the ten members of the team are convening for a final meeting to adjourn. This is an informal gathering that should feel more like a celebration than a meeting, so there is no need to record the proceedings.

Agenda	Process Design Notes
Welcome and agenda overview (5 minutes)	• Welcome members to the session. • Provide an overview of the meeting.
Personal reflections (40 minutes)	• Invite each member to share his or her reminiscence of the best thing about the team and also the most valuable thing he or she personally learned from time as a member.
Strength bombardment (40 minutes)	• Have each team member write his or her name on a sheet of paper. Ask each person to pass his or her sheet to the person to the right. Members write notes to the person whose name is on the sheet under two headings: What you did that was really effective, keep doing it. The greatest contribution you made to the team. • Sheets are passed until everyone has written on each person's sheet. • Start with one sheet to pass around the group. Have each person read aloud what he or she wrote about that person. • Repeat until every sheet has been passed around and read out. Each person leaves with his or her sheet.
Networking and socializing (30 minutes)	• Allow time for exchange of future contact information. • Adjourn to socialize.

Session Planning Worksheet

To aid you in planning your next session, consider the following:

Purpose of the session: ____

____

____

Number of members: ____________ Do they need to be introduced? Y / N

1. What will you do to warm up the group?

____

____

____

____

2. Do you need to develop special norms for this activity? If yes, what should the norming questions be?

____

____

____

____

3. Will buy-in be a problem? If yes, what's the buy-in question to ask?

____

____

____

____

4. What background information, empowerment parameters, or other constraints do members need to know?

____

____

____

____

____

____

____

____

5. What are the key questions that must be answered in order to arrive at the answers the group will be seeking?

____

____

____

____

____

____

____

____

6. What activities/process tools do you expect to be using at the session?

7. What could go wrong at the session? (Possible considerations: interpersonal conflicts, cynicism, lack of energy, overwhelming task, unable to achieve closure, lack of skills, etc.) For each possible problem, also identify strategies to overcome it.

Session Barriers	Solutions

8. What evaluation questions should you plan to ask at the start?

At the mid-point check?

On the final evaluation form?

9. What audiovisual aids, videos, and other props will you need?

About the Author

INGRID BENS is a consultant and trainer with a master's degree in adult education and more than twenty-five years of experience as a facilitator. Over the years Ingrid has designed and led numerous strategic change initiatives. She has also consulted on many team implementation projects and helped with the implementation of a variety of projects aimed at creating more collaborative workplaces.

While Ingrid is an experienced organization development consultant, she now spends most of her time writing about facilitation skills and teaching workshops. In addition to *Facilitating with Ease!* Ingrid is also the author of two other Jossey-Bass publications: *Advanced Facilitation Strategies* and *Facilitating to Lead.*

In 2009 the Pfeiffer Company asked Ingrid Bens to create a competency model for facilitation. The result was the *Facilitation Skills Inventory* (FSI). More information about implementing this assessment in your organization can be obtained at www.pfeiffer.com/fsi.

In 2010 Ingrid Bens created the first and only online facilitation skills e-learning program. This program teaches core skills and can be found at www.facilitationtutor.com.

For more information about the author and her publications and go to the web page established to support this book at www.josseybass.com/go/ingridbens.

Acknowledgments

The development of this third edition would not have been possible without the generous input and advice of a very diverse group of people who practice as facilitators in several countries. This group includes Ewa Malia, Ronnie McEwan, Mark Vilbert, Sieglinde Hinger, Adriano Pianesi, Sandy Benz, Stephanie Carol, Ian Maddell, and Krister Forsberg,

I wish to also mention those who provided their wisdom and insight to the earlier editions, including Marilyn Laiken, Michael Goldman, Jan Means, Charles Bens, Bev Davids, Carl Aspler, Chris Boyd, and Charlotte de Heinrich.

Facilitation Certification

Certifying the members of your team has never been easier. Now you can determine the facilitation skill level of your staff with the Facilitation Skills Inventory (FSI). The FSI is based on actual observation and creates detailed and specific feedback for improving performance. For more information about the FSI go to the following website pages:

www.pfeiffer/go/facilitationskills.

http://www.pfeiffer.com/WileyCDA/PfeifferTitle/productCd-PCOL4870.html

About the Website

The materials listed below are available in electric format on the Jossey-Bass website.

Throughout the book these items were indicated by the icon in the margins.

There is no charge for accessing these resources. Whether you're a facilitator, a manager, or someone who is teaching facilitation skills to others, we hope you find these materials to be truly helpful.

To access these *Facilitating with Ease!* resources, go to

www. josseybass.com/go/ingridbens
password: professional

Facilitation Cue Card

Core Practices Observation Sheet

Process Flow Observation Sheet

Best and Worst Facilitation Practices for Leaders

Assessment Questions

Group Assessment Survey

Facilitation Strategies Chart

Team Effectiveness Survey

Group Behaviors Handout

Peer Review Instructions

Peer Review Worksheet

The Empowerment Continuum

Decision Options Chart

Decision Effectiveness Survey

The Eight-Step Feedback Process

Wording an Intervention

Conflict Effectiveness Survey

Meeting Effectiveness Survey

Shared Facilitation

Bibliography

Chapter 1

Argyris, C. (1970) *Intervention Theory and Method.* Addison-Wesley. Reading, Mass.

Beckhard, R. (1969) *Organization Development: Strategies and Models.* Addison-Wesley. Reading, Mass.

Bennis, W.G. (1966) *Changing Organizations.* McGraw-Hill. New York.

Block, P. (1987) *The Empowered Manager.* Jossey-Bass. San Francisco.

Block, P. (1999) *Flawless Consulting* (2nd ed.). Pfeiffer. San Francisco.

French, W.L., & Bell, C. H., Jr. (1978) *Organization Development.* Prentice Hall. Englewood Cliffs, N.J.

Hargrove, R. (1995) *Masterful Coaching.* Pfeiffer. San Francisco.

Jongewood, D., & James, M. (1973) *Winning with People.* Addison-Wesley. Reading, Mass.

Kayser, T. A. (1990) *Mining Group Gold.* Serif Publishing. Segundo, Calif.

Lewin, K., & Hanson, P. (1976) Giving Feedback: An Interpersonal Skill. In W. G. Bennis and others (Eds.), *The Planning of Change* (3rd ed.). Holt Rinehart & Winston. New York.

Lippitt, G.L. (1969) *Organization Renewal.* Appleton, Century, Crofts. New York.

McKroskey, J.C., Larson, C.E., & Knapp, M.L. (1971) *An Introduction to Interpersonal Communication.* Prentice Hall. Englewood Cliffs, N.J.

Nadler, D.A. (1977) *Feedback and Organization Development.* Addison-Wesley. Reading, Mass.

Schein, E. H. (1969) *Process Consultation: Its Role in Organization Development.* Addison-Wesley. Reading, Mass.

Schein, E. H. (1987) *Process Consultation: Lessons for Managers and Consultants.* Addison-Wesley. Reading, Mass.

Schein, E. H., & Bennis, W. G. (1965) *Personal and Organization Change Through Group Methods: The Laboratory Approach.* John Wiley & Sons. Hoboken, N.J.

Chapter 2

Anderson, T. D. (1992) *Transforming Leadership.* Human Resource Development Press. Amherst, Mass.

Autry, J. A. (2001) *The Servant Leader.* Prima Publishing. Roseville, Calif.

Bennis, W., & Goldsmith, J. (2003) *Learning to Lead.* Perseus Books. New York.

Belasco, J., & Stayer, R. (1993) *Flight of the Buffalo.* Warner Books. New York.

Block, P. (1990) *The Empowered Manager.* Jossey-Bass. San Francisco.

Burns, J. M. (1978). *Leadership.* Harper & Row. New York.

Hesselbein, F., Goldsmith, M., & Beckhard, R. (Eds.) (1997) *The Organization of the Future.* Jossey-Bass. San Francisco.

Hunsaker, P., & Alessandra, A. (1980) *The Art of Managing People.* Prentice-Hall. Englewood Cliffs, N.J.

Katzenbach, J., & Smith, D. (1993) *The Wisdom of Teams.* HarperCollins. New York.

Kinlaw, D. C. (1993) *Team-Managed Facilitation.* Pfeiffer. San Francisco.

Pfeiffer, J. W., & Jones, J. E. (1972) *A Handbook of Structured Experiences for Human Relations Training* (Vols. I–X). Pfeiffer. San Francisco.

Rees, F. (1991). *How to Lead Work Teams.* Pfeiffer. San Francisco.

Tagliere, D. A. (1992) *How to Meet, Think, and Work to Consensus.* Pfeiffer. San Francisco.

Weaver, R. G., & Farrell, J. D. (1997) *Managers as Facilitators.* Berrett-Koehler. San Francisco.

Chapter 3

Argyris, C. (1970) *Intervention Theory and Method.* Addison-Wesley. Reading, Mass.

Beckhard, R. (1969) *Organization Development: Strategies and Models.* Addison-Wesley. Reading, Mass.

Blake, R. R., & Mouton, J. S. (1968) *Corporate Excellence Through Grid Organization Development.* Gulf. Houston, Tex.

Block, P. (1999) *Flawless Consulting* (2nd ed.). Pfeiffer. San Francisco.

Lewin, K., & Hanson, P. (1976) Giving Feedback: An Interpersonal Skill. In W. G. Bennis and others (Eds.), *The Planning of Change* (3rd ed.). Holt Rinehart & Winston. New York.

Likert, R. (1967) *The Human Organization.* McGraw-Hill. New York.

Lippitt, G., & Lippitt, R. (1978) *The Consulting Process in Action.* Pfeiffer. San Francisco.

Margulies, N., & Wallace, J. (1973) *Organizational Change: Techniques and Applications.* Scott, Foresman. Glenview, Ill.

Nadler, D. A. (1977) *Feedback and Organization Development.* Addison-Wesley. Reading, Mass.

Reddy, B. (1994) *Intervention Skills: Process Consultation for Small Groups and Teams.* Pfeiffer. San Francisco.

Schein, E. H. (1969) *Process Consultation: Its Role in Organization Development.* Addison-Wesley. Reading, Mass.

Schein, E. H. (1987) *Process Consultation: Lessons for Managers and Consultants.* Addison-Wesley. Reading, Mass.

Chapter 4

Argyris, C. (1964) *Integrating the Individual and the Organization.* John Wiley & Sons. Hoboken, N.J.

Beckhard, R., & Harris, R. T. (1969) *Organizational Transitions: Managing Complex Change.* Addison-Wesley. Reading, Mass.

Dyer, W. G. (1987) *Team Building.* Addison-Wesley. Reading, Mass.

Likert, R. (1961) *New Patterns of Management.* McGraw-Hill. New York.

McGregor, D. (1960) *The Human Side of Enterprise.* McGraw-Hill. New York.

Pfeiffer, J. W., & Jones, J. E. (1972) *A Handbook of Structured Experiences for Human Relations Training* (Vols. I–X). Pfeiffer. San Francisco.

Schein, E. H. (1969) *Process Consultation.* Addison-Wesley. Reading, Mass.

Schutz, W. C. (1966) *The Interpersonal Underworld.* Science and Behavior Books. Palo Alto, Calif.

Tuckman, B. W. (1965) Development Sequences in Small Groups. *Psychological Bulletin.*

Weisbord, M. M. (1991) *Productive Workplaces.* Jossey-Bass. San Francisco.

Chapter 5

Bennis, W. G. (1966) *Changing Organizations.* McGraw-Hill. New York.

Bennis, W. G., and others. (1976) *The Planning of Change* (3rd ed.). Holt Rinehart & Winston. New York.

French, W. L., & Bell, C. H., Jr. (1978) *Organization Development.* Prentice Hall. Englewood Cliffs, N.J.

Kayser, T. A. (1990) *Mining Group Gold.* Serif Publishing. Segundo, Calif.

Pfeiffer, J. W., & Jones, J. E. (1972) *A Handbook of Structured Experiences for Human Relations Training* (Vol. I–X). Pfeiffer. San Francisco.

Scannell, E. E., & Newstrom, J. (1991) *Still More Games Trainers Play.* McGraw-Hill. New York.

Schein, E. H. (1969) *Process Consultation: Its Role in Organization Development.* Addison-Wesley. Reading, Mass.

Schein, E. H. (1987) *Process Consultation: Lessons for Managers and Consultants.* Addison-Wesley. Reading, Mass.

Schein, E. H., & Bennis, W. G. (1965) *Personal and Organization Change Through Group Methods: The Laboratory Approach.* John Wiley & Sons. Hoboken, N.J.

Senge, P., and others. (1994) *Fifth Discipline Fieldbook.* Doubleday. New York.

Wood, J. T., Phillips, G., & Pederson, D. J. (1986) *Group Discussion: A Practical Guide to Participation and Leadership.* Harper & Row. New York.

Chapter 6

Avery, M., Auvine, B., Streiel, B., & Weiss, L. (1981) *Building United Judgment: A Handbook for Consensus Decision Making.* The Center for Conflict Resolution. Madison, Wis.

DeBono, E. (1985) *Six Thinking Hats.* Key Porter Books. Toronto.

DeBono, E. (1993) *Serious Creativity.* HarperCollins. New York.

Fisher, A. B. (1974) *Small Group Decision Making: Communication and Group Process.* McGraw-Hill. New York.

Fisher, R., & Ury, W. (1983) *Getting to Yes.* Penguin Books. New York.

Harvey, J. B. (1988) *The Abilene Paradox and Other Meditations on Management.* Heath. Lexington, Mass.

Kuhn, T. S. (1970) *The Structure of Scientific Revolutions.* University of Chicago Press. Chicago.

Saint, S., & Lawson, J. R. (1994) *Rules for Reaching Consensus.* Jossey-Bass. San Fransisco.

Schneider, W. E. (1994) *The Reengineering Alternative: A Plan for Making Your Current Culture Work.* Irwin. Burr Ridge, Ill.

Van Gundy, A. B. (1981) *Techniques of Structured Problem Solving.* Van Nostrand Reinhold. New York.

Chapter 7

Beckhard, R. (1967, March) The Confrontation Meeting. *Harvard Business Review, 45.*

Beckhard, R. (1969) *Organization Development: Strategies and Models.* Addison-Wesley. Reading, Mass.

Blake, R. R., Shepard, H., & Mouton, J. S. (1965) *Managing Intergroup Conflict in Industry.* Gulf. Houston, Tex.

Filley, A. C. (1975) *Interpersonal Conflict Resolution.* Scott, Foresman. Glenview, Ill.

Fisher, R., & Ury, W. (1983) *Getting to Yes.* Penguin Books. New York.

Kilmann, R. H., & Thomas, K. W. (1978) Four Perspectives on Conflict Management: An Attributional Framework for Organizing Descriptive and Normative Theory. *Academy of Management Review.*

Kindler, H. S. (1988) *Managing Disagreement Constructively.* Crisp Publications. Los Altos, Calif.

Likert, R., & Likert, J. G. (1976) *New Ways of Managing Conflict.* McGraw-Hill. New York.

Thomas, K. W., & Kilmann, R. H. (1974) *The Thomas-Kilmann Conflict Mode Instrument.* Xicom. Tuxedo, N.Y.

Walton, R. E. (1987) *Managing Conflict: Interpersonal Dialogue and Third Party Roles.* Addison-Wesley. Reading, Mass.

Zander, A. (1983) *Making Groups Effective.* Jossey-Bass. San Francisco.

Chapter 8

Bradford, L. P. (1976) *Making Meetings Work.* Pfeiffer. San Francisco.

Doyle, M., & Straus, D. (1976) *How to Make Meetings Work: The New Interaction Method.* Berkley Publishing Group. New York.

Dyer, W. G. (1987) *Team Building.* Addison-Wesley. Reading, Mass.

Frank, M. O. (1989) *How to Run a Meeting in Half the Time.* Simon and Schuster. New York.

Haynes, M. E. (1988) *Effective Meeting Skills: A Practical Guide for More Productive Meetings.* Crisp Publications. Los Altos, Calif.

Jones, J. E. (1980) Dealing with Disruptive Individuals in Meetings. *The 1980 Annual Handbook for Group Facilitators.* Pfeiffer. San Francisco.

Chapter 9

Beckhard, R. (1969) *Organization Development: Strategies and Models.* Addison-Wesley. Reading, Mass.

Cooperrider, D. L., & Whitney, D. (1999) *Appreciative Inquiry.* Berrett-Koehler. San Francisco.

Delbecq, A. L., & Van de Ven, A. H. (1971) A Group Process Model for Problem Identification and Problem Planning. *Journal of Applied Behavioral Science.*

Deming, W. E. (1986) *Out of Crisis.* MIT Center for Advanced Engineering Study. Cambridge, Mass.

Fritz, R. (1989) *The Path of Least Resistance.* Ballantine. New York.

Fritz, R. (1991) *Creating.* Fawcett Columbine. New York.

Green, T. B., & D.F.R. (1973) Management in an Age of Rapid Technological and Social Change. *Southern Management Association Proceedings.* Houston, Tex.

Ingle, S. (1982) *Quality Circle Masters Guide.* Prentice Hall. Englewood Cliffs, N.J.

Ishikawa, K. (1990) *Introduction to Quality Control.* 3A Corporation. Tokyo.

Johnson, D.W., & Johnson, R.T. (2005) *Teaching Students to Be Peacemakers.* Interaction Book Company. Edina, Minn.

Massarik, F. (1990) *Advances in Organization Development.* Ablex Publishing Corporation. Orwood, N.J.

Ohno, T. (1988) *Toyota Production System: Beyond Large Scale Production.* Productivity Press. Portland, Ore.

Ouchi, W. (1981) *Theory Z.* Addison-Wesley. Reading, Mass.

Pfeiffer, J. W., & Jones, J. E. (1972) *A Handbook of Structured Experiences for Human Relations Training* (Vol. I–X). Pfeiffer. San Francisco.

Senge, P., and others. (1994) *Fifth Discipline Fieldbook.* Doubleday. New York.

Stavros, J., & Hinricks, G. (2009) *The Thin Book of SOAR: Building Strengths-Based Strategy.* Thin Book Publishing Co. Bend OR.